Restoration of Reason

The Eclipse and Recovery of Truth, Goodness, and Beauty

Montague Brown

D1468639

B
Baker Academic
Grand Rapids, Michigan

©2006 by Montague Brown

Published by Baker Academic
a division of Baker Publishing Group
P.O. Box 6287, Grand Rapids, MI 49516-6287
www.bakeracademic.com

Printed in the United States of America

Library of Congress Cataloging-in-Publication Data
Brown, Montague, 1952–
    Restoration of reason : the eclipse and recovery of truth, goodness, and beauty / Montague Brown.
        p.   cm.
    Includes bibliographical references and index.
    ISBN 10: 0-8010-3154-0 (pbk.)
    ISBN 978-0-8010-3154-0 (pbk.)
    1. Thought and thinking—Religious aspects—Christianity. 2. Reasoning.
I. Title.
BV4598.4.B76 2006
190—dc22   2006014400

Restoration of Reason

In memory of Olaf Tollefsen,
whose love of wisdom, clarity of thought,
and breadth of knowledge were an inspiration to me.

Contents

Acknowledgments

I would like to thank all those who have helped bring this project to fruition. First and foremost I am indebted to my colleagues and students at Saint Anselm College for providing an intellectual community in which such a broad pursuit of intelligibility is possible and for providing the occasions of many fruitful discussions. I am also grateful to the college for providing the initial funding for this project and for continuing to support my work. A special word of thanks is due Professor Fred Lawrence of Boston College, who read the manuscript and made many valuable suggestions for improvement, in particular concerning the passages on Bernard Lonergan's thought. The misinterpretations and mistakes that remain are my own. Finally, I am grateful to my wife, who patiently permitted such unproductive work when I could have been painting the house or generally making myself useful.

Introduction

The Great Instauration

Being convinced that the human intellect makes its own difficulties, not using the true helps which are at man's disposal soberly and judiciously—whence follows manifold ignorance of things, and by reason of that ignorance mischiefs innumerable—he thought all trial should be made, whether that commerce between the mind of man and the nature of things, which is more precious than anything on earth, or at least anything that is of the earth, might be by any means restored to its perfect and original condition.[1]

So Francis Bacon begins the Proem to his major work, *The Great Instauration*. And so begins a new age. Gone are the days of scholastic disputation about obscure metaphysical themes. Gone are the days when moral disagreement disrupts the common good. The age of progress has dawned. All that is needed is a new way of looking at things, a new method to restore human reason to its privileged position in the divine plan.

Bacon recognizes a serious problem: the schools of philosophy dominated by the thought of Aristotle and Aquinas seem unable to make sense of the new science introduced by Copernicus and Galileo. Many

---

1. Francis Bacon, *The Great Instauration*, in *The New Organon and Related Writings*, ed. Fulton H. Anderson (New York: Liberal Arts, 1960), p. 3. *The Great Instauration* was published in 1620. It represents Bacon's mature thought. However, Bacon had expressed his general idea of a renewal of a new way of advancing knowledge as early as 1603 in his work *On the Interpretation of Nature*.

of the old school masters refuse to accept the findings of the new science even against clear evidence. The result is much controversy and
little progress in the arts and sciences. According to Bacon, the old ways
need to be abandoned and a new method introduced that will allow all
intelligent and well-meaning people to move ahead with the project of
understanding the world and applying that understanding to improve
the human condition.

The theme Bacon invokes is moral and even biblical. Bacon believes
his new method is a return to the proper use of reason. If followed, it
will restore humanity to its unfallen condition. Reason will operate
within just bounds, and the progress that will result will return our
estate to something rivaling the garden of Eden. Indeed, the word *instauration* means "restoration." Bacon's motive for publishing his work
is noble—to help humanity return to a state of flourishing in which we
assume our rightful role as rulers over nature so that nature may work
for our benefit.

All that is needed for this restoration is careful attention to Bacon's
new method and a refusal to let the mind pursue tasks that are beyond
it (again a biblical ring).[2] The present state of intellectual knowledge
is stagnant and confused: there are disagreements and disputations,
which not only waste time, since they concern fictitious topics, but
also create discord among people. This is what happens when reason
is given free reign to pursue answers to its many questions. The solution is to confine reason to a sphere in which it can serve the common
good. "There was but one course left, therefore—to try the whole thing
anew upon a better plan, and to commence a total reconstruction
of sciences, arts, and all human knowledge, raised upon the proper
foundations."[3]

What we need, in place of the confused jumble that is the present
condition of knowledge in the arts and sciences, is an ordering principle
that can turn an education of controversy and debate into fruitful and
progressive science. For this we must all enter upon "the one path which
is alone open to the human mind."[4] In general, Bacon proposes as this
ordering principle what we would call the scientific method of hypothesis
and verification through experiment. Although such a complete overhaul
of the sciences might seem daunting, it is the only legitimate course of
action. Comparing his new way with the old, Bacon writes: "the one,
arduous and difficult in the beginning, leads out at last into the open

2. See Psalm 131: "O Lord, my heart is not lifted up, / my eyes are not raised too high; /
I do not occupy myself with things / too great and too marvelous for me" (RSV).
3. *Great Instauration*, p. 4.
4. Ibid.

country, while the other, seeming at first sight easy and free from obstruction, leads to pathless and precipitous places."[5]

However, far from being the panacea for all human ills, Bacon's *Great Instauration* was, in fact, a great violation of reason from which the modern world has not yet recovered; hence, a restoration of reason in its many dimensions is in order. Bacon's solution of restricting reason to one method was unwarranted and has led to absurdities in almost every area of human thought. Contrary to Bacon's thesis, it is clear that more than one path is open to the human mind. Besides the ability to operate in terms of scientific method (that is, to provide hypotheses whose adequacy is tested by experiments), reason also yields metaphysical, moral, and aesthetic knowledge.[6] These kinds of knowledge are not obtained by scientific method; in fact, restricting reason to scientific method makes metaphysical, moral, and aesthetic knowledge impossible. There is no way of proving the existence of God or even the validity of thought through scientific method, for neither God nor rational principles can be verified by sense experience. Nor is it possible to show scientifically why the intentional killing of innocent people is always wrong since right and wrong, justice and injustice, are not material things. Nor, finally, can one show why a particular object or work of art is beautiful merely by referring to statistical laws of matter in motion.

Thus, as to Bacon's assessment of the two ways open to the human mind, I would agree with Bacon's analogy, except that I would reverse the application and say that it is Bacon's new method that is bound for "pathless and precipitous places." Ironically, Bacon's plan to restore that precious "commerce between the mind of man and the nature of things" will succeed in doing just the opposite. Bacon points human thinking in

5. Ibid.

6. Thomas Nagel's book *The Last Word* (Oxford: Oxford University Press, 1997) deals in many ways with this same theme. Nagel is at pains to refute contemporary forms of relativism born from the kind of restrictions on reason that Bacon suggests. Nagel holds that arguments against the validity of reason are all ultimately self-refuting. Although he focuses mostly on the theoretical disciplines of logic, mathematics, and science, he says that the same principles apply to moral reasoning and perhaps even to aesthetics (pp. 20–25). "The defender of reason must therefore mount his defense in each domain of thought separately, by trying to show, from within a form of reasoning, that its methods are inescapable and that first order engagement with them resists displacement by an explanation of the practice in other terms that do not employ those methods" (p. 27). In other words, each sphere of reason has its own method. Although Nagel suggests that ethics and aesthetics are distinct from theoretical disciplines, he does not penetrate to their distinctive features. Nagel's treatment of ethics falls short of distinguishing its first principles, and his treatment of aesthetics is just a suggestion that its method might be able to be specified in the same way he has specified those of logic, physics, and ethics. Thus my treatment goes beyond Nagel's in trying to specify distinct methods and principles for the realms of the true, the good, and the beautiful.

a direction that leads to the impossibility of any commerce at all between the mind and things. What is needed today is the frank admission that Bacon's plan was wrongheaded and a consequent restoration of reason to its full richness.

In an attempt to show the seriousness of Bacon's error and what is needed to correct it, we shall begin with an analysis of the features of Bacon's thought, along with the thought of two other major players in the inauguration of this new age: René Descartes and Thomas Hobbes (chapter 1). Having witnessed the startling change in the mode of explanation presented by these philosophers, we shall then consider the immediate background and context of this dramatic shift (chapter 2) and some of the reasons why ancient and medieval thinkers did not make it (chapter 3).

Following these general considerations, we shall explore the power of this new approach, and its limitations, through an examination of the disciples of Bacon, Descartes, and Hobbes. In chapter 4 we shall consider thinkers in the Empiricist tradition and in chapter 5 those in the Rationalist tradition. In both cases we shall find that, if one follows the principles of Bacon, Descartes, and Hobbes consistently, one ends in the twin absurdities of solipsism and skepticism.

With chapter 6, we shall trace the beginnings of a recovery process. We shall examine the thought of Kant and Hegel who, while sharing with Bacon and Descartes the ideal of having one method to unify our understanding of reality, were aware of the arbitrariness of some of the restrictions put on reason by Bacon, Descartes, and their followers. In the thought of Kant and Hegel, we witness a commitment to expand the range of reason.

Chapter 7 traces the further recovery of reason's riches in the thought of two twentieth-century thinkers—Alfred North Whitehead and Bernard Lonergan, S.J. These thinkers, in addition to knowing the modern philosophers well, explicitly hark back to some of the thinkers in the Greek and medieval worlds who had been, for the most part, fiercely rejected by the moderns. While clearly interested in recovering the multidimensionality of reason, these thinkers are still bound by the ideal of a single method to unify all knowledge and hence fall short, in some ways, of honoring the full range of reason.

In the last two chapters, we get to the heart of the matter. Here we present the alternative to the modern ideal of one method for all knowledge through an examination of the thought of the great ancient and medieval thinkers—Plato, Aristotle, Augustine, and Aquinas. Central to this philosophical tradition is the understanding that method should be adapted to the object rather than object to the method. There are three distinct objects of the human mind—the true, the good, and the beautiful. Therefore, there must be three distinct methods, each guided by its own first principles. Specifically, chapter 8 will distinguish systematically the three realms of reason, and chapter 9 will address the question of how these realms are related in the unity of human intelligence.

Although this book involves a fair amount of work in the history of philosophy, its central concern is primarily systematic. That is, the focus is reason, its subject areas (objects), and the principles and methods appropriate to each area. I contend that reason operates according to distinct principles and methods according to whether it pursues the true, the good, or the beautiful. My concern is at once to argue for this rich vision of reason and to see what happens when reason is restricted to the principles and method of one realm or another. I begin with Bacon, Descartes, and Hobbes because they introduce the scientific model of reason which dominates our world and because they enthusiastically tout this model as an unambiguous advance over the ancient and medieval model I seek to restore. Indeed, they see their contribution as the overthrow of learned ignorance and the rebirth of enlightened humanism.

In my discussions of historical figures, I have not tried to be comprehensive either by including all important thinkers or by analyzing in detail the thinkers that are included. Thus, much of importance in the history of philosophy and in the thought of the philosophers examined has been left out. Since my interest is in restoring the rich diversity of reason and in understanding how this diversity was lost, my focus will be on the first principles and methods of the thinkers I do discuss, and on the implications of holding these principles and methods. As Aristotle says, "a principle is thought to be more than half the whole, and through it many of the things sought become apparent also."[7]

One might ask why I treat historical figures at all, and not rather dispense with them completely in favor of a strictly systematic approach to the problem. Why not just present straight philosophical distinctions? There are two answers to this question. In the first place, we are educationally and culturally influenced by the history of philosophy in more ways than we know. To study these thinkers is to understand better our own thinking. Such a study also reveals the dynamic of ideas to be not just a set of abstract relations but the energetic efforts of human beings involved in a great conversation. Tracing this conversation adds a certain excitement and vitality to the systematic problematic. In the

---

7. Aristotle, *Nicomachean Ethics* (hereafter *NE*) 1.7.1098b7–9, trans. Hippocrates G. Apostle (Grinnell, IA: Peripatetic Press, 1984), p. 11.

second place, studying the history of philosophy is a systematic study in itself, for philosophers have a way of making clear the implications of their predecessors' principles, either by following them or rejecting them. As Etienne Gilson points out, there is a kind of unity of philosophical experience which shows that, given certain first principles, certain conclusions logically follow.[8]

Finally, it must be said that, in the following chapters, I never argue that the scientific method itself is bad. With its continuous reevaluation of hypotheses and attention to data, scientific method has shown and continues to show itself to be a powerful and effective instrument for exploring and understanding the material universe. However, scientific method is not the only way we know. To insist that it is violates our humanity by truncating the truth arbitrarily and by removing from our lives the intelligible riches specific to the realms of the good and the beautiful.

8. See Etienne Gilson, *The Unity of Philosophical Experience* (New York: Charles Scribner's Sons, 1937).

1

The Responsible Restriction of Reason

One of the hallmarks of the early modern movement in philosophy is an ethical concern for the improvement of the human lot. Although other motives clearly come into play (e.g., excitement over the new discoveries of science, attraction to the power over nature promised by the new science), there is no reason to doubt the genuineness of the moderns when they claim to be acting in the service of humanity. Thus the restriction of reason that Bacon initiates, and Descartes and Hobbes imitate in their own ways, is seen by these thinkers as a responsible move designed to counteract the irresponsibility of letting reason run wild, the consequence of which is endless controversy and even skepticism. Ironically, however, such a seemingly responsible restriction of reason proves to be grossly irresponsible, for it implies the impossibility of grounding any moral responsibility at all.

In this chapter we shall consider the major features of Bacon's project along with the somewhat different proposals of Descartes and Hobbes. After clarifying what these thinkers see as the problem to be solved, we shall examine their solutions. Then we shall have to ask ourselves what has been gained and what, if anything, lost in the philosophical revolution.

Bacon

As we said above, Bacon is concerned that the present state of human knowledge is in a quagmire. No progress is being made, and the best minds are wasting time debating issues of no importance. The Aristotelian tradition, which dominates university education, is more concerned with winning arguments than with finding the truth. Such disputation is all very well as training for argumentation (perhaps for a career in the law courts), but as a vehicle for discovering the truth, it is worthless. "For its value and utility it must be plainly avowed that that wisdom which we have derived principally from the Greeks is but like the boyhood of knowledge, and has the characteristic property of boys: it can talk, but it cannot generate, for it is fruitful of controversies but barren of works."[1]

The trouble, as Bacon sees it, is that the mind is flawed and requires a new method (his new organon) to set it straight. The mind cannot be trusted on its own to come to true knowledge. Thus, the mistake that the Greeks made was in trusting reason. It is not that Bacon blames the Greeks: they could not help themselves. For without Bacon's method, which is "totally new,"[2] how could they have avoided falling into such petty, immature disputes? The mind is not a blank tablet, able to know all things, as Aristotle held. Rather, it is an uneven mirror, distorting the information it receives from the senses. "For let men please themselves as they will in admiring and almost adoring the human mind, this is certain: that as an uneven mirror distorts the rays of objects according to its own figure and section, so the mind, when it receives impressions of objects through the sense, cannot be trusted to report them truly, but in forming its notions mixes up its own nature with the nature of things."[3] When this happens, the "commerce between the mind and things" clearly breaks down. Bacon believes that his new method will correct or at least compensate for the "uneven mirror" of the mind.

1. Francis Bacon, *The Great Instauration*, pp. 7–8. This emphasis on works and progress can be found in Bacon's earlier works, too. As early as 1603 Bacon writes, "Now among all the benefits that could be conferred upon mankind, I found none so great as the discovery of new arts, endowments, and commodities for the bettering of man's life" (*On the Interpretation of Nature*, proem, in *Selected Writings of Francis Bacon*, ed. Hugh G. Dick [New York: Random House, 1955], p. 150). In *Of the Proficience and Advancement of Learning, Divine and Human*, published in 1605, he writes, "Neither is my meaning, as was spoken by Socrates, to call philosophy down from heaven to converse upon the earth; that is, to leave natural philosophy aside, and to apply knowledge only to manners and policy. But as both heaven and earth do conspire and contribute to the use and benefit of man, so the end ought to be, from both philosophies to separate and reject vain speculations and whatsoever is empty and void, and to preserve and augment whatsoever is solid and fruitful; that knowledge may not be as a curtesan, for pleasure and vanity only, or as a bond-woman, to acquire and gain to her master's use; but as a spouse, for generation, fruit, and comfort" (*Of the Proficience and Advancement of Learning, Divine and Human*, bk. 1, in *Selected Writings*, pp. 193–94).
2. *Great Instauration*, p. 5.
3. Ibid., p. 22.

However, a question readily presents itself: if the mind is flawed, how can it be trusted to come up with the appropriate method to guide itself? Might not Bacon's method itself be the product of a ray of light distorted by the uneven mirror of the mind? This question is, by definition, unanswerable from within Bacon's system. Of course, Bacon may be serious when he speaks of his discovery as an accident or a matter of luck (as opposed to reason), ascribing it ultimately to the "infinite mercy and goodness of God."[4] However, this claim sits ill with Bacon's assertion that the worst kind of philosophy is one which allows an admixture of religion. And if the activity of God is invoked at any point, there arises the peculiar problem of judging when to trust and when not to trust a correction of reason by faith or grace, given that the power of reason itself is flawed.

Let us consider briefly the distortions that Bacon claims accompany our thinking, what Bacon calls the "Idols of the human mind."[5] There are four general classes of idols: the idols of the tribe, the idols of the cave, the idols of the marketplace, and the idols of the theater. The first three are inevitable stumbling blocks for the human mind; the last we manufacture for ourselves.

The most deeply rooted in our nature, and hence the most universal, are the idols of the tribe. They belong inevitably to all members of the human race and have the effect of skewing all our knowledge. Because of these idols, we cannot trust the mind. "The human understanding is like a false mirror, which, receiving rays irregularly, distorts and discolors the nature of things by mingling its own nature in it."[6] As we said above, were what Bacon says true, it is hard to see how one could come up with a method to solve the problem since any method itself would have to be a product of a distorting mind.

In addition to distorting the nature of things, the human mind is defective in supposing more order in nature than really exists, in stubbornly defending its opinions, in being subject to the imagination, in jumping to hasty conclusions, and in being moved by the will and the emotions.[7] All these additional tendencies of the mind are well known and must be admitted, but they certainly are not decisive defects; for they all can be discovered by the mind and corrected by a will guided by the understanding. Bacon admits as much: the correction of these defects is to be found in his new method—"the interpretation of nature."[8]

4. Ibid., p. 5.
5. *New Organon*, bk. 1, aphorism 23, p. 44.
6. Ibid., bk. 1, aphorism 41, p. 48.
7. Ibid., bk. 1, aphorism 41–49, pp. 48–52.
8. *Great Instauration*, p. 19. Also, note that the full title of Bacon's *New Organon* (the second part of his *Great Instauration*) is *The New Organon or True Directions Concerning the Interpretation of Nature* (*The New Organon and Related Writings*, p. 31).

However, Bacon undercuts his corrections once again when he goes on to say that the senses deceive the mind. "The sense by itself is a thing infirm and erring."[9] If one accepts this as true, the success of Bacon's interpretation of nature is cut off. Bacon claims that what is needed are experiments to mediate between the senses and the things. However, if the senses are unreliable, why should one accept the testimony of the senses when reading the results of the experiment any more than when experiencing the original sensation? These idols of the tribe are the biggest stumbling block to Bacon's new method, for if neither reason nor sense can be trusted, it seems impossible to have any certain knowledge about the world or, indeed, about anything at all.[10]

The other three classes of idols that Bacon discusses are legitimate critiques of external and internal influences on human thinking that, unlike the idols of the tribe, are in principle correctable.

The idols of the cave are the individual quirks and limitations in each one of us that are the inevitable results of our mental and bodily particularities as well as our upbringing, experiences, and education. Because of these individual limitations, people often tend to reduce the scheme of things to one particular discipline. As an example, Bacon accuses Aristotle of reducing natural philosophy to logic. This accusation, however, is clearly without warrant. Aristotle holds that logic is not a science with a particular subject matter, and he insists on the need for each science to have its own method, suited to its subject matter.[11] Ironically, it seems that Bacon himself falls prey to this idol since he wants all aspects of the world and humanity to be understood according to his empirical method, which is his new organon (i.e., new logic).

The idols of the marketplace have to do with misuse of words. These idols are the most troublesome, according to Bacon, for people confuse words with reality. "Men believe that their reason governs words; but it is also true that words react on the understanding; and this it is that has rendered philosophy and the sciences sophistical and inactive."[12] Words can be idols in two ways: either they refer to nothing at all, such as words like fortune, prime mover, and the element of fire, or they refer to things that exist but are misunderstood because of a lack of clear

---

9. *New Organon*, bk. 1, aphorism 50, p. 53.

10. As we shall see in chapter 3, the two things that the tradition of Aristotle and Aquinas holds to be self-evidently trustworthy are the intellect and the senses when concerned with their proper objects. When Bacon denies the trustworthiness of these two, he is committed to skepticism if he is consistent.

11. Aristotle's position will be discussed more fully in chapters 3 and 4.

12. *New Organon*, bk. 1, aphorism 59, p. 56.

definitions.[13] Bacon is right that we can think we know something just because we have a word for it.[14] We ought to be careful not to let words direct our thoughts. But Bacon is arbitrary in his choice of criteria for accepting words as meaningful or not. As Bacon adopts an empirical method, those words are fictitious whose objects cannot be verified by sense experience. This rules out many abstract terms (good, just, right, form, thing) as well as words referring to immaterial realities. This is an arbitrary restriction unless Bacon can show that empirical verification is the only standard for affirming something as meaningful, which he cannot do and still claim that his new idea (which like all ideas is not verifiable by the senses) is to be affirmed as meaningful.

The idols of the theater are philosophical systems. These idols are neither innate (like the idols of the tribe) nor inevitable (like the idols of the tribe, cave, and marketplace) but are drawn up at will according to certain principles and demonstrations. He divides these systems into three groups: the sophistical or rational school (those who from the experience of a few facts spin out complete theories), the empirical school (those who experiment in one area thoroughly and then apply their findings to all other areas), and the superstitious school (those who mix theology with philosophy to the destruction of natural science).[15] Aristotle would be an example of the first, Democritus and the atomists examples of the second, and Aquinas an example of the third. Bacon's short answer to refuting these schools is simply to say that, since he disagrees with them on principles and method, there is no basis for rational debate. "To attempt refutations in this case would be merely inconsistent with what I have already said, for since we agree neither upon principles nor upon demonstrations there is no place for argument."[16]

According to Bacon, each of these philosophical schools is inadequate to the advancement of science and technology. The rational or sophistical

13. This interest in language and how it affects thought is picked up by Hobbes and Locke and becomes a continuing concern for the British empirical tradition to this day.

14. This is not a new idea. Thomas Aquinas insists that, although we have a word "God," we do not know what God is, only that he exists (*Summa theologiae* 1, prologue to Q. 2).

15. *New Organon*, bk. 1, aphorism 62, pp. 59–60.

16. Ibid., bk. 1, aphorism 61, p. 58. In some sense Bacon is right: a system is essentially bound up with its principles and method. For this reason, as I mentioned in the introduction, this work focuses on an examination of principles and methods when analyzing and comparing theories. However, unlike Bacon, I think that comparison can be made between theories that differ in principles. This is done in two ways: first, by examining the internal coherence and consistency of the theories, and second, by seeing the degree to which the theories support or violate those self-evident aspects of human experience that it would be absurd to deny. My contention is that Bacon's principles and method, although appropriate for addressing scientific questions about the material world, are dismally inadequate when applied to other dimensions of human experience, such as ultimate questions about reality (metaphysics), questions about morality, or questions about beauty.

school moves too quickly from data to generalizations about the causes governing the data. The empirical school dwells deeply on the data in one small area, but then tries to apply principles of causality drawn from that area to all reality. Thus, it also moves too quickly to general principles. However, by far the worst kind of philosophical school is the superstitious. At least the first two schools begin with sense experience and move from there to general principles. The superstitious school borrows principles from faith that, by definition, are not drawn from natural reason at all. Whatever science is, it is not revelation, and the attempt to bring the two together spells disaster for both.

Bacon likens the three plausible philosophical theories—empirical, rational, and Bacon's—to the ant, the spider, and the bee, respectively. Bacon claims that his method combines what is best in the others while avoiding their shortcomings. Since the aphorism which presents this analogy is a fairly concise presentation of Bacon's method, I quote it in full here.

> Those who have handled sciences have been either men of experiment or men of dogmas. The men of experiment are like the ant, they only collect and use; the reasoners resemble spiders, who make cobwebs out of their own substance. But the bee takes a middle course: it gathers its material from the flowers of the garden and of the field, but transforms and digests it by a power of its own. Not unlike this is the true business of philosophy; for it neither relies solely or chiefly on the powers of the mind, nor does it take the matter which it gathers from natural history and mechanical experiments and lay it up in the memory whole, as it finds it, but lays it up in the understanding altered and digested. Therefore from a closer and purer league between these two faculties, the experimental and the rational (such has never yet been made), much may be hoped.[17]

Thus Bacon's solution to these idols of the mind is to restrict reason to what he calls interpretation of nature,[18] which is the study of material nature through hypothesis and verification, what we know as the scientific method. This is his "new organon," the new logic that will restore human knowledge to its original purity and bring prosperity to humanity. He compares this new logic with the old syllogistic logic of Aristotle.[19]

17. Ibid., bk. 1, aphorism 95, p. 93.
18. *Great Instauration*, p. 19. This is in opposition to the ancient philosophers' "anticipations of the mind."
19. Again, this idea that Aristotle holds logic to be the key to all knowledge—a kind of metascience—is clearly false. Although Aristotle thinks (sensibly) that true arguments must follow valid logical forms, he does not think that the various sciences (fields of knowledge) are derived from logic. Against this, Bacon holds that there is only one acceptable method for all fields of knowledge, and that is his interpretation of nature (scientific method).

In order to clarify his revolutionary method, Bacon says that his logic differs from Aristotle's logic in three ways: "in the end aimed at, in the order of demonstration, and in the starting point of the inquiry."[20] While he considers the end of the old logic (or philosophy in general, since Bacon sees logic as foundational) to be the overcoming of an opponent in argument, the purpose of his new logic is "to command nature in action."[21] Thus Bacon sees his logic as having a practical orientation. The old logic not only wastes time and intellectual talent but is also positively destructive (since it is the basis for disputes); the new logic will bring thinkers together in a cooperative venture to help mankind.

As to the order of demonstration, Bacon considers the old logic to be basically deductive even though, in collecting data, it is briefly inductive. Thus he allows that Aristotle does have a brief inductive stage in his logic as it is applied to physical things. Against this, the new logic is to be thoroughly inductive. Bacon's is a "form of induction which shall analyze experience and take it to pieces, and by a due process of exclusion and rejection lead to an inevitable conclusion."[22] As far as recommending greater patience in collecting data, Bacon's method seems eminently suitable for the empirical sciences. However, it is hard to understand how a science could be thoroughly inductive—just gathering and analyzing without drawing general conclusions. And in fact, Bacon himself complains that the empirical philosophers do not rise to general principles.

Lastly, Bacon proposes a different beginning for the sciences. Here he specifies three points of disagreement between his new method and the old logic. He complains about the drawbacks of the old logic: "first, the logicians borrow the principles of each science from the science itself; secondly, they hold in reverence the first notions of the mind; and lastly, they receive as conclusive the immediate informations of the senses, when well disposed."[23]

As to the first point, while the old logic assumes the principles of each science (assuming different principles for different sciences), Bacon proposes his method as a metascience that is somehow prior (or should be prior) to the others. "The true logic ought to enter the several provinces of science armed with a higher authority than belongs to the principles of those sciences themselves, and ought to call those putative principles to account until they are fully established."[24] This is a clever move. If the only way to establish acceptable principles is through the new method

20. *Great Instauration*, p. 19.
21. Ibid.
22. Ibid.
23. Ibid.
24. Ibid.

or metascience, then there cannot be distinct principles of any science that are not reducible to Bacon's "interpretation of nature." According to Bacon, only by adopting his method could one enter into the discussion of which method is appropriate to which science. On these grounds, Bacon's position is, of course, unassailable.

The second point concerns first principles of the mind. While the traditional logicians "hold in reverence the first notions of the mind," Bacon intends to consider these first notions of the mind all "suspect" until they have passed the test of the new logic. Thus something as basic and obvious as the law of noncontradiction (something cannot be and not be at the same time and in the same respect[25]) is to be challenged: if it cannot be empirically verified, it is not to be accepted. However, how one might challenge such a first principle is unclear. For to say that all notions must be subject to the new method is presumably *not* to say that such notions are not to be subject to the new method, and this is simply to follow the law of noncontradiction.[26]

Bacon's third point of disagreement with the beginnings of traditional logic concerns trusting the senses. While Aristotle and his followers hold that the senses, when well disposed (not sick or damaged or defective) provide accurate information, Bacon suspects the senses. Just as he distrusts the intellect, so he distrusts the senses. "The testimony and information of the sense has reference always to man, not to the universe; and it is a great error to assert that the sense is the measure of things."[27] All this is quite odd for an empirical philosopher who holds that all knowledge must come through the senses. We can begin to see the metamorphosis of Bacon's claim that his method would reestablish the commerce between the mind and things. For if all knowledge comes from the senses, and the senses are about man, not the things of the universe, then all knowledge must be about man, not the things of the universe.

Let us turn now to some of the ways that Bacon's method will restrict reason. As noted, Bacon is very clear on his limitation of legitimate

25. Formulated by Aristotle in *Metaphysics* 4.3.1005b19–21.

26. Fulton H. Anderson says that Bacon does not challenge the law of noncontradiction, that he is concerned only with showing that the content of the empirical sciences cannot be deduced from such a first principle (editor's introduction in *The New Organon and Related Writings*, p. xxiv). If this is all Bacon means, then Aristotle (and I) would agree. However, that is not what he says: "With regard to the first notions of the intellect, there is not one of the impressions taken by the intellect when left to go its own way, but I hold it as suspect and no way established until it has submitted to a new trial and a fresh judgment has been thereupon pronounced" (p. 21). Although in practice Bacon must honor the law of noncontradiction or be unintelligible, the fact that his radical empirical method does not allow for it (since such a law cannot be empirically verified) counts against his theory.

27. *Great Instauration*, p. 21.

human thought to the study of material things by the so-called scientific method of hypothesis and verification. He bemoans the fact that in natural history as it stands, there is "nothing duly investigated, nothing verified, nothing counted, weighed, or measured."[28] If things are not weighed and measured, then things are not known. Thus, Bacon restricts the legitimate activity of reason to mathematics and physics,[29] thereby denying the realm of traditional metaphysics (whose ultimate object is the first principle of being, which is not material), eliminating traditional morality (since moral norms are not susceptible to sense verification), and removing the possibility of an aesthetics in which beauty is an object of knowledge (since any universal criterion of beauty would also not be susceptible to sense verification).

In his new dispensation, natural philosophy replaces metaphysics as first philosophy, and his natural philosophy is to be understood as interpretation of nature, the analysis of matter in motion. "Matter rather than forms should be the object of our attention, its configuration and the changes of configuration, and simple action, the law of action or motion; for forms are figments of the human mind, unless you will call those laws of action forms."[30] Bacon accepts a restricted idea of forms, one familiar to the modern scientific mind: that is, he accepts the notion of universal laws or forces, but not the idea that individual things (such as daisies and dogs) have particular forms that serve as intrinsic principles of activity.[31] All talk about ultimate first causes, formal causes, or final causes is to be eliminated, being but the importation of superstitious philosophy.[32]

This, again, effectively does away with all metaphysical thought as well as all traditional moral thought (where virtues and self-evident precepts are held to be central) and any objective aesthetics. If we are not to speak of first causes, then we are not to speak of God or providence; if we are not to speak of final causes, then we are not to speak of the final end of mankind, the purpose of our being here, or the ideal standards toward which we ought to strive. If we are not to speak of forms, we must give up any discussion of the beautiful, for beauty, insofar as it is an object of reason, is found essentially in form (structures, integrity, proportion, unity).[33]

Bacon, however, is not primarily seeking scientific knowledge of the material world for its own sake. Behind his choice of the scientific method

28. *New Organon*, bk. 1, aphorism 98, p. 95.
29. *Great Instauration*, p. 279.
30. *New Organon*, bk. 1, aphorism 51, p. 53.
31. Thus today physicists speak of the four great forces (gravity, electromagnetism, the strong force, and the weak force) that are supposed to explain the things of the universe and their activities.
32. See *New Organon*, bk. 1, aphorism 65, p. 62.
33. Beauty will be discussed more fully in chapter 8.

as the sole path open to the human mind is a quest for technological progress, for the purpose of making nature serve the ends of mankind. "A way must be opened for the human understanding entirely different from any hitherto known, and other helps provided, in order that the mind may exercise over the nature of things the authority which properly belongs to it."[34] Technology ("the mechanical arts")[35] is his greatest interest. Speaking of his project, Bacon says: "I entreat men to believe that it is not an opinion to be held, but a work to be done; and to be well assured that I am laboring to lay the foundation, not of any sect or doctrine, but of human utility and power."[36]

Thus behind the move to make natural science the queen of the sciences is the more fundamental desire for technological progress—a practical end. But such a practical end (or moral imperative) cannot be justified by his method for two reasons. First, it precedes the method in importance. The method does not imply the end but serves the end. Second, as a universal norm or ideal, his method cannot be verified in any collection of data, however extensive. Here Bacon's system strains to accommodate an area of reason that his method effectively rules out—the realm of the good and of obligation.

How does Bacon's revolutionary theory affect his moral thought in practice? This is hard to say, since Bacon wrote very little of an ethical nature. It belonged to his disciples to explain how such an application might be done.[37] However, he does say that the moral and political sciences are stagnant and lack depth[38] and that these sciences, too, ought to follow the new method.[39]

Of course there is, as we have mentioned, a moral presupposition at the root of his whole system: the goodness of improving human life. Technology is to serve humankind, to make lives better. Two things should be noted about this position. In the first place, the human life in question must be limited to our material existence; for with the abandonment of all formal, final, and first efficient causes, Bacon has ruled out the possibility of human goods such as wisdom and virtue, as well as the possibility that human beings transcend material influences (that is, are free). With no ultimate moral norms and no freedom of choice to pursue them, the project of creating an ethics looks pretty bleak. Second, and more destructive of the consistency of his project as a whole, it is hard

34. *Great Instauration*, p. 7.
35. Ibid., p. 8.
36. Ibid., p. 16.
37. We shall discuss one of them (Hobbes) later in this chapter and others (Locke and Hume) in chapter 4.
38. *New Organon*, bk. 1, aphorism 80, p. 77.
39. Ibid., aphorism 127, p. 115.

to see how the moral obligation to improve human life can be derived from a study of matter in motion.

Just as the denial of final causality rules out morality as an object of reason, so the denial of formal causality rules out beauty as an object of reason. If Bacon is to have a philosophy of the beautiful, it will have to be a matter of sense or feeling only, for he restricts reason to the activities of collecting data and drawing up very general laws, while beauty concerns the individual thing. Formal structure, balance, unity: all the characteristics of a beautiful thing are incompatible with Bacon's theory of reason and his method. Consistent with his principles, Bacon has very little to say about beauty.

Bacon, indeed, is mostly concerned with practical matters, and he recognizes that beauty is not about practicality. Thus he notes that the beauty of a building is clearly secondary in importance to its function. "Houses are built to live in, not to look on; therefore let use be preferred before uniformity, except where both may be had. Leave the goodly fabrics of houses, for beauty only, to the enchanted palaces of the poets; who build them with small cost."[40]

Nor is the appreciation of beauty an activity of reason (which is reserved for the sciences). Rather, beauty is a function of the imagination.[41] Bacon holds that poetry and the arts are more a matter of chance than of rules. "There is no excellent beauty that hath not some strangeness in the proportion."[42] Although Bacon is right that there is something undefinable and unique about a beautiful thing, it is the "strangeness" in the context of order and proportion (not just strangeness itself) that makes a thing beautiful. Elsewhere he writes that poetry is more a matter of instinct or emotion than of reason. "For being as a plant that cometh of the lust of the earth, without a formal seed, it hath sprung up and spread abroad more than any other kind. But to ascribe unto it that which is due, for the expressing of affections, passions, corruptions, and customs, we are beholding to poets more than to the philosophers' works; and for wit and eloquence not much less than to orators' harangues."[43] Bacon is a source of the distinctively modern idea that what makes art good is its introduction of something new.[44] This indeed is of a piece with his emphasis on progress.

40. Essay 45, "Of Building," in *Essays or Counsels Civil and Moral*, in *Selected Writings*, p. 114.
41. *Of the Proficience and Advancement of Learning*, pt. 2, in *Selected Writings*, p. 230.
42. Essay 43, "Of Beauty," in *Essays or Counsels*, in *Selected Writings*, p. 112.
43. *Of the Proficience and Advancement of Learning*, pt. 2, in *Selected Writings*, pp. 246–47.
44. This idea will be taken up by Nietzsche and Hegel (to be discussed in chapters 5 and 6, respectively) and again by Whitehead (to be discussed in chapter 7).

Bacon says little about beauty in nature. Indeed, to do so would be incompatible with his rejection of intrinsic form and with his ideal of conquering nature. Of course, we could take pleasure in various sights and sounds in nature as well as in painting and music, but this appreciation would be, like pleasure, merely subjective. Bacon does include beauty in his practical scheme by suggesting that it is good for us to exercise the imagination, perhaps for reasons of general health. But the idea of beauty as appreciated for its own sake is completely foreign to his thought.

Descartes

Across the English Channel, René Descartes heard Bacon's call for a practical solution to the problems facing mankind. Although Descartes is thought to be the beginning of the rationalist school and Bacon (for all his protestations of uniting the rational and empirical) the source of the empirical, they are surprisingly alike in the general direction of their thought. Like Bacon, Descartes complains of the disputatious and useless education taught in the universities. And like Bacon, he seems to see human reason as naturally bound to drift in a bad direction—ultimately into skepticism. In his *Discourse*, he writes of his own drift in that direction.[45] Unhappy with the education he has received, he finds himself full of doubts. The time is right for introducing the proper rational method, one that will set all knowledge on a firm foundation.

Descartes' purpose, like Bacon's, is to help mankind by opening a new way to progress.[46] And like Bacon, the way is through following a new method to correct the infirmity of the human mind. The full title of his work is *Discourse on the Method of Rightly Conducting One's Reason and of Seeking Truth in the Sciences*. In it he introduces treatises on optics, geometry, and meteorology. In the *Discourse*, reason is primarily viewed as a technique for getting somewhere; thus the idea of a useful tool is built into Descartes' as well as Bacon's conception of reason. Studies are commended insofar as they are useful: languages and morals are useful;[47] mathematics is useful.[48]

Although he does not go as far as Bacon in explicitly equating utility and truth,[49] Descartes does judge thinking according to its effects. "It

45. René Descartes, *Discourse on the Method of Rightly Conducting One's Reason and of Seeking Truth in the Sciences*, pt. 1, trans. Donald A. Cress (Indianapolis and Cambridge: Hackett, 1980).
46. *Discourse*, pt. 1, p. 2.
47. Ibid., pt. 1, p. 3.
48. Ibid., pt. 1, p. 4.
49. Bacon, *New Organon*, bk. 1, aphorism 124, p. 114.

seemed to me that I could discover much more truth in the reasonings that each person makes concerning matters that are important to him, whose outcome ought to cost himself dearly later on if he has judged incorrectly, than in those reasonings that a man of letters makes in his private room, which touch on speculations producing no effect. . . ."[50] Descartes' purpose is to replace the speculative science of the schools with a practical one that will make us "masters and possessors of nature."[51] Although there is a good deal of theoretical discussion about the metaphysical topics of the soul and God in Descartes' work (for which discussion he is most famous), it is subservient to practical purposes, to the sciences and the technological advances that they will bring.[52]

However, although Descartes and Bacon share the same practical purposes in their projects, their models for achieving this purpose differ significantly. For Descartes, the paradigmatic science is mathematics, for it has the clarity and distinctness necessary to overcome skepticism. Just as Bacon allows mathematics a role in his philosophical method, so Descartes allows a place for experiment. However, the ways they blend these two features of scientific method differ radically. Bacon names his paradigmatic science "the interpretation of nature," and it involves a patient empirical study of nature, moving to general laws only very slowly and almost as a last resort (since laws of any sort conjure up the idea of formal causality, which Bacon thinks is, in its common meaning, a fictitious idea). Descartes, on the other hand, thinks that the true principles of all knowledge are innate—even the knowledge of the material world. In the same way that geometrical knowledge is deduced from axioms, so all human knowledge is deductive, at least in principle. "All things of human knowledge follow in the same way as geometrical deduction."[53] This is the reason (at least in the scientific view of Descartes) that Descartes needs God in his system: he requires a first principle perfect enough to be the principle from which all actuality is deduced.[54]

50. *Discourse*, pt. 1, p. 5.
51. Ibid., pt. 6, p. 33.
52. Ultimately, his practical purpose is to find a science of medicine that will ensure "the maintenance of health, which unquestionably is the first good and the foundation of all the other goods in this life" (*Discourse*, pt. 6, p. 33). "I have resolved to spend my remaining lifetime only in trying to acquire a knowledge of nature which is such that one could deduce from it rules for medicine that are more certain than those in use at present" (*Discourse*, pt. 6, p. 41).
53. *Discourse*, pt. 2, p. 10.
54. There is the famous remark of Pascal on this point: "I cannot forgive Descartes. In all his philosophy he would have been quite willing to dispense with God. But he had to make Him give a fillip to set the world in motion; beyond this, he has no further need of God" (Blaise Pascal, *Pensées*, 77, trans. W. F. Trotter [New York: E. P. Dutton, 1931], p. 23).

Let us trace very briefly the underpinnings of Descartes' science. As he wishes to meet the challenges of skepticism, Descartes begins with radical doubt. What he discovers is that, even if he is unsure about everything, he at least knows with certainty that he exists; for in order to doubt, he must exist. Hence, he arrives at his famous *cogito, ergo sum* (I think, therefore I am).[55] No matter what arguments the skeptics offer, I at least know that I exist. I cannot even doubt whether I exist without existing. But if all that I can be sure of is that I doubt and therefore exist, then all I can be sure of is that I am a thinking thing.

What else do I, as a thinking thing, know? I know that I am imperfect, for if I were perfect, I would not be in doubt. However, one can judge that something falls short only if one knows the standard. Therefore, I have an idea of perfection. Since neither I (the imperfect doubter) nor any other limited being can be the cause of this idea of infinite perfection, the source of this idea must be the infinitely perfect God. Thus Descartes proves the existence of God.[56]

How does knowing that God exists help me to know the world? Since I know God to be perfect, I now know that God cannot be a deceiver. Thus whatever I know with certainty, that is, with the same kind of clarity and distinctness present in knowing that I exist as a thinking thing, must be true. Matter understood as an object of mathematics (that is, as extension) is such an object. For I find innumerable ideas in my mind which are not the same as the mind itself and which are not simple modes of thought since they come to me against my will. When I open my eyes, I cannot help but see pen and paper, table, window, trees, etc. Therefore, since God as perfect does not deceive me, I know that there are some things besides myself and God, which can be understood mathematically, that is, as extension in motion.[57] Although experiments are useful for corroboration, all scientific knowledge can theoretically be deduced from the above principles.

55. Descartes, *Discourse*, pt. 4, p. 17. Nagel thinks that Descartes' *cogito* is a bastion for realism, "a limit to the kind of self-criticism that begins when one looks at oneself from the outside and considers the ways in which one's convictions might have been produced by causes which fail to justify or validate them" (*The Last Word*, p. 19). Although Nagel interprets the *cogito* in this way, he is critical of Descartes for entertaining the radical doubt which Nagel thinks is contradictory; for ultimately, there is no good reason to doubt reason.

56. See Descartes, *Discourse*, pt. 4, pp. 18–19, and the third meditation in *Meditations on First Philosophy*, trans. Donald Cress (Indianapolis: Hackett, 1983), pp. 28–30. There are two other proofs of God's existence which he presents in the *Meditations*, one later in the third meditation and the other in the fifth meditation.

57. See the sixth meditation in *Meditations*, pp. 49–50. The laws of motion will be better developed by Newton in the next century.

Descartes' metaphysical view, which is more fully developed in his *Meditations on First Philosophy*, seems to offer the possibility for both an ethics and an aesthetics since it places the immaterial reality of thought at the center of things. Descartes' theory, indeed, allows for a serious discussion of the traditional objects of metaphysics, God and the soul.[58] These he treats as prior to and better known than physical things. Hence Descartes' philosophy seems to offer the possibility of an intelligible ethics, for freedom of choice is possible (given that the soul is a distinct substance from the body and therefore is not subject to the determination of physical laws), and there is a transcendent object of choice (God) which moves us by its intelligibility, not by its physical attractiveness. An intelligible aesthetics would also seem possible, given that there is a locus of intelligent appreciation and free creativity—the mind.

How does Descartes actually relate his new method to other traditional areas of reason? Like Bacon, Descartes sees his new method as applicable to all areas of reason. Just as geometrical method had helped Descartes to combine algebra and geometry, he thinks it can be "applied just as profitably to the other sciences."[59]

Apparently this applies to ethics as well. Like Bacon, Descartes disparages the moral writings of the ancients: "I compared the writings of the ancient pagans who discuss morals to very proud and magnificent palaces that are built on nothing but sand and mud. They place virtues on a high plateau and make them appear to be valued more than anything else in the world, but they do not sufficiently instruct us about how to know them."[60] Evidently Descartes hopes that his new method will help us know what virtues are. In fact, he refers in one place to governing his moral conduct by means of the reason that his method taught him.[61] However, like Bacon, Descartes never gets to a discussion of morals. He adopts as provisional the morals of his society and church in part 3 of the *Discourse* and never revisits the issue. Just how ethics might be a deductive science is left to his disciples to develop. We shall revisit the issue in chapter 5.[62]

It seems that Descartes' principles would permit him to develop some kind of philosophical account of beauty. Since formal cause is central to Descartes' method (I am a thinking thing) and since form (structure, proportion, integrity) is essential to an explication of what makes something beautiful, Descartes has a better chance than Bacon of developing

58. The full title of Descartes' work is *Meditations on First Philosophy: In which the Existence of God and the Distinction of the Soul from the Body Are Demonstrated*.

59. *Discourse*, pt. 2, p. 12.

60. Ibid., pt. 1, p. 4.

61. Ibid., pt. 6, p. 33.

62. Spinoza, in particular, will apply Descartes' method of geometry to ethics.

a meaningful aesthetics. However, he says very little about beauty. Perhaps, as in Bacon's case, this is due to his fundamentally practical concern. However, this is not all that stands in his way. Given his deductive method, it seems that he would not be able to account for the particular beautiful thing (flower, landscape, painting, musical composition) in all its particular concreteness. Indeed, Descartes does not speak of beauty in either the *Discourse* or the *Meditations*.

When he does speak of beauty in a letter to his friend Mersenne in 1630, Descartes dismisses any kind of notion that beauty is objective. "Neither the beautiful nor the pleasant signifies anything other than the attitude of our judgment to the object in question."[63] Descartes goes on to say in this passage that the criterion for what makes good music is majority opinion. Thus beauty is subjective and relative, a matter of personal opinion and not based on objective criteria found in things. Again, this is compatible with Descartes' theory, for the reality of material things as it can be known objectively is merely quantitative extension in space according to principles of geometry. All qualities are added to things by the mind.

When it comes to speaking of the production of beauty or art, Descartes does so in a surprisingly mechanistic way. "I would say that this disposition to write verse stems from a powerful stimulus of organic impulses, one which might completely close off the imaginations of those whose brains are not well-balanced, but which in other cases merely warms the imagination and disposes it to poetry."[64] Beauty seems to be a function of our bodies, not our minds. Like Bacon, Descartes attributes the recognition of beauty to feeling and imagination rather than reason.

The fact that Descartes does not develop a genuine ethics or aesthetics should not be surprising. After all, the realm of the good (ethics) and the realm of the beautiful (aesthetics) are distinct areas of reason with their own first principles and appropriate methods. A metaphysics that is open to such developments because it allows for immaterial realities does not itself provide principles and method for those areas. This is especially true if the metaphysics is deductive, for it is hard to understand how the distinct characters of ethics and aesthetics can be deduced from the first principles of metaphysics. As distinct, the realms of the good and the beautiful have their own first principles and require their own methods.

However, not only does Descartes fail to develop a genuine ethics or aesthetics (thus neglecting the good and the beautiful), but his metaphys-

63. Descartes to Mersenne, March 18, 1630, in Wladyslaw Tatarkiewicz, *History of Aesthetics* (The Hague: Mouton, 1974), vol. 3, p. 373.
64. Descartes to Princesse Elizabeth of the Palatinate, February 22, 1649, in Tatarkiewicz, *History of Aesthetics*, vol. 3, p. 375.

ics itself fails; that is, he fails to give an adequate account of the realm of the true. In order to show the deep problems in Descartes' theory of the real, it is helpful to retrace the stages of his metaphysical deduction from self and God to the world, only in reverse.

The last major stage in the deduction is the proof of the existence of a material world of extended matter in motion. Recall that Descartes has recourse to a nondeceiving God as guarantor that his clear and distinct ideas about the physical world (as extension to be understood mathematically) really do apply to that world. Thus, his knowledge of the world depends on his knowledge of God. However, arguing from God to the world is never metaphysically legitimate for the simple reason that we do not know the nature of God. Given the standard notion of God as unlimited perfection (to which Descartes subscribes), it is clear that we cannot know God's essence, for our concepts must be, by definition, limited. Descartes himself seems to admit this when he says that he knows himself to be imperfect.

But, one might say, has not Descartes succeeded in proving the existence of a perfect God? If so, then it seems that we can know the nature of God and hence can deduce conclusions from that knowledge. However, even if Descartes' proofs for the existence of God are successful (I shall argue shortly that, given his presuppositions, they are not), to know that God exists is not the same as to know what God is. Just as one can know that something causes the tides to rise and fall without knowing the universal nature of gravity, so one can know that something is the cause of one's ideas without knowing the nature of that cause. And just as one cannot deduce truths about the relations of all material things simply from knowing that there must be a cause for the rise and fall of the tides (without understanding the nature of gravity), so one cannot deduce truths about the world of things simply by knowing that there is a perfect creating cause (without knowing the nature of the perfect God).

But again we might ask, as Descartes does, how one can know that one is imperfect without knowing perfection. It seems that to judge that something falls short of a standard, one must know the standard. Thus to judge that a pen is defective, one needs to know what a good pen would be. In other words, the effect that Descartes says needs to be explained is his idea of perfection. Since there must be as much in the cause as in the effect (since one cannot get more from less), the cause of this idea must itself be perfect.

There are three critical points to be made here. In the first place, judging something to be defective does not require an absolute standard. One does not need to know what a perfect pen would be to know that this blotting one is imperfect. So also, one does not need to know the nature of perfection in itself (God) to judge that one is imperfect. Merely to know oneself as limited in some way is enough.

In the second place, given that all Descartes knows is himself, he does not have the basis for knowing himself to be imperfect. To judge something as imperfect, one must have some knowledge of what more perfect and less perfect mean. This does not seem such a problem if one takes a commonsense view of reality: birds are more perfect than flowers, which are more perfect than mud, and I am more perfect than any of them. But this simple source is not available to Descartes. This is where his method distorts irrevocably his metaphysics. Recall that Descartes knows only that he thinks and therefore exists. Knowing only the self, he has no means of comparing levels of perfection. Indeed, if one recognizes that things are more or less perfect, one can argue to the need for a cause of what they have in common—perfection. But by the terms of Descartes' method of radical doubt, he does not know things as more or less perfect. He knows only that he exists. Hence he cannot even conclude to the existence of an absolutely perfect being, never mind to its essence.

But there is more. Even to know that he thinks, Descartes must refer to something other than himself, and this for two reasons. In the first place, the notion of self is meaningless unless there is something else. One becomes aware of oneself as a self only in relation to another. If there were no other (if all were really just the mind), one would not be aware of having a self. In the second place, knowing that one is think-ing is a second act of the mind. One can know that one knows only if knowing is already going on, and knowing always requires something to be known. To begin with "I think, therefore I am" and then reason to the rest of reality is logically out of order. Thinking of one's thinking is a second act of the mind, an act of reflection. But this second act of the mind logically presupposes a first act of the mind, some interaction between the mind and world.[65] Self-awareness presupposes a process of thought that is already going on—doubting the senses, entertaining the idea that we might be dreaming—which process is a reflection on one's relations to other things.[66]

Thus Descartes gets his starting point wrong. Instead of "I think, therefore I am," it should be "the world of which I am a part is, there-fore I think." Even doubting presupposes my existing in a world. Far from the world of existing things being a deduction from my existence

65. On the two acts of the mind, see Thomas Aquinas, *Summa theologiae* 1.87.1.

66. One might say that Descartes is merely following Augustine here, who argues against the skeptics that there is at least one truth for one who is deceived—the truth that one is deceived and so must exist (*City of God* 11.26). But in affirming this truth, Augustine does not presuppose the impossible task of putting everything out of his mind.

and the existence of God, it is a prerequisite for my awareness of my existence (knowing that I know) and for any legitimate argument for the existence of God.

This brings us to the context for Descartes' momentous discovery of the *cogito*—his radical doubt. Despite what Descartes (also Bacon) says, there are no good reasons to doubt reason, and there are no reasons to doubt the trustworthiness of the senses. Obviously, one cannot settle (or even entertain) the doubt about reason without using reason. But if one is not confident about reason, how can one trust any insight—even the *cogito*? Nor is the idea that the senses are intrinsically flawed any more plausible. If they are flawed, we cannot know that they are. Consider the kinds of arguments raised by Descartes against the senses (e.g., that a square tower looks round in the distance or that the sun appears to be the size of a coin). The mistake can easily be shown to be not a deception of the senses but a failure to apply our reason properly. It can be shown that over distance, the atmosphere affects the way light travels. This is why the tower looks round. And since the sun is so far away (93 million miles), to the naked eye it looks to be the size of a coin. How, indeed, will one correct the senses if in doubt? One must go up closer and examine the tower with one's senses, or read a delicate instrument: at some point the senses must be trusted. We do not need the guarantee of a nondeceiving God for this.

Logically, if one were seriously to doubt reason and the senses, such doubt could never be overcome; for the sole means we have of affirming reality are the senses and the intellect. If these are no help, there is no help: the twin absurdities of solipsism (self alone) and skepticism (nothing can be known) are inevitable.

Perhaps the most serious problem for Bacon and Descartes is the apparent inability of their methods to justify the responsibility they impose on themselves to benefit mankind and their expectation that others ought to help them complete their self-appointed tasks. The idea that we have a universal obligation to promote the common good is not an empirically verifiable fact. As universal, it cannot be derived from particular bits of data. Thus Bacon's method must fail to provide foundations for moral obligation. With Descartes' method, there is at least room for the possibility of universal obligation since Descartes holds that there are immaterial realities (God and the soul) which, like moral absolutes, are not verifiable by scientific method. However, how specific obligations might be derived from the idea of God or from God's guarantee of the truth of what one knows clearly and distinctly to be the case is hard to say. Even less clear is how Descartes' deductive method can give us the specific circumstances of a situation (an essential ingredient in making a specific moral judgment).

Thus neither Bacon nor Descartes successfully accounts for ethical obligation. However, since neither took explicit interest in moral philosophy, perhaps our judgment on the insufficiency of their methods and principles for grounding morality is premature. Perhaps if we consider the philosophy of Hobbes, who is influenced by the ideas of Bacon and Descartes and also focuses explicitly on ethical and political matters, we shall find a solution to the problem of how obligation can be derived from the methods of science.

Hobbes

In Thomas Hobbes we find someone who has intimate connections with both Bacon and Descartes, who shares their enthusiasm for the new science, and who has an explicit interest in moral and political matters. Perhaps some of the questions about ethics left unanswered by Bacon and Descartes will be addressed and put to rest by Hobbes. Hobbes was connected personally as well as philosophically with Bacon. As Bacon's sometime amanuensis, he inherited Bacon's disdain for Aristotelianism and Catholicism as well as Bacon's conviction that only what is empirically verifiable is real. With Descartes, Hobbes embraces the ideal of using the method of geometrical deduction.[67] Hobbes was also influenced, as were Bacon and Descartes, by Galileo, whom he met on a trip to Italy in 1634–1637. Following Galileo's lead, Hobbes attempts to explain everything in terms of matter in motion ordered by geometrical deduction.

Beyond having a common interest in geometry and a common influence in Galileo, Hobbes and Descartes were intimately connected by philosophical debate. In book 6 of the *Discourse*, Descartes solicited objections to the metaphysical underpinnings of his new science. These objections and his replies were attached to Descartes' *Meditations*, which was an expanded version of the metaphysical principles of the *Discourse*. Hobbes's contribution forms the third set of objections. It is instructive and rather entertaining to read the debate between the two philosophers, for they utterly fail to connect on principles. Although he agrees with Descartes on the ideal of geometrical deduction as science, Hobbes disagrees with Descartes on the nature of reality. Hobbes begins with matter in motion: he is an avowed materialist and mechanist.[68] Descartes

67. In his *Brief Lives*, Aubrey tells of Hobbes's reading of Euclid's *Elements*, which "made him in love with Geometry." *Aubrey's Brief Lives*, ed. O. L. Dick (London: Secher and Warburg, 1950), p. 18.

68. Hobbes is clearly influential on the line of continental materialism, which moves from the Encyclopaedists of the Enlightenment (La Mettrie, Diderot, and d'Holbach) through the positivism of Auguste Comte (1798–1857).

begins with the immaterial realities of mind and God and counts these to be most real. True enough, when Descartes gets to material reality, his theory is nearly identical to Hobbes's mechanistic materialism: Descartes holds that the human body and animals are machines.[69] But Descartes holds that there are two distinct substances, mind and body, while Hobbes holds that there is only one: body.

As with Bacon and Descartes, Hobbes finds the world in trouble, and the ultimate purpose of his proposal (like theirs) is practical. Hobbes notes that the current education leads to nothing but endless disputations about the meaning of words. Like Bacon and Descartes, Hobbes decries the Aristotelians and their scholastics followers, holding with Bacon that their systems of philosophy are full of insignificant words.[70] This explains not only the lack of all progress in the sciences, but also the lack of progress in ethics and political thought. Application of the scientific method to the data will end the debate and open the doors to new discoveries in all fields of study.

> To conclude, the light of human minds is perspicuous words, but by exact definitions first snuffed, and purged from ambiguity; reason is the pace; increase of science the way, and the benefit of mankind, the end. And on the contrary, metaphors, and senseless and ambiguous words, are like *ignes fatui*; and reasoning upon them, is wandering among innumerable absurdities; and their end, contention, and sedition, or contempt.[71]

Like Bacon and Descartes, Hobbes believes that the principle cause for the confusion is lack of a proper method. The philosophy of the schools, dealing as it does with universal truths, is meaningless; for there is "nothing in the world universal but names."[72] Hobbes inherits this nominalism (the idea that things are not universally related in reality but only in name) from Bacon. Also like Bacon and Descartes, he is skeptical about the value of book-learning in general, and he specifically rejects the authorities of Aristotle, Cicero, and Aquinas.[73] All one needs for success is the geometrical method and the common sense natural to us all. Geometry is "the only science that it has pleased God hitherto to bestow on mankind."[74] Thus all valid knowledge must be deduced from

69. *Discourse*, pt. 5.
70. Thomas Hobbes, *Leviathan*, pt. 1, ch. 4, ed. C. B. Macpherson (London: Penguin, 1985), p. 101.
71. Ibid., pt. 1, ch. 5, pp. 116–17. For ease of reading, I have normalized the spelling used by Hobbes and followed by Macpherson.
72. Ibid., pt. 1, ch. 4, p. 102. Hobbes follows a long tradition of English nominalism going back to William of Ockham, which we shall discuss briefly in chapter 2.
73. Ibid., pt. 1, ch. 4, p. 106.
74. Ibid., pt. 1, ch. 4, p. 105.

first principles which, for Hobbes, are those of Galileo and Bacon: matter in motion. Unlike Bacon's empiricism, however, Hobbes's is strictly mechanical. Whereas Bacon warns against jumping to conclusions about the order of matter in motion, Hobbes insists that all can be explained, in principle, deductively. While there are mysterious principles of action in Bacon that leave scientific knowledge open to further qualifications and progress,[75] for Hobbes, all is determined according to mechanical laws.

The theme of power, stressed by Bacon and Descartes in terms of technological progress for the domination of nature, rises to the position of first principle for Hobbes. Everything is reducible to the effects of power, from the origins of sensation and thought in the power of matter in motion affecting our senses,[76] to the political community in which "justice" is whatever the sovereign power says it is.[77]

Our sensations are caused by external particles in motion setting particles moving in us, and all our thoughts are merely copies of our sensations. Following Galileo, Hobbes holds that all qualities are nothing but matter in motion; ideas of different kinds of things, either known by the senses or understood by the mind, are fictions. "All which qualities called sensible, are in the object that causes them, but so many several motions of the matter, by which it presses our organs diversely. Neither in us that are pressed, are they anything else, but divers motions (for motion produces nothing but motion)."[78] All is to be explained by Galileo's laws of motion. Under such laws, interactions are to be understood in mechanical terms, and just as the motion of a ball moved by a boy is separate from the boy, so sensation in us is separate in time and space from the motion in the object sensed. The implication of such a model is that we cannot know for certain the relationship between a sense impression and the object that caused it.

Even more radical are the implications for thought. If motion produces nothing but motion, then our understanding of the material universe is nothing but a certain kind of motion. But since what is in motion changes through time and space, no insights or judgments can be affirmed across time, nor can any thoughts be universal. Only particular things exist: universals are just words. This position is somewhat problematic, for Hobbes is claiming to lay out for us a true, and hence universal, theory. If, however, his theory is taken with all its implications, it can have no meaning (since meaning, as universal and unchanging, cannot be ex-

75. This made Bacon's thought attractive to Whitehead, whose position we shall discuss in chapter 7.
76. *Leviathan*, pt. 1, ch. 1, p. 85.
77. Ibid., pt. 1, ch. 18, p. 234.
78. Ibid., pt. 1, ch. 1, p. 86

plained by particular matter in motion), nor are we free to accept or not accept it (since our choices themselves are mere reactions to external actions of matter in motion).

How does Hobbes's method apply to the other realms of reason—the good and the beautiful? Following the suggestion of Bacon that the new method should apply to all sciences, Hobbes extends his theory of matter in motion to the realms of ethics and politics. Since motivation is traceable to the original motions of external matter on our senses, it can be explained, in theory, as one more instance of mechanism. Since fear and the self-interested desire for protection seem to be basic to human existence, Hobbes treats these as the most real of human motivations. And because they are the most natural and basic of our motivations, Hobbes will, in good geometrical method, deduce all other motivations from these. As power is the way to guarantee our protection, the search for power underlies all action.

Although we may use terms of moral obligation and virtue that seem to transcend this basic motivation, they are all reducible to the search for power. Power is the measure of everything, from the physical level to the moral level. Even the value of a human being is equivalent to the value of the use of his power.[79] All virtue is reducible to power: "*Honourable* is whatsoever possession, action, or quality, is an argument and sign of Power. . . . Magnanimity, Liberality, Hope, Courage, Confidence, are honourable; for they proceed from the conscience of Power."[80] Thus for Hobbes the moral question becomes how best to maximize one's power so as to get what one wants. This may involve compromise with others, but only if the compromise is likely to benefit one in the long run.

Hobbes does insist that some natural laws apply to us all. These are based on our knowledge of self. "Whosoever looks into himself, and considers what he does when he does think, opine, reason, hope, fear, etc., and upon what grounds; he shall thereby read and know, what are the thoughts, and passions of all other men, upon the like occasions."[81] One must beware, however, of granting to Hobbes's natural laws any of the moral absolutes (i.e., exceptionless moral norms) found in what is commonly known as the natural law tradition of ethics stemming from Plato and Aristotle and continuing through Cicero to Augustine and Aquinas. Rather, Hobbes's most basic natural laws merely take seriously the implications of being motivated by a desire to get power. His first law concerns the power to survive: we should seek peace if available or fight if it is not. The second shows us how to reach this peace: lay down one's

79. Ibid., pt. 1, ch. 10, p. 151.
80. Ibid., p. 155.
81. Ibid., pt. 1, ch. 1, p. 82.

arms and enter a social contract (compromise) if and only if others are willing to do the same. Thus a community (social contract) comes into being. The third law provides for keeping the peace: one must honor one's covenants.[82] Basically, reason, as it applies to morality, is a technique for getting what one wants. In Hobbes's mind, such a technique leads ultimately to peace: if only we would be consistently self-interested, moral and political problems would be at an end.

However, with the third of his natural laws, Hobbes runs into trouble with consistency; for it is not at all clear that keeping one's covenants or promises is always an act of self-interest. If one calculates that power can be maximized by breaking one's covenants, then according to Hobbes's mechanism, one will do so—end of story. If one says (as I think Hobbes meant to say on a deeper level) that one *should not* break one's covenants because it would endanger the common good, then one must hold the obligation to promote the common good (and not just self-interest) to be a principle of morality. It seems clear that such an ethical principle is behind Hobbes's entire enterprise: he wants to provide a resolution to the senseless killing and cruelty of the English Civil War (as well as to provide a universal way of resolving other wars). This is indeed a noble cause, but it is not derivable from the mechanics of matter in motion, or from the mediate principle of acting always from self-interest.

Given the parameters Hobbes has set for explanation (geometrical deduction applied to matter in motion), he cannot legitimately conclude to moral obligation. If obligation is to be binding, it must be universal, and Hobbes begins by insisting that only particular matter in motion is real. This problem is not unique to Hobbes: anyone who tries to derive ethics by scientific method is doomed to fail. This is because the principles of moral obligation are not derivable from principles of theoretical reason, whether these principles be logical, scientific, or even metaphysical. Thus Hobbes's project, while explicitly addressed to moral and political questions, fails to justify the insight of Bacon and Descartes that the methods of science (mathematics, empirical study, or a combination of the two) can be successfully applied as universal methods. There is simply no way to derive moral obligation from premises about what is true or false, whether these be empirical or mathematical.

David Hume will make this very clear when he objects to the practice of modulating from "is" statements to "ought" statements in philosophical arguments.[83] Hume's insight is based on the simple rule of logic that it is illegitimate to have more in the conclusion than is contained in the

---

82. For the first three laws, see ibid., pt. 1, ch. 14 and 15, pp. 189–208.

83. David Hume, *Treatise*, bk. 3, pt. 1, sec. 1, ed. L. A. Selby-Bigge, 2nd ed., revised by P. H. Nidditch (Oxford: Clarendon, 1978), pp. 468–69. Hume's thought will be discussed in more depth in chapter 4.

premises. If all one's premises are mathematical or scientific truths about the way things *are*, then no valid conclusions can be drawn about the way things *ought to be*. Essential to ethics is insight into the good as what *ought* to be promoted and not violated. If there are no first principles of obligation, then there can be no conclusions of obligation. The move by Bacon, Descartes, and Hobbes to make scientific method foundational for all knowledge ensures their inability to handle moral questions successfully. Such a method can handle only the technical and hence incidental aspects of moral questions (means to end analysis, tabulation of consequences). The heart of morality (obligation and intention) is simply outside the ken of science; "justice" is really just a name, a meaningless universal that cannot be verified by sense experience.

About beauty, Hobbes says very little, even less than Bacon or Descartes. He does call beauty "the good in the promise,"[84] sounding a bit like Bacon by suggesting that beauty is not real but a projection of the imagination, something new to come. As may be expected, Hobbes deduces the production of beauty in art from experience. "Time and Education beget Experience; Experience begets Memory; Memory begets Judgment and Fancy; Judgment begets the strength and structure, and Fancy begets the Ornament of a Poem."[85] Prior to "Time and Education," one should read in Hobbes's other stages explaining the origin of sensation that we have noted. Ultimately all is traced back to matter in motion. Thus the appreciation of beauty and the production of art are equally necessary products of matter in motion (as are all things, even thought and choice). As moral obligation is reduced to matter in motion, so are aesthetic appreciation and creativity. Any idea of value as something freely to be pursued (morality) or appreciated (aesthetics) is systematically excluded from Hobbes's mechanistic materialism.

The fact is, none of our three thinkers says much about beauty. In some ways this is rather odd, for both Plato and the modern scientists influenced by him—Copernicus and Kepler—consider order, harmony, and beauty to be fundamental to reality. Plato identifies it with the Good, which is the source of all reality, and the scientists refer to the beauty of creation stirring them on to more perfect explanations of reality.[86]

84. *Leviathan*, pt. 1, ch. 6, p. 49.
85. Hobbes, "The Answer to Davenant, 1650," in Tatarkiewicz, *History of Aesthetics*, vol. 3, p. 381.
86. For Plato's identification of the beautiful with the good, see *Republic* 5.452e and *Symposium* 201c. Copernicus speaks of growing "disgusted that no more certain theory of the motions of the mechanism of the universe, which has been established for us by the best and most systematic craftsman of all, was agreed by philosophers. . ." (Nicolaus Copernicus, *On the Revolutions of the Heavenly Spheres*, trans. A. M. Duncan [New York: Barnes & Noble, 1976], p. 25). Kepler speaks of the harmony created by the artisan (Johannes Kepler, *The Harmonies of the World*, bk. 5, ch. 9, trans. Charles Glenn Wallis in

Two reasons for such a lacuna come readily to mind. First, the impetus for all three of our philosophers' positions is practical, and beauty is anything but practical. Beauty is to be appreciated for its own sake. Science for its own sake is closer to the notion of beauty than science for the sake of technology to improve human material well-being. Second, all three philosophers begin with the self, if not explicitly like Descartes, then at least in the sense that method is primary and is the lens through which we consider reality. Things are to be accepted, not on their own terms (an essential characteristic of beautiful things), but on the terms of the method. Thus, although it is true than none of our philosophers speaks of beauty in any detail, it is also true that, given their presuppositions, it would seem to be impossible that any should be able to speak of beauty as distinct from the truth discovered by his method. Or if any would speak of beauty, it could not be in reference to reason, but would have to refer to imagination or feeling.

Costs of the Revolution

It is, perhaps, a bit hard for us to be startled by the idea of limiting reason to the operations of mathematics and the analysis of matter in motion (the scientific method). After all, the ascendancy of such a method has been a cultural constant for some three hundred years now. That such a move was made in the name of improving the lot of mankind through technology makes the move seem even less troubling, for who can object to making things better for others? However, when one examines what such a move rules out, the enormity of the revolution becomes apparent and, it seems to me, appalling.

The cost of such a revolution is most obvious in the case of Bacon and Hobbes, who insist on sense verification as the ultimate criterion for truth. It is true that both Bacon and Hobbes allow for mathematics, but they understand it as subserving physics. Hence, unlike Plato, they are not led by the universal and unchanging character of mathematical objects to ask questions about immaterial realities. In fact, their method logically excludes discussion of immaterial realities. For Bacon and Hobbes, reality is matter in motion.

Given this assumption, discussions of immaterial realities are meaningless. But if this is so, then not only can there be no traditional metaphysics (with its discussions of God and the soul); there also can be no intelligible ethics or aesthetics. Terms such as good, virtue, justice, and

Great Books of the Western World, 2nd ed., ed. Mortimer J. Adler [Chicago: Encyclopaedia Britannica, 1990]), vol. 15, pp. 1049–50).

beauty, since they are not verifiable by the senses, are meaningless, and freedom—a prerequisite for meaningful choice and artistic creation—is not possible. Since all that is real is material, and material things are determined according to laws of matter in motion, there is no real freedom. Thus ethics is impossible. Aesthetics as a meaningful discipline fares no better. Just as the denial of final causes rules out ethics, so also the denial of formal causes rules out aesthetics. According to the method of Bacon and Hobbes, any universal characteristics of beauty must be denied, and one is left with raw particularity. The principles of order and proportion that have traditionally been associated with the beautiful can have no place. Nor is there room for the freedom of the artist's conscious creativity. Our appreciation of beauty, if there is any, is reduced to a function of feeling and imagination.

While precluding metaphysical ideas such as God and the soul would not bother Bacon and Hobbes (in fact they are pleased to deny the philosophical meaningfulness of such words), nor would the denial of objective aesthetics, the impossibility of a normative ethics, at least, should give them pause. After all, one of the foundational reasons for searching for a new method was moral—the ideal of helping mankind. But this ideal is not susceptible to sense verification. Given the new method's account of reason, such a moral ideal is irrational. The same is true, ultimately, of all ideas, whether they be moral ideas such as friendship and justice, or aesthetic ideas such as beauty and integrated order, or metaphysical ideas such as God and the soul. Truth of any kind is ruled out since ultimately it must come down to meaning, and meaning is not material.

This last point is a real problem for the new method. If the method insists that truth is relative to the verification of matter in motion, then the judgment that the new method is the only way to truth cannot itself legitimately be said to be true; for it is an idea of proper procedure, not just matter in motion (some physical presence or force to be seen, touched, or otherwise verified). Or if it is just matter in motion, then it is meaningless. Thus not only metaphysics, aesthetics, and normative ethics must go, but also physical science as bringing truth—that precious commerce between the mind and things that Bacon so desires.

One might think that the method of Descartes can succeed where that of Bacon and Hobbes fails. Since Descartes' view of reality begins with immaterial things (the mind and God), the possibility of there being other realities irreducible to matter—such as virtue, justice, and beauty—is left open. However, Descartes' deductive derivation of the world from the mind and the idea of perfection (God) also fails.

In the first place, if we accept Descartes' deduction, we are left with a material world of mere extension. This is not a suitable object of aesthetic appreciation, for it lacks the particularity of intrinsic form. Appreciating beauty implies (objectively) particular things and (subjectively) sense and intellect. Although a meaningful aesthetics is out, the worldview of Descartes might allow for an ethics, for it seems that first principles of moral obligation are not gained through experience of things. However, although it seems possible that Descartes could develop an ethics based on self-evident first principles, he never does so.[87]

In the second place, Descartes' deduction is unacceptable in itself and hence cannot, under any circumstances, yield an objective ethics or aesthetics. Since we have (and can have) no concept of God, adopting geometrical analysis (a form of deduction) as a metaphysical method cannot work. If we claim to have a workable starting point (one that we can define), then we are not starting from God, for God is not a limited thing, subject to classification. Such a metaphysics spells the loss of God as ultimate cause and the loss of the world in its fullness. It spells the loss of God since we define something only by limiting it in some way. But a limited being is not what we mean by the word "God." It spells the loss of the world in its fullness because, if we deduce the world from a limited concept (and all concepts are limited), we shall end up with a world limited to fit our concept of its origin. Hence all the philosophical systems that claim to explain the world of things as deductions from a first principle begin by narrowing the possibilities of what the world could be like.

A legitimate metaphysics, such as that of Aristotle or Aquinas, always moves from effect (the world of things) to cause (God), never from cause (God) to effect (the world of things). The latter way is not open to us since we do not know *what* God is, but only *that* God is. It is possible to prove that God exists from unexplained elements of our experience that require an ultimate explanation or cause, but this knowledge of God's existence does not show us the essence of God. Such knowledge could come only through direct experience of God (which we do not have) or by deduction from some prior being. This latter way, of course, is not possible, given what we mean by the name we give to this ultimate cause "God." For if there is a prior being, then that would be what we mean by "God." In short, since we do not know the essence of God, we cannot make deductions from that essence: Descartes' deductive metaphysics from the perfection of God is impossible.

Neither the inductive/empirical method of Bacon and Hobbes nor the deductive/rationalistic method of Descartes can ground the obligation to serve mankind, nor can either establish that commerce between human beings and the world of things that both methods hope to establish. In

87. Spinoza's or Kant's ethics, which we shall discuss in chapters 5 and 6, respectively, are perhaps examples of such an ethics.

the end, the debate about whether the roots of our knowledge are empirical or rationalistic may not be important, for if both empiricists and rationalists doubt reason and the senses, then both are headed toward skepticism and solipsism. This is the most radical problem for all our thinkers as they try to correct the defects in sensation and reason with a new method. Beginning with the self (and a defective one at that), there is no way to get out of self to know anything about the world, one's friends, or beauty. This is the tyranny of method: by narrowing reason, it fails to do justice to the full range of intelligibility. As a lens invented to correct our vision of reality, it remakes reality in our own image.

Given the dramatic cost of restricting reason to scientific method and the ultimate absurdity of such a move, why was it made? How can one explain a choice that implies the ultimate denial of explanation and choice? In the next chapter we shall consider some of the influences, cultural and intellectual, that may have inspired our three thinkers (and with them the modern world) to move in such a dangerous direction.

2

Background to a Revolution

Since Bacon, Descartes, and Hobbes all believed that they were bringing some kind of salvation to humanity, it might be worthwhile to consider the troubled world they intended to save. Understanding the context and background of the "new ideas" introduced by Bacon, Descartes, and Hobbes may help us to see why such a philosophical revolution was deemed necessary. We may also find, in the event, that these "new ideas" were not always as brand-new as their proponents claimed but had, on the contrary, a rather extensive history in some quarters.[1]

As everybody knows, the world Bacon, Descartes, and Hobbes inhabited was one of multiple problems and new adventures. The old structures of authority were breaking down, in part as a moral response to abuses, but also due to a certain restlessness and impatience. Scientific discoveries and the recovery of some key ancient texts presented new challenges for the academic community. In addition, the discovery of the Americas, the Renaissance in literature and art, and the Reformation in religion all prompted changes of direction, and all of them were considered by their proponents to be real advances over what had been the status quo. In this chapter, we shall first consider the ways in which

1. The consideration here of this troubled world will be rather broad brush. Our purpose is not to settle difficult questions of historical scholarship, but merely to gain some perspective on why such a dramatic change (with such dire implications in many quarters) could have been made by numbers of highly intelligent people.

47

the old structures of authority were breaking down. Then we shall turn to the scientific and textual discoveries that led to the ascendancy of the new authorities of science and individualism.

Breakdown of Authority

The breakdown in authority was occurring in three main areas: spiritual, educational, and political. A consequence of these breakdowns was the rise of a general skepticism and individualism—characteristics that will feature in the modern experiment for years to come, even to the present day. The thinkers try to overcome this skepticism, but they do not do so by returning to the realist tradition of ancient and medieval thinkers. On the contrary, they try to defeat skepticism through a kind of individualism in the form of new methods to be applied without reliance on any of the old structures or traditions.

Spiritual authority was weakening both pastorally and theologically. It is well known that the late medieval and Renaissance popes were rather worldly, often wielding the authority of their office for such secular ends as power, wealth, and fame. Philip Hughes argues that the decline of the church began shortly after the death of Thomas Aquinas in 1274.[2] He cites numerous reasons for the decline, chief among them the temporal interests of the papacy and the rising power of the curia (sometimes dominating even the papacy). The papacy owned lands and levied taxes to raise armies in order to secure its own position.[3] In fact, the centralized papacy was criticized widely throughout the church.[4] When Martin Luther traveled to Rome on a mission in 1510, he was appalled at the corruption of the church administration, especially as to the selling of spiritual indulgences. In 1517, preachers of a scandalous papal indulgence came to Wittenberg.[5] Luther's response was his *Ninety-five Theses* criticizing the practice of indulgences and other corruption in the church. Not all of these theses may be theologically sound, but there is no doubt that the credibility of the church of Rome had been

2. Philip Hughes, "The Decline," ch. 6 in *A Popular History of the Catholic Church* (New York: MacMillan, 1966).

3. See Machiavelli's discussion of Pope Alexander VI in *The Prince*, esp. ch. 11 and 18. Alexander led armies and arranged for the rise to power of his son Caesare Borgia, whom Machiavelli holds up as the model of the new prince (ch. 12). This was not new to the sixteenth century. Consider Dante's strong criticisms of papal secular power in his *Divine Comedy*, written in the early fourteenth century.

4. Hughes, *History*, p.145.

5. Hughes notes that a main reason for the indulgence was to raise money to repay principle and interest that the archbishop of Mainz had to pay in order to become archbishop of Magdeburg (*History*, fn. 1, p. 176).

harmed by its worldliness and corruption and that these abuses contributed to a whole host of reformers separating from the church of Rome, from Luther to Calvin and Zwingli, to Henry VIII of England. Thus was Christianity divided in Europe.

Not only was the authority of the church weakened by the Reformation; the authority of reason itself was also challenged. Both Luther and Calvin held that the fall (original sin) had irreparably corrupted reason so that faith is our only reliable guide. Although this notion gained prominence as a tenet of the Reformers, its seeds had been sown in late medieval theology. Well before the time of Luther and Calvin a movement challenged the authority of reason in theology. The mainstream tradition stemming from Saint Paul, Justin Martyr, Saint Augustine, Boethius, Saint Anselm, and Saint Thomas Aquinas, which held that reason and revelation were compatible, had been challenged ever since the end of the thirteenth century.[6] Thomas Aquinas had held that, although the central doctrines of the faith (such as the Trinity and the incarnation) can be known only by faith, a number of doctrines of the faith can be proven by natural reason (e.g., that God exists, that God is good, omnipotent, eternal, and provident). While Thomas thought that we can know both that the world is created (that God exists) and the nature of that world (its intrinsic intelligibility), the late medieval movement thought that one had to choose between God and the universe. They reasoned that whatever intrinsic reality is accorded to creatures comes at the expense of the reality and power of God. Either God is in charge or he is not. If we allow creatures their own existence and activity, then God's omnipotence as creator is denied. Hence, in the name of giving more glory to God, these thinkers diminished the intelligibility of the universe.

The seeds of this late medieval movement can be found in the work of two contemporaries of Thomas Aquinas: Alexander of Hales and Bonaventure. These thinkers were heirs to a tradition, apparently traceable back to Augustine, that held that creatures were just barely real, having within themselves a tendency to revert to the nonexistence from which they came.[7] In other words, of themselves, creatures are not; they exist

---

6. Actually, there were always tendencies to what we might call fundamentalism within the church. Thus as early as the second century, Tertullian (c. 160–c. 240) had asked what Athens has to do with Jerusalem (*Prescription against Heretics* 7).

7. This was not actually the view of Augustine but was construed as such. In his *Summa Theologica*, Alexander of Hales writes: "In every creature, to the extent that it is from nothing and so has been changed from non-being to being, it is changeable to non-being" (1.30). Alexander considers creation to be a kind of change, and since all change requires some substratum, he introduces the notion of spiritual matter to explain how immaterial creatures came to be and to indicate in them the possibility of their changing out of being. In his commentary on Peter Lombard's *Sententia*, Bonaventure makes similar distinctions. "Everything which has changed has in itself mutability; but every creature

only in God. This presents an obvious problem for natural reason. For how can one argue from things to God if things are real only because of God and not also somehow in themselves? One is caught in a vicious circle—trying to prove the existence of the first cause (God) from the existence of other things (creatures) that are intelligible only in the first cause (God). Thus natural reason's ability to know the things of the world is cast into doubt, and hence also its ability to know that God exists, is all-powerful, all-knowing, all-good, provident, etc.

By denying any intrinsic being to created things, Bonaventure and Alexander of Hales had opened the door to the denial of reason's access to the world. However, they did not go too far down this road, nor did Duns Scotus of the next generation. They still believed that reason could argue from the world to the existence of God. However, the trend was for more and more power and intelligibility to be given to God (and thus mistakenly taken from creatures). It was just a matter of time before someone would claim that natural reason can say nothing meaningful about the world, nor consequently about the Creator of the world. This someone came along in the generation after Duns Scotus.

William of Ockham, who was a great logician, wasted no time in drawing the implications of placing all intelligibility in God. If all intelligibility is in God, then there is none in things. This position is known as nominalism, which we noted in the last chapter was adopted by Bacon and Hobbes. The word "nominalism" refers to a central tenet of Ockham and other late medieval thinkers that universals are mere names (*nomina*). Only individual things exist, and the intelligibility (universal knowledge) that we seem to find in things is not really there. Obviously such a position is going to affect the attempt to prove anything about the faith. For example, Aquinas's proofs for the existence of God all begin with the intelligibility of things and conclude by stating that God exists. But if there is no intelligibility in things, then obviously there can be no proof of the existence of God. Nor can there be a proof about anything. True, we can understand logical structures, but since we have no access to real universal characteristics of things, we can make no judgments about the essences of things or their interrelations. The denial of formal and final causality in Bacon and Hobbes is really just a consequence of this theological position of Ockham.

Such a position not only made theoretical knowledge of the world impossible; it also spelled the end of all natural moral knowledge. Since all intelligibility is rolled back into God, we have no way of knowing

---

has been made; therefore, every creature has been changed: therefore, none is immutable" (*I Sententia* 8.1.2.2.c). Since every creature comes from nothing, every creature naturally tends toward nothingness. "It must be said that every creature is *vertibilis* by nature if left to itself" (ibid., ad 7).

(save by divine revelation) what is right and what is wrong. This is the origin of the divine command theory: right and wrong depend entirely on God's will. The seeds for this position can be found in the thought of Duns Scotus, who held that God's will is the source of ethics.[8] Practically speaking, however, Duns Scotus never denied natural reason's ability to know right from wrong. But Ockham draws the ultimate implications of such a position. If God is the absolute source of morality in every sense, then God could change the natural law. He could, if he chose, make murder and adultery permissible and even obligatory. He could even make it right for us to hate him.[9] Given that "God" means the principle of all existence and goodness, if God ought to be hated (which according to Ockham is possible if God says so), then we have abandoned reason, for the contradiction in considering perfect goodness as something to be hated (something bad) is obvious.

This placing of all intelligibility in one source to which we have no access becomes the model for Bacon's idea of science and, in general, the contemporary view of science. We must withhold judgment about the things we experience, for their apparent structures are not really real, only constructions of our imperfect minds. The only real structures are the highest laws. Thus we have a world of things unintelligible in themselves, only to be explained by the most universal principles. For the moderns (Galileo as well as Bacon and Descartes), God plays the role of the ultimate principle from which all knowledge of the world can be deduced.

This model of reducing all power or intelligibility to one unintelligible first principle affects spheres other than science. It becomes a model for the church in Protestantism: there is no hierarchy in the church; rather, all individuals are equal in authority under God. And it also, very obviously, becomes the model for political theory, whether the structure be the reduction of the political community to the prince as in Machiavelli, or to the Leviathan (common will) as in Hobbes.

The breakdown of authority in education was equally profound. In some ways such a revolution seems justified. All three of our philosophers (Bacon, Descartes, and Hobbes) complain bitterly about the state of higher education in their day, as indeed will almost all of their followers. Although there are a few factors that might indicate that such a judgment was not purely disinterested (which I shall discuss below), it is hard to believe that such a widespread complaint had no justifica-

8. John Duns Scotus, *Quaestiones super libros Sententiarum* (*Ordinatio*, also known as *Opus Oxoniense*) 3.37, in *Opera Omnia* (Paris: Vivès, 1891–1895), vol. 8–21. This theory also goes back to Tertullian.

9. William of Ockham, *Quaestiones super libros Sententiarum* (also known as *Reportatio*) 4.16.

tion. The education in the schools was modeled on the philosophy of Aristotle as handed down by the scholastics (chief among them Thomas Aquinas). However, rather than reading original works of Aristotle and Aquinas, students were taught from textbooks, which could often be commentaries on commentaries on the masters, or even further removed. Thus what was presented by Aristotle and Aquinas as a living philosophy opening up to first principles of the true, the good, and the beautiful was taught as a deductive system where particular truths were deduced from general principles.

Although such a system of education might be able to teach an enormous amount of material efficiently through this well-ordered format, it must have been deadly dull and, moreover, ultimately false to the nature of the philosophy of the masters. For excepting logic, which is merely a tool for understanding and has in itself no content, Aristotle always begins any subject where it originates—with a question, in wonder. Only after first raising the appropriate question and considering a wide range of answers does he begin to sort out the better from the worse answers and arrive at his conclusions. These conclusions have only as much certainty as the subject matter allows, not always the absolute certainty of a conclusion deduced from perfectly known premises.[10] Without a doubt, some of the complaints leveled at university education were well founded.

Some of the complaints, however, can be put down to the impetuous nature of youth and the restless spirit of the age. After all, Francis Bacon completed his higher education at Cambridge by the age of 14; Descartes finished his education at La Flêche at age 18; and Hobbes finished his work at Oxford at age 19. Even allowing for the more thorough instruction given at the lower levels in Europe, none of these philosophers spent anywhere near the kind of time trying to understand the material they were studying as did any medieval master of arts or indeed Aristotle himself (who studied under Plato for 19 years). All three philosophers of the new education would, of course, have said that such a lengthy education was just the problem: common sense does just as well. The point here is that, as it is unlikely that these three were able to master the philosophy they were rejecting in the time they had to spend on it, their judgment as to its inadequacies must not be taken as a fully informed opinion.

An additional influence on both the spiritual life and the educational life of the era was the teaching of the Humanists, who were involved in the reclamation of ancient texts of Greek and Roman literature and rhetoric. Their criticism of the scholastic teaching was based first of all on style. Compared to the Latin of the great writers of the Roman era,

10. See Aristotle, *NE* 1.1.

the late scholastic prose was dreadfully dull and ugly. Erasmus, while never directly condemning Aquinas, is very critical of Duns Scotus and the late scholastic way of writing. In both his *Praise of Folly* and his *Handbook for the Militant Christian*, he attacks the scholastics for their horrible style and recommends a return to the Romans for rhetoric and the Fathers of the church for theology. In the words of Folly:

> For myself, I often have a good laugh when they particularly fancy them-
> selves as theologians if they speak in a specially uncouth and slovenly
> style, and while they mumble so haltingly as to be unintelligible except to
> a fellow-stammerer, they refer to their powers of perception which can't
> be attained by the common man. They insist that it detracts from the
> grandeur of the holy scriptures if they're obliged to obey the laws of gram-
> mar. It seems a peculiar prerogative of theologians, to be the only people
> permitted to speak ungrammatically; however, they share this privilege
> with a lot of working men.[11]

How much of the Humanist preference for the Fathers is based on style and how much on content is hard to say. But certainly both the Humanists and the Reformers consciously reject the scholastic theology in favor of the theology of the Fathers. This is true even though the Neoplatonism of the Fathers (Erasmus particularly commends Origen) is less compatible with Christianity and its incarnational center than the Aristotelianism of the scholastics. Such Neoplatonic notions as that the material world and the body are evil, and that all things emanate by necessity from the One to be eventually reabsorbed by the One (again by necessity), clearly go against the incarnational and sacramental life of the church and the idea of a good and free creation. The extent of the influence of the stylistic critique on the philosophical and theological thought of the day is hard to determine. But certainly disdain for the scholastics on stylistic grounds reinforced disdain on other fronts.

Europe's political life was in turmoil. Based in large part on religious differences between Lutherans and Catholics, the nobles of Germany fought incessantly, and in France the bloody Wars of Religion were being waged between Calvinists and Catholics. In Italy power struggles contin-ued between the Italian city-states, the papacy, and the nations—France, Spain; Machiavelli reports on these struggles in *The Prince*.[12] There seemed to be no legitimate authority that could claim the respect of all

11. Erasmus, *Praise of Folly*, trans. Betty Radice (London: Penguin, 1985), p. 163.
12. As we mentioned above, these problems in Italy were long-standing. See Dante's *Divine Comedy*, particularly *Inferno*, for an account of the strife between papacy, city-states, France, Spain, and the German emperor in the late thirteenth and early fourteenth centuries.

parties. In addition to this, the latest handbook on politics—Machiavelli's *The Prince*—presents an amoral guide to power politics. According to Machiavelli, the good prince must be willing and able to make use of traditional virtues when suitable for protecting his position of power but also be willing to make use of cruelty and injustice when they serve. Since human beings are really only animals seeking self-preservation, glory, and fame, the most essential virtues for the good prince are force (like the lion) and deception (like the fox).[13]

Thus not only was there a de facto lack of leadership in Europe, but there was also a moral vacuum: the traditional ideas of what makes a good leader were gone. It is well known that Henry VIII's faithful Lord Great Chamberlain, Thomas Cromwell, placed a copy of Machiavelli's *The Prince* in his hands when he was involved in his controversy with Rome. It was precisely this continuing lack of stable and legitimate leadership that Hobbes tries to rectify in his *Leviathan*.

Skepticism

Given the breakdown in authority of these spiritual, educational, and political structures, it was natural for people to wonder who, if anyone, should be followed. People disagree. Who is to say who is right? On the spiritual front, Catholics and Protestants disagree, and the Protestants disagree among themselves. New cultures have been discovered with new customs sometimes radically different from European culture: who are we to say our customs are right? Scholasticism, if we are to trust the reports from Bacon, Descartes, and Hobbes, has formalized disagreement and controversy as central to the educational system. As Bacon says, one cannot think of any proposition so strange that a philosopher has not held it, nor is there any thesis, metaphysical or moral, that is not disputed by one party or another. Politically, we have the parliamentarians against the royalists. Who is right?

Thus arose a fourth and more radical challenge to authority: skepticism, the challenge to the authority of reason itself. To fuel this challenge, new translations of the works of the Roman skeptic Sextus Empiricus were made available in the 1560s. The skepticism presented by Sextus Empiricus was that of the ancient Greek philosopher Pyrrho.[14] Pyrrhonism involves presenting arguments for and against every proposition, not indeed to find out the truth of the matter (which was the ostensible point of scholastic disputations), but to arrive at *ataraxia*, that is, a state

13. *The Prince*, ch. 18; cf. Hobbes's "cardinal virtues": force and fraud (*Leviathan*, pt. 1, ch. 13, p. 188).

14. C. 360–270 BCE.

of peace reached by realizing that the question, being unanswerable, is not worth asking. Intellectual pursuits, be they about metaphysics or ethics or politics, are not worth entering, for all they do is upset one. Better to stand aside, preserving one's inner peace.

Michel de Montaigne was the most eminent spokesman for this skeptical position in the Renaissance.[15] His works were widely read on the Continent and translated into English in Bacon's time by John Florio, a friend of Philip Sidney's. In the face of apparently irresolvable controversies over truth and morality, Montaigne suggests a new method. Instead of searching for definitive answers to objective questions, Montaigne turns to the study of himself. As he claims in his preface, "I am myself the substance of my book."[16] In himself he finds innumerable ideas that he tests out in an exploratory way (hence the origin of the term essay, from the French essayer, to try). Montaigne's works are full of references to conflicting ideas—philosophical, historical, moral, theological—with no ultimate resolution.[17] "I allow my own ideas to run their course, feeble and trivial as when I first conceived them, without plastering and patching defects revealed to me by this comparison."[18]

Given the recognition of defects, one might ask why the next step would not be to correct those defects. There seem to be two answers to this question. One is the conviction of the skeptics that the mind is incapable of correcting the defects—that the mind is incorrigibly flawed (a theme we have encountered in Bacon and Descartes). The other is that, even if the answer could be found, it would be found only after much work and controversy, and these dissolve the tranquillity that is the ultimate purpose of all philosophy.

> The most manifest sign of wisdom is a constant happiness; its state is like that of things above the moon: always serene. . . . Why, Philosophy's object is to calm the tempests of the soul, not by a few imaginary epicycles but by natural and palpable arguments! Its aim is virtue, which does not, as the schoolmen allege, stand on the top of a sheer mountain, rugged and inaccessible. . . . Anyone who knows the way can get there by shady, grassy, and sweetly flowering paths, pleasantly and up an easy and smooth incline, like that of the vault of heaven.[19]

Although tranquillity might come by discovering the answer to one's questions, by far the easier path is to deny that the questions are worth

15. Montaigne (1533–1592) was born a generation before Francis Bacon.
16. Michel de Montaigne, Essays, trans. J. M. Cohen (London: Penguin, 1988), p. 23.
17. See especially his most famous essay, "An Apology for Raymond Sebond," in Essays, bk. 2, ch. 12, trans. M. A. Screech (London: Penguin, 1993).
18. "On the Education of Children," in Essays, bk. 1, ch. 26, p. 50.
19. Ibid., pp. 67–68.

asking. The proper attitude to adopt vis-à-vis the difficulties one faces in life is a kind of carelessness.[20]

Individualism

Although Bacon, Descartes, and Hobbes do not share Montaigne's general skepticism, they do adopt features of his method—chief among them the implicit individualism. In contrast to the attitude of the ancient and medieval philosophers who saw themselves in a long philosophical tradition that had painstakingly worked its way toward the truth, each of our modern philosophers is self-consciously announcing a brand new way to truth discovered by himself alone. Whereas Aristotle and Aquinas hold that the method must suit the object, the modern philosophers make method primary. The new method is, in fact, necessary if one is to discover the object. Since one method is supposed to do for all, it is only fitting that one person should provide this method and, through it, the general direction for all future work.

Of course, the skepticism of Montaigne was not the only impetus to individualism at the time. If the authorities are no longer in place, then one has to make up one's own mind. This is an obvious feature of the theology of the Reformers. One is saved by faith alone, and faith is an immediate consciousness of being saved rather than the elaborate creed, theology, and sacramental life that had been developed over the centuries in the Roman Catholic Church. But even within the Catholic Church, with the scandals of many church leaders (including popes), one had to decide whether or not one would remain a faithful follower of the church. Thus there was an emphasis on the individual conscience in religious matters.

A great example of this movement toward individual piety is to be found in the book *The Imitation of Christ*, by Thomas à Kempis, which was a strong influence on Erasmus, among others (including, at a later time, Immanuel Kant). The moral rigor and call to individual responsibility of this work are impressive indeed. However, the emphasis on developing the inward or spiritual man is sometimes made at the expense of the recognition of the good of creation and community. Turning away from the external world is not just a matter of avoiding desire for material possessions; it is sometimes also a call to give up all nature, including such fundamental human goods as knowledge and friendship.[21] This conflicts with the incarnation of

20. Ibid., p. 80.
21. "All worldly delights are either hollow or base." Thomas à Kempis, *Imitation of Christ*, trans. Edgar Daplan (New York: Sheed and Ward, 1950), p. 65. There is a kind of

Christ, the resurrection of the body, the church as the body of Christ, and the sacraments.[22]

Educationally, if the old structures of education were insufficient, then one had to do what one could on one's own, by studying oneself or the book of the world. Descartes claims the privilege of setting aside all his former education. Bacon describes all the theories he studied in school as so many idols of the theater, plays spun from wayward imaginations. Protestants like Bacon and Hobbes had an additional reason to reject the Aristotelian structures of education: the introduction of Aristotle into theology was considered by Protestants as one of the grave mistakes of the Catholic Church. To be free of Aristotle was to be free of the structures and mistakes of the rejected religion.[23]

Finally, the question of political loyalty was difficult. How was one to know to whom one should be true? After all, the tradition of citizens' rights was long-standing in England, going back to the Magna Carta of 1215. And in fact, Hobbes's solution in his *Leviathan* is that the sovereign power really is just the individual will (transmuted through the logic of following Hobbes's natural laws of self-interest). This idea has its difficulties in terms of articulating the freedom and responsibility of sovereign and citizen, but the ideal is that individual consent is the basis for legitimate power.

Of course, individualism is good in many ways. In terms of learning, one does have to make an idea one's own to understand it. Morally speaking, every individual is intrinsically valuable, and conscience is inviolable. Given this intrinsic value of every individual, political sovereignty ought to depend on free assent. And theologically, Christ died to save every person, and everyone must personally assent to the faith and accept God's grace.

The danger of individualism is that the individual will not bother to consult others or try to understand the position that he or she immediately thinks is mistaken. This, I think, was part of the problem of Bacon, Descartes, and Hobbes, and understanding it helps to explain why each followed his method to the end, even though it quite obviously was insufficient to handle all aspects of human knowledge.

---

anti-intellectualism in the *Imitation*; see bk. 3, § 44, p. 125 and bk. 4, § 18, pp. 183–84. There is also a good deal of focus on solitude and suspicion of friendship; see bk. 1, § 20, pp. 39–40.

22. In book 4, the author calls one to participate in communion and confession, honor the priesthood, and show a great devotion to the holy church. However, the first three books focus on the individual and private piety rather than on the sacramental and mystical community that is the church. Erasmus and the Reformers embrace this individualism and the relative unimportance of sacraments and theology.

23. See Hobbes, *Leviathan*, pt. 1, ch. 12, p. 182.

Discoveries

So far, we have spoken of a breakdown of authority in the spiritual, educational, and political arenas which provided the opportunity for some new authority to arise and address the problems of a troubled time. Besides these trends, which explain the possibility of a new dominant authority (and hence could be said to be indirect causes of the ascendancy of the scientific method), unprecedented successes of the scientific method in various fields directly fueled its rise to prominence. These numerous successes revealed the real promise of science and individualism. There was the discovery of a new world in the Americas, with all the opportunities such a discovery promised. There was the rediscovery of ancient texts of mathematics and mathematical cosmology. And there was the discovery of new technologies which promised to revolutionize human life and bring about great progress in human well-being.

With the discovery of the Americas came new economic resources as well as an explosion of new knowledge of plants, animals, and cultures. Here individual enterprise had clearly paid off. If the explorers had been content to rest in the current knowledge of geography, they would never have attempted to cross the seas. The great success of their enterprises showed the importance of individual initiative.

With the renewed interest in ancient texts came the discovery of two seminal works for the modern movement: the *Elements* of Euclid, and the dialogues of Plato, especially the *Timaeus*.[24] The growth of scientific method with its mathematical understanding of the physical world owed much of its impetus to these texts. University education since the thirteenth century had been dominated philosophically by the work of Aristotle. Although Aristotle has something to say about mathematics, the paradigm for his philosophy is more biological than mathematical. With Plato, mathematics takes pride of place. In the *Timaeus*, the universe is said to be constructed of triangles and can be understood mathematically. The geometry of Euclid provided a coherent and intricate model for a mathematical interpretation of nature as well as a method of deducing scientific truth.

There was great optimism about applying the new mathematical method to all areas of study. Just as the application of scientific method helped Copernicus replace the cumbersome Ptolemaic astronomy and its odd epicycles with a simpler and clearer heliocentric model of the solar system, so this same method, applied to other fields of study, should bring us out of skepticism to other new advances that will improve the

---

24. The year 1505 saw the first Latin translation of Euclid taken directly from the Greek (Vienna). The Platonic works were translated from the Greek in the 1400s.

general well-being of humanity. The successful revolution in astronomy could be the model for revolutionizing all human knowledge.

Finally, certain empirical discoveries and inventions were dramatically changing the direction of modern Europe and fueling the great optimism in progress. Bacon speaks of three such fundamental inventions that had already contributed to the well-being of humanity and that he sees as promises of more to come if his empirical and experimental method is followed. These are the magnet, the printing press, and gunpowder.[25] We have already discussed the fruit of the first—its contribution to the invention of the compass and the consequent navigational feat of crossing an ocean.[26] At about the same time, the printing press was invented.[27] Gunpowder was introduced in the West around 1400. These three inventions opened up enormous opportunities. With the compass, exploration, trade, and colonization increased dramatically. The printing press made for the possibility of a wide distribution of books, thus taking education out of the university and into the lap of the public. Gunpowder increased the military might of those who had it—providing the means for the defense and expansion of civilization.

Of course, as C. S. Lewis points out so ably in *The Abolition of Man*, these kinds of technological advances are double-edged. None of them carries its own moral justification. Thus improvements in sea travel are good if one's purpose in traveling is good, but it would be hard to say that sea travel to exploit or enslave a people is good. So also, the increased communication brought about by the printing press is good if one has something good to communicate, but how if the communication is not worth reading or is false or degrading? The additional power granted by gunpowder is positive if used for a worthy cause such as defending an innocent people against an unjust aggressor, or for nonmilitary purposes such as building roads. But it is easy to see that greater power in the hands of one bent on destroying or enslaving results in greater evil. These problems are all too apparent. When coupled with the new amoral political agenda of Machiavelli, they present a morally ambiguous and perhaps dangerous social context.

Galileo

Let us conclude this chapter with a discussion of the Galileo controversy. In it most of the themes we have discussed come together:

25. *New Organon*, bk. 1, aphorism 129, p. 118.
26. The compass in a suitable form for long-range navigation had appeared in Europe around 1450.
27. The Gutenberg Bible was published about 1456.

the misuse of authority, the challenge of individualism, the application of mathematics to nature, and technological invention in the form of the telescope, which extended humanity's reach into nature. As is well known, Galileo's last work, *Dialogue on the Great World Systems*, led to his condemnation by the Roman Catholic Church, and Galileo was forced to recant. The case is usually cited to show the incompatibility of religion and science. Interestingly, neither the church nor Galileo thought that religion and science were incompatible. The compatibility of revelation and natural reason had long been one of the tenets of the Catholic tradition, and Galileo was aware of and basically subscribed to this position. He did not consider the account of creation in Genesis to be science, nor scientific method to be a replacement for faith. That there should have been such a breach of this tradition, apparently on both sides, indicates the deep fragmentation of human reason occurring at the time and the confidence some people had in the new method to settle controversies.

Excited by the work of Copernicus and Kepler, which involved the application of mathematics to the material of experience, Galileo was clearly on the bandwagon of the new science.[28] Developing the insights of the Pythagoreans and Plato, Galileo claimed that the book of the universe "is written in the language of mathematics, and its characters are triangles, circles, and other geometric figures without which it is humanly impossible to understand a single word of it."[29] He also shared Bacon's interest in the practical; he himself perfected the telescope, which helped confirm Copernicus's insights concerning the naturalness of the heavenly bodies and the structure of motion in the universe.

However, Galileo did not see these discoveries as antithetical to the Aristotelian spirit of natural philosophy. Galileo thought that the natural philosophy of Aristotle and the new science were not necessarily incompatible; rather, they involved looking at the data of experience in two different ways.[30] Using his telescope, Galileo had discovered that the moon was made of rock and that there were sunspots on the sun, which indicated that the sun changed. This contradicted the Aristotelian claim that the heavenly bodies were made of an unchanging substance different in kind from material things on earth. However, Galileo rightly saw that Aristotle's conclusions were based on empirical data of the unaided

28. "Now, in order that we may harvest some fruit from the unexpected marvels that have remained hidden until this age of ours, it will be well if in the future we once again lend ear to those wise philosophers whose opinion of the celestial substance differed from Aristotle's" (Galileo Galilei, "Letters on Sunspots," trans. Stillman Drake, in *Discoveries and Opinions of Galileo* [Garden City, NJ: Doubleday Anchor, 1957], p. 118).

29. Galileo, *The Assayer*, in *Discoveries*, p. 238.

30. "Letters on Sunspots," p. 118.

senses. If Aristotle had had the benefit of a telescope and witnessed the changes in the sun, he surely would not have continued to claim that the sun does not change. "I should even think that in making the celestial material alterable, I contradict the doctrine of Aristotle much less than do those people who still want to keep the sky inalterable; for I am sure that he never took its inalterability to be as certain as the fact that all human reasoning must be placed second to direct experience."[31]

This is clearly true. In fact, when judging the number of unmoved movers in the *Metaphysics*, Aristotle allows that if more heavenly motions were to be discovered, there would need to be more unmoved movers.[32] Aristotle was always one to consult experience. If he was wrong scientifically (and clearly he was on this and other issues), the reason was not methodological or metaphysical but empirical. Galileo's point is that technology has provided us with better tools for data gathering, and such tools have discovered things that the unaided senses could not.

Many of the contemporary scientists (who were also clerics) refused even to consider the new data that Galileo had discovered. Galileo shares the following outrageous scene with his fellow scientist Kepler. "Here at Padua is the principal professor of philosophy, whom I have repeatedly and urgently requested to look at the moon and planets through my glass, which he pertinaciously refuses to do."[33] Such blind obedience to authority in natural reason is certainly not the attitude of either Aristotle or Aquinas. Galileo knew this and was able to distinguish the decadence of the schools from the teaching of the masters.

Why did the church condemn Galileo and force him to recant? This is a fairly complicated issue, but some general points seem clear. The Catholic Church was embroiled in controversies with the Protestants, who rejected the teaching authority of the church in theology and the interpretation of Scripture. In addition, the new science apparently threatened the centrality of the human being in God's plan. I say "apparently," because obviously the importance of the human being is not spatial (to be at the center of a material universe), but metaphysical, moral, and spiritual. Perhaps the claims of some to have found a method that would revolutionize all thought (and even Galileo sounds this way at times) worried the authorities, leading them into a position of confusion on the appropriate methods for different inquiries. In other words, the authorities forgot their own tradition, the very tradition which this book seeks to recover and which the modern scientific revolution threatened, i.e., that there are distinct realms of reason whose

31. Ibid.
32. Aristotle, *Metaphysics* 12.8.
33. Galileo to Kepler, 1610, quoted by Robert M. Augros and George N. Stanciu in *The New Story of Science* (New York: Bantam, 1986), p. 176.

characteristic differences and limits must be carefully recognized and honored. Galileo, more than Bacon, understood this tradition, which was why (at first, at least) he did not see any incompatibility even between the Aristotelian view of natural philosophy and his own, never mind between the much more distinct disciplines of natural philosophy and ethics, or metaphysics, or theology.

To consider that all knowledge is based on one method is to open the doors to confusion and animosity, for if there is to be only one method, each discipline, not wanting to cease to exist, would lay claim to having the one method. This is a problem whether the science be the mathematical-physical science of Galileo or the theology of the church. Since they do not treat the same object in the same way, they cannot, if held within their reasonable limits, contradict each other. One considers material reality insofar as it is quantifiable; the other considers all reality (material and spiritual) according to the principles of revealed truth.

The Galileo affair is particularly important for its influence on our three philosophers. Bacon, as we have said, was a contemporary of Galileo and the two share a general interest in the new scientific method, though Galileo puts more emphasis on mathematical hypotheses and Bacon on empirical foundations. Hobbes actually met Galileo, and Galileo's theory of motion is clearly a central influence on Hobbes's work. Descartes withheld the publication of his work *Le Monde* for fear of encountering the same fate as Galileo. He mentions this at the beginning of part 6 of the *Discourse*, and attaches to the *Discourse* a few, although not all, of the treatises from the original work. What is noteworthy is Descartes' early interest in science (*Le Monde* was ready for publication three years before the *Discourse*) and the secondary importance, at least in his original plan, of metaphysical themes. Although the *Meditations* has become Descartes' most famous work, its metaphysics was conceived in large part as a basis for refuting skepticism and getting on with the work of the new science.

Such, in very broad brush, is the world into which Bacon, Descartes, and Hobbes were born. It is well to be aware of the context and background to such a world, not only so that we do not judge too harshly the motives of those who, I argue, limited reason without warrant, but also so that we may begin to see how influences that are not directly pertinent to a particular field of study may encroach upon that field to the detriment of both areas of thought. If theology, for example, is asked to settle questions of empirical science, or if mathematics is called upon to settle moral questions, we are in trouble. Both science and ethics will suffer at the hands of inappropriate and hence damaging methods, and the methods of theology and mathematics will be distorted in a hopeless attempt to cover areas beyond their jurisdictions.

Of course, historical and cultural context and background do not justify the positions espoused by Bacon, Descartes, and Hobbes. Ultimately, their positions must be judged as philosophically adequate or inadequate. So judged, we have found them inadequate. Before tracing the implications of the new methods through an examination of the disciples of Bacon, Descartes, and Hobbes, let us pause to ask why the revolution occurred so late in the history of Western thought. In the next chapter, we shall consider briefly why earlier periods of thought did not make science and technological progress paradigms for human intellectual activity.

3

Technology—The Road Not Taken

I t is a fact that technology did not develop very fast or very far in either the ancient or medieval worlds. Why didn't the ancients and medievals make scientific method and technology central to their intellectual efforts? It does not seem to be a matter of inferior intelligence, for these eras were not at all inferior to the modern era in terms of moral and metaphysical thinking, and even the rudiments of scientific method are taken from ancient texts of mathematics and philosophy. Besides, Bacon, Descartes, and Hobbes all agree that the application of their methods does not require superior intelligence for success. How, then, does one account for the lack of interest in applying science to dominate nature for the good of mankind? I suggest that this was not just oversight or ignorance. There was at least an ambivalence toward the promise of technology, if not a conscious rejection of it, within the ancient and medieval cultures. The roots of this ambivalence or animosity lie largely in their religious, moral, and political traditions. However, there are also metaphysical and aesthetic reasons for such ambivalence. Let us consider the mythical and religious reasons first.

Prometheus

In ancient Greece, the god Prometheus was said to have stolen fire from Zeus and given it to mankind. Fire allowed human beings to develop technology, which gave them self-sufficiency and independence from the

gods. In Aeschylus's play *Prometheus Bound*, using words sounding quite
a bit like Bacon, Prometheus claims to have shown human beings the
proper use of their minds: "I found them witless and gave them the use of
their wits and made them masters of their minds."[1] He brought to them
the arts of building, of calculating from the stars, of numbering, and of
grammar. He taught them the art of taming beasts to work for them, and
he taught them shipbuilding and sailing. More importantly, he brought
them the arts of medicine (that great good which also moved Descartes
so profoundly) and prophecy. And he brought them the hidden blessings
of the earth—copper, iron, silver, and gold. "One brief word will tell the
whole story: all arts that mortals have come from Prometheus."[2]

All these arts are indeed good, as are the technological advances foreseen and promoted by Bacon and Descartes. However, it is also true
that these goods have been in some way the bane of human existence,
especially those last mentioned—silver and gold. They are not bad in
themselves, but the overzealous love for them and for the independence
their possession promises has led humanity away from the more important goods, those moral and spiritual goods represented, in Aeschylus's
play, by Zeus.

Thus one finds in *Prometheus Bound* a tension between Prometheus
and Zeus, Prometheus representing mercy and compassion for mankind,
Zeus representing justice. What Prometheus did for mankind was to
provide comfort—primarily physical comfort. This, of course, is good;
however, such comfort is attended with the danger that human beings
will turn away from the gods and from justice. Prometheus himself seems
to be aware of his sin: "I knew when I transgressed nor will deny it."[3] In
defending his act of stealing fire from the gods, Prometheus declares:
"I caused mortals to cease foreseeing doom. . . . I placed in them blind
hopes. . . . Besides this, I gave them fire."[4] It may indeed be a comfort not
to dwell on death and judgment; however, it is a false comfort since all
will die and come to judgment. Such blind hopes may lead to a kind of
forgetfulness and insouciance concerning our choices and deeds in this
life, which lack of concern is bad for us now as well as at the moment of
judgment. To trust in one's own technology is ultimately a false hope. In
the end, "the plans of man shall never pass the ordered law of Zeus."[5]

1. Aeschylus, *Prometheus Bound*, lines 442–43, in *Greek Tragedies*, vol. 1, ed. David
Grene and Richmond Lattimore, trans. David Grene (Chicago and London: University of
Chicago Press, 1968), p. 81.

2. Ibid., lines 503–4, p. 83.

3. Ibid., line 268, p. 75. Elsewhere he speaks of his "excessive love for man" (line 122,
vol. 1, p. 69).

4. Ibid., lines 250–54, p. 74.

5. Ibid., lines 552–53, p. 84.

In writing his play, Aeschylus was drawing on the work of the poet Hesiod.[6] In Hesiod's account of the relations between Prometheus and Zeus, one finds the same ambivalence toward the good Prometheus brings. Indeed, Hesiod blames Prometheus and his behavior rather more than Aeschylus does. According to Hesiod, Prometheus deceives Zeus into accepting the less desirable parts of a sacrificial animal, thus leaving the better parts for mankind. When Zeus, who is portrayed by Hesiod as "Father of Gods and of Men"[7] and hence to be honored and obeyed, punishes mankind by taking back the gift of fire, Prometheus steals fire from Zeus and returns it to mankind. From one point of view the actions of Prometheus are seen as kind and noble. From another, however, they are foolish and disastrous. Prometheus (whose name means forethought) must have known that he could not ultimately deceive Zeus, "whose plans are unfailing."[8] Ultimately, his act brings misery to himself (in the form of being chained to a column and having his liver eaten daily by an eagle), and to mankind (through the creation of the first woman Pandora and the miseries she lets loose).[9] Only hope is left, which is a poor substitute for the blessedness that had been the state of humanity under the rule of Zeus prior to Prometheus's act.

Leaving aside the tangential question of who is to blame for human misery (male or female), it is clear that Hesiod thinks the miseries we face are due to Prometheus's acts of deception and theft. Hence there was for Hesiod, as well as for Aeschylus, a kind of ambivalence about the ultimate value of technology and the comfort it brings, particularly when achieved through injustice.

Of course, in Aeschylus's play there are passages focusing on Zeus's failings as well—on the injustice of his punishing Prometheus. From this perspective, Prometheus is seen as a suffering servant, willing to endure torture for the sake of mankind, while Zeus is the unjust tyrant who imposes his arbitrary will by violence. Indeed, the play would fail to achieve its dramatic intensity were not the claims of Prometheus and Zeus given nearly equal weight. My point is not to show that the play is an apology for Zeus. It clearly is not. In Homer, Hesiod, and the playwrights, the gods are never treated as unambiguously good (this was one of Plato's complaints about Greek religion). I wish merely to indicate that the ideal of technology that Prometheus represents, with all its material advantages, was viewed with suspicion by the Greeks.

6. Aeschylus lived from 525–456 BCE. Hesiod flourished in the eighth century BCE.

7. Hesiod, *Theogony*, line 542, in *The Poems of Hesiod*, trans. R. M. Frazer (Norman: University of Oklahoma Press, 1983), p. 64.

8. *Theogony*, line 545, p. 64.

9. For the story of Pandora, see Hesiod, *Works and Days*, lines 53–105, in *Poems*, pp. 98–100.

It is interesting to compare this ancient ambivalence with Percy Bysshe Shelley's *Prometheus Unbound*, a treatment of the myth written on the other side of the technological revolution.[10] In Shelley's version, Prometheus is unambiguously the hero, and God (Jupiter, Zeus) unambiguously the villain.[11] Not only is Prometheus praised for what he brings to mankind, but his rebellion itself is commended. While final reconciliation and order between Zeus and Prometheus is presupposed by Aeschylus, this is not the case with Shelley. On such a reconciliation, Shelley writes: "But, in truth, I was adverse from a catastrophe so feeble as that of reconciling the Champion with the Oppressor of mankind. The moral interest of the fable, which is so powerfully sustained by the sufferings and endurance of Prometheus, would be annihilated if we could conceive of him as unsaying his high language and quailing before his successful and perfidious adversary."[12] And indeed, the play ends with a tone of confirmed rebellion:

> Neither to change, nor falter, nor repent:
> This, like thy glory, Titan, is to be
> Good, great and joyous, beautiful and free;
> This is alone Life, Joy, Empire, and Victory.[13]

That rebellion against authority is considered good in itself is, I have suggested, one of the features of the modern movement. Such a position would seem to be highly questionable. For if the authority is wise and just, rebellion must be foolish and unjust. Hence, the moral issue comes to the fore: rebellion against unjust authority is good but not against just authority. Given Shelley's portrayal of God as entirely bad and Prometheus as entirely good, one is likely to go along with his glorification of Prometheus's rebellion. But why should one think that God's authority is arbitrary and not grounded in justice? I suppose that the problem of evil (human suffering under a providential God) may be the reason for setting up God as merely powerful and uncaring, but a

10. Shelley first published *Prometheus Unbound* in 1820. Shelley belonged to the Romantic movement, which was in many ways a reaction to the narrowing of reason in the Renaissance and Enlightenment.

11. In the poem Shelley often uses the term "God" for Jupiter. Thus, Jupiter stands for the one God and Creator, at least in some form. In his blistering criticism of God (Jupiter, Zeus) in the poem, Shelley shares in the anti-Catholicism of Bacon and Hobbes as he indicates in his preface: "We owe the great writers of the golden age of our literature to that fervid awakening of the public mind which shook to dust the oldest and most oppressive form of the Christian religion" (Lawrence John Zillman, ed., *Shelley's Prometheus Unbound: The Text and the Drafts* [New Haven and London: Yale University Press, 1968], p. 39).

12. Ibid., lines 26–33, p. 35.

13. Ibid., act 4, lines 575–78, p. 233.

richer and more adequate notion of the Christian God (and even Zeus) and of God's relation to man calls for a more subtle treatment of the relative moral goodness of God and Prometheus.[14]

If the wrongfulness of rebelling against divine providence is a reason for distrusting technology in the Greek world, how much more is it for the medieval world where culture is dominated by the revealed religions, all of which have a strong sense of the one, eternal, omnipotent, and providential God. Although this one God remains a mystery and the goodness of his actions is not always clear to us, his goodness and justice would never be questioned the way Zeus's goodness and justice were in Aeschylus's play. Technology as the attempt to free ourselves from the providence of God, or at least to view such providence as less necessary, would be viewed as a temptation that threatens to destroy our chance for eternal happiness.

A Question of Means and Ends

This religious antagonism toward science and technology is more or less influential on the philosophers of the ancient and medieval periods: more, for example, on Plato and Augustine than on Aristotle and Aquinas. What is more to the point for all these thinkers (and for us in this book on reason, not revelation) is the moral unsuitability of devoting one's life to technological progress aimed at securing material well-being. As Bacon, Descartes, and Hobbes all begin with a moral reason for introducing their new methods (the conquering of nature for the good of mankind, much like the ideal of Prometheus), it would be fitting to consider the moral reasons of the ancient and medieval thinkers for not making science and technology their central aim.

It is well known that Plato held the rational soul to be the human being and the body an impediment to human happiness.[15] Given this position, it is not surprising to find Plato emphasizing the goods of the soul over those of the body. In his search for the meaning of justice in the *Republic*, Plato draws an analogy between the proper order within the state and that within the individual. Although Plato finds a place for the craftsman within the state, it is clearly an inferior place, and the craftsman's job is

14. The importance of man's inventive powers in terms of science and technology is also emphasized in the play, especially in the fourth act. "In it Shelley depicts the joy of a liberated universe. The forces of nature, twisted to maleficent ends by the evil will of Jupiter, are now free to work beneficently at man's bequest" (Carl Grabo, *A Newton among Poets: Shelley's Use of Science in Prometheus Unbound* [New York: Cooper Square, 1968], p. 139).

15. See Plato, *Phaedo* 64a–67e.

to provide the necessities for the state so that those members who can understand ethical, political, and metaphysical realities may have the time and security to do so. As the craftsman's well-being is important for its contribution to the order of justice in the *polis*, so the individual's body is to be fed and taken care of just so much as is conducive to the mind participating in the world of the forms. To spend time flattering the body with extra comforts would not only be a waste of time; it would also hinder one's achieving happiness. Likewise, an emphasis on technological progress for the comfort of our bodily lives would hinder the achievement of happiness in our communal life.

Aristotle, who holds that the human being is the unity of body and soul, would not have such an obvious reason for rejecting technology. Indeed, although Aristotle does not seem to encourage technology to any great extent, he is certainly interested in scientific progress; for the material world is really real and worth understanding for it own sake. However, even as Aristotle includes material well-being as part of happiness, it is the least important part. The essence of happiness is to be found in activities of the rational soul—knowing the truth and choosing well.[16] Human beings are distinguished from the other animals by their reason; thus human happiness is specifically intellectual.

> Nature, as we say, does nothing without some purpose; and for the purpose of making man a political animal she has endowed him alone among the animals with the power of reasoned speech. Speech is something different from voice, which is possessed by other animals also and used by them to express pain and pleasure; for the natural powers of some animals do indeed enable them both to feel pleasure and pain and to communicate these to each other. Speech on the other hand serves to indicate what is useful and what is harmful and so also what is right and what is wrong. For the real difference between man and other animals is that humans alone have perception of good and evil, right and wrong, just and unjust.[17]

To overemphasize bodily care (which care to a degree is good since the soul cannot function without the body) is to neglect the development of the moral and intellectual virtues. To do so is at once wrong and destructive of happiness.

As far as the political state is concerned, its end, too, is something higher than subsistence or material comfort. Although it is necessary that material goods be present and that there be some people who are suited to such work, the purpose of the state is to provide a basis for the

16. See Aristotle, *NE* 10.9.
17. Aristotle, *Politics* 1.2.1253a8–17, trans. T. A. Sinclair (Middlesex, England: Penguin, 1976), pp. 28–29.

doing of philosophy—political and metaphysical. The primary purpose of government is to help the citizens be good. Aristotle appreciates what science and technology have brought to the state but warns against changing laws to encourage extensive technological progress.[18]

> If the mind is to be regarded as part of a living creature even more than its body, then too in cities we must regard the corresponding parts as more important than what merely conduces to utility and necessity; I mean such things as fighting-qualities and all that belongs to the administration of justice, and over and above these, that counseling faculty which is political wisdom in action.[19]

Thus, Aristotle holds technology to be a good, but not the greatest good; too much emphasis on material well-being threatens the happiness of the individual and the state. "That life is best, both for individuals and for cities, which has virtue sufficiently supported by material wealth to enable it to perform the actions that virtue calls for."[20] Nobility is more important than skill or material prosperity, and therefore technology and wealth must be for the sake of nobility in the individual and the city. In the best state "the citizens must not live a banausic or commercial life. Such a life is not noble and not conducive to virtue."[21] Proper order should always be observed among the goods of the soul and the state.

> All life can be divided into work and leisure, war and peace, and of things done some belong to the class of actions that have moral worth, while others are necessary but have no such value. In the choice of these the same principle, the lesser for the sake of the greater, must be followed in actions as in parts of the soul; that is to say, we choose war for the sake of peace, work for the sake of leisure, menial and useful acts for the sake of the noble.[22]

18. *Politics* 2.8, pp. 81–83.
19. Ibid., 4.4.1291a24–29, p. 157.
20. Ibid., 7.1.1323b40–1324a2, pp. 257–58.
21. Ibid., 7.9.1328b39–40, p. 273. In her book *The Human Condition* (Chicago: University of Chicago Press, 1958), Hannah Arendt underlines the dangers that the Greek world saw in emphasizing promotion of wealth over virtue. "To own property meant here to be master over one's own necessities of life and therefore potentially to be a free person, free to transcend his own life and enter the world all have in common" (p. 65). To focus on property, as opposed to choosing freely to enter the life of the community, would be to renounce one's freedom and citizenship. "If the property-owner chose to enlarge his property instead of using it up leading a political life, it was as though he willingly sacrificed his freedom and became voluntarily what the slave was against his will, a servant of necessity" (p. 65).
22. *Politics* 7.14.1333a30–38, p. 287.

Turning to the medieval tradition of natural law, we find Augustine and Aquinas espousing views similar to Plato and Aristotle, respectively. Augustine, while never agreeing completely with Plato's idea that the human being is just the rational soul, certainly considers the soul to be more important than the body and eternal things more important than temporal things. This he holds both philosophically, following Plato, and theologically. Although temporal goods (those goods of the body which technology can provide) are really good, they are so much less good than the goods of the soul and the ultimate good (God) that Augustine is impatient to get on with the ascent from lowly material goods to the intellectual and spiritual goods. "The eternal law, therefore, orders us to turn our love away from temporal things, and to turn it in its purity to the eternal."[23] Material goods that serve the body are clearly less good than the body itself, which in turn is less good than the soul. Of the three human goods—the body, the powers of the soul, and the virtues—the body is the least good and the virtues the greatest. Like Plato and Aristotle, Augustine holds that any quest for external goods to serve the body that gets in the way of virtue would be wrong.

In the *City of God*, Augustine compares the earthly city with the heavenly city. The latter is clearly superior, and even in the former the goods that technology can bring are not the greatest goods but serve other higher goods.

> In the earthly city, then, temporal goods are to be used with a view to the enjoyment of earthly peace, whereas, in the heavenly City, they are used with a view to the enjoyment of eternal peace. Hence, if we were merely unthinking brutes, we should pursue nothing beyond the orderly interrelationship of our bodily part and the appeasing of our appetites, nothing, that is, beyond the comfort of the flesh and plenty of pleasures. . . . Because, however, man has a rational soul, he makes everything he shares with brutes subserve the peace of his rational soul so that he first measures things with his mind before he acts, in order to achieve that harmonious correspondence of conduct and conviction which I called the peace of the rational soul.[24]

Thus, for Augustine, technology serves the body within this life so that the human being may be virtuous while living within a human society and may make preparation for eternal life. To overemphasize technology would be to make living virtuously in this life very difficult and the achievement of eternal happiness with God even more unlikely.

23. *On Free Choice of the Will* 1.15, trans. Anna S. Benjamin and L. H. Hackstaff (Indianapolis and New York: Bobbs-Merrill, 1964), p. 31.
24. *City of God* 19.14, trans. Gerald G. Walsh et al. (Garden City, NY: Doubleday, 1958), p. 459; see also *On Free Choice of the Will* 1.15, p. 31.

Thomas Aquinas, following Aristotle, pays more attention than Augustine to the physical world and to the ways we know that world, i.e., the various sciences. To study the world is not to ignore our ultimate end, God; for by studying God's effects, we learn about God and glorify him for the wonder of his creation and our ability to know it. Thus technology, as the application of reason to the material world, is not intrinsically a temptation to be avoided. However, like Aristotle, Aquinas recognizes a hierarchy of importance among goods. Goods may be virtuous, pleasant, or useful: all are worthy of our attention, but the virtuous more so than the pleasant and the pleasant more so than the useful. "Goodness is not divided into these three as something univocal to be predicated equally of them all, but as something analogical to be predicated of them according to priority and posteriority. Hence it is predicated chiefly of the virtuous, then of the pleasant, and lastly of the useful."[25] In the same place, Aquinas distinguishes further between the three kinds of goods.

> Those things are called pleasing which have no other formality under which they are desirable except the pleasant, being sometimes hurtful and contrary to virtue. Whereas the useful applies to such as have nothing desirable in themselves, but are desired only as helpful to something further, as the taking of bitter medicine, while the virtuous is predicated of such as are desirable in themselves.[26]

Technology, which develops out of a desire for some other useful end, is thus not a very good model for moral perfection since, as a means, it is clearly less good than the end.

The key ingredient in morality is intention, not consequences. Sometimes, of course, a proper concern for consequences is part of rightful intention, but the quality of a moral act is not drawn from the consequences but from the purpose of the agent. "Good that is loved has the nature of an end, and . . . the motion of the will is designated good or evil in terms of the end it pursues."[27] And the most important end is clearly not useful for the attaining of some further good but is something to be delighted in for its own sake. "Augustine says: No one rightly uses God, but one enjoys Him. But God alone is the last end. Therefore we cannot use the last end."[28]

---

25. Thomas Aquinas, *Summa Theologica* (hereafter, *ST*) 1.5.6 ad 3, trans. Fathers of the English Dominican Province (Westminster, MD: Christian Classics, 1981), vol. 1, p. 28.
26. *ST* 1.5.6 ad 2, vol. 1, p. 28.
27. Thomas Aquinas, *Compendium Theologiae* 47, trans. Cyril Vollert, S.J. (St. Louis: B. Herder, 1958), p. 42.
28. *ST* 1–2.16.3 sed contra, vol. 2, pp. 654–65.

Limitations of the Scientific Method

So far, after some cultural and religious considerations, we have focused on the ethical reasons of the ancient and medieval worlds for not embracing science and technology as guiding lights. Thus the criteria for objecting to overemphasizing science and technology have been claims from the realm of the good. But there are also theoretical reasons (from the realm of the true) why the great ancient and medieval thinkers did not place scientific method at the core of their intellectual lives. To make scientific method central would be metaphysically unsound. Plato, Aristotle, Augustine, and Aquinas would all agree on this point, even though their metaphysical positions differ substantially. Since the medievals (Augustine and Aquinas) follow their ancient models fairly closely on this point, we shall focus in this section on the thought of Plato and Aristotle.

Recall Bacon's declaration that natural philosophy is the rightful queen of the sciences and that all other sciences are to be judged ultimately by this authority. The same is basically true for Descartes and Hobbes even though mathematics figures more prominently in their thinking. For not only the certainty of mathematics, but also its usefulness, attracts Descartes and Hobbes. We have already seen how Descartes' metaphysics and method are aimed at the sciences and how he has the practical purpose of making nature serve mankind. And while Hobbes takes geometry as the model for reasoning, his theory of reality derives from the mechanics of matter in motion.

The idea of natural philosophy as queen of the sciences would have seemed absurd to these ancient and medieval thinkers. As important as physics might be, it cannot be the most important subject, for it is not the last word in understanding reality. For thinkers in the ancient and medieval tradition, metaphysics or natural theology is the queen of the sciences (though, of course, for believers, revealed theology as the direct word of God is given an even higher status).

In the thought of Plato, studying material things is not a focus, for their changeableness renders knowledge of them uncertain. If we have any certain understanding, it must come from knowing unchanging realities. Material things are real only insofar as they participate in immaterial paradigms. The ideal of the intellectual life, and indeed of the happy life, is to ascend from the many things that are not quite real (since they are in stages of becoming) to the one first principle that is the intrinsic intelligibility of everything: the Good. Not to do so is to abandon intelligibility. How could the queen of the sciences be a science of opinion?

Although it is true that mathematics figures in Plato's thought in almost as big a way as in that of Descartes and Hobbes, the role of mathematics is quite different. Usually, Plato regards mathematics as a stepping stone to dialectic, which is how we approach the forms.[29] Its purpose is to wean us away from this world of change and to help us realize that truth is unchanging. Even when, in the *Timaeus*, the universe is explained in terms of number and geometrical forms, Plato never tries to dominate the material world through the application of mathematics. Rather, he consistently places mathematics between the unreal world of changing material things and the fully real world of the forms. The Demiurge looks to the forms for his patterns in making the world. Thus the prime intelligibility of things is not matter in motion, nor mathematics, but metaphysical forms and ultimately the one single principle of all reality: the form of the Good.

Unlike Plato, Aristotle has a developed natural philosophy as well as a metaphysics, and both his natural philosophy and his metaphysics take issue with the position of the moderns. In fact, the natural philosophy and metaphysics of Aristotle are very much of a piece, for it is only by beginning with natural philosophy that one gets to metaphysics. Since Aristotle's natural philosophy begins with sense experience, as do the philosophies of Bacon and Hobbes, it would be interesting to consider why he would reject their project.

Aristotle thought that explanation must be intelligible (a sensible thing to think). To argue (as the atomists did, and as Bacon and Hobbes thought) that the question of why things are as they are is answerable ultimately by reference to matter in random motion is not to give an intelligible account, for intelligibility is universal and unchanging, not particular and changing. Aristotle's account of explanation involves four distinct elements—his famous four causes.[30]

When we ask why something is, there are four different kinds of answers we may give. Consider an investigation of a manufactured item, say a ship. If we want to give a purely materialistic explanation of the ship, we will give a list of the materials of which it is made. We can do this on many levels—invoking ordinary names (steel and aluminum), or giving the chemical analysis of the metals, or proceeding to give their atomic or subatomic makeup. This would be to address the material cause. However, this kind of an explanation does not tell us much about the ship, for other things are made of metals and atoms, etc. So we refer to what Aristotle calls the formal cause of the ship—the structure whereby it is different from an automobile or an airplane. This tells us the kind of thing it is, which in this case might minimally be defined as something that floats and can carry things. We are still left with only

29. See Plato's discussion of the divided line, *Republic* 6.509d–511d.
30. See Aristotle, *Physics* 2.3–7.

a partial explanation, for how did it come to be? Metallic elements do not spontaneously form themselves into ships. We can answer our question "Why this ship?" by pointing to the company that built it or the chief naval architect or the engineers. Thus we have recourse to a third kind of explanation, what Aristotle calls the moving cause, the cause of something coming to be. But even this cause does not seem sufficient, for companies, naval architects, and engineers do not build ships by necessity, but for some purpose, whether that purpose be to transport goods somewhere, or to make money, or to defend a nation. This last cause Aristotle calls the final cause, final because it is ultimate in the realm of explanation. For none of the other causes would feature in this ship were it not for the choice to build it, and the choice would not have been made without some end or purpose in mind.

When applied to manufactured items like the ship, I do not think that anyone would have any difficulty accepting Aristotle's four kinds of explanation, not even our modern philosophers. However, Aristotle thought that natural things as well as artificial things were to be explained by the four causes, and that the ultimate explanation of natural things is also a final cause. Bacon and the adherents to scientific method (as we saw in chapter 1) deny the significance of formal or final causes in the explanation of the physical universe. They accept only the material and moving causes along with some very general causes such as the most universal scientific laws. Taking Hobbes's mechanism as an example (or Descartes' view of material reality, which is very much the same), everything can be explained in terms of quantifiable stuff and the laws of motion. What is lost is the notion of a thing, that is, a distinct kind of being with its own unique function and purpose.

It is precisely this notion of thing or substance that Aristotle thinks cannot be left out of an explanation of the natural world without draining that world of meaning. And it is upon this notion of thing (and the attendant distinctions and relations between things) that Aristotle grounds his metaphysics. The collapsing of things into one generalized stuff in random motion is precisely what the atomists had done before Aristotle. His complaint is that such a world is almost unintelligible. How can undifferentiated matter and random motion (chance) be better explanations than intelligible form and purpose? To say that something happens by chance is to say that there is no explanation. In this light, it is a practical absurdity for scientists to continue to try to explain a universe that is intrinsically unintelligible. More immediately, there is the theoretical absurdity of claiming (universally and unchangeably) that all explanations are based on the random flux of radical particularity.

It is true that, by treating things as if they were matter moving according to general laws, one may advance in the ability to manipulate nature.

Nor is there anything wrong with doing this, so long as one understands that one's explanation is only partial. The idea that consideration of formal and final causes is not helpful to the advance of modern science or technology does not necessarily imply that formal and final causes are mere fictions of the mind, as Bacon and his followers thought. This would follow only if the scientific method were the only valid explanation. But it seems that it is not, given our example of the ship. Why should we limit such explanations to artificial things and deny them to natural things? Why, in short, should we limit reason?

The kinds of justifications for limiting reason to the elements of scientific method (mathematics and empirical verification) given in the last two chapters are insufficient. The fact that people disagree about what are the true formal and final causes is no indication that such causes are unreal, for disagreement does not necessarily mean that no one is right. The fact that late medieval theology and the theology of the Reformers tended to a nominalism, where formal distinctions were denied between things and all explanations rolled back into God, is no proof that such a limitation of reason is well-taken; for if nominalism is taken seriously, no universal account (and all accounts are either universal to some extent or meaningless) can be accepted, not even that limited one given by science. Just because we cannot have experimental verification of formal or final causes does not mean that we should ignore them. After all, neither do we have experimental verification of the claim that the scientific method is the only valid method.

When we ignore these other kinds of explanations we ignore meaning. We arbitrarily shut down our intelligence. Unless a question can be shown to involve a contradiction, there is no reason to ignore it. In short, there can be no good reasons for limiting reason. This is Aristotle's point. The materialist's explanation is one explanation, and at least partially true, but it is not the only one, nor ultimately the most important one.

Aristotle makes activity or function, rather than the smallest particle, the primary element in explaining what something is. Thus, although it is true that chemicals, atoms, and subatomic particles have particular characteristics as they follow the universal (mathematical) laws of science, each thing has its own distinctive activity, which is the primary way of explaining what it is. This is more obvious in living things and most obvious in the human being. Aristotle explains the difference between the atomist position and his own in the following way:

> Now if each animal and each of its parts were to exist by virtue of its shape and color, what Democritus says would be right, and such appears to be his belief. At any rate, he says that it is clear to everyone that a man is a thing such as his shape, seeing that he is recognized by his shape and

his color. But the form of a dead man, too, has the same shape, and yet a dead man is not a man.[31]

Although the chemical and atomic composition might be the same, clearly a dead human being and a living human being are not the same. The difference is in terms of act, not matter.

Of the two causes (final and material), the final is clearly more basic. For just as, if one intends to make a saw (final cause), then it is necessary for it to be made of something hard and sharp like metal (material cause) and not cheese or Styrofoam, so too, if there is to be such and such a thing (granite, rose, dog, human being), then it is necessary for it to be made of such and such a material. The idea that ordered things come about because matter accidentally falls into this or that shape leaves one with no explanation, for the thing is being explained by its matter, whose motion and composition are being explained by chance.

Aristotle's complaint to Bacon and Descartes would not be that they are completely wrong. Pursuing the material or mathematical causes of things are legitimate avenues to knowing them. However, these avenues are not the only ones. To limit reason to these empirical and mathematical methods is arbitrary, and the cost of such limitation is high, as we shall see in chapters 4 and 5.

When Aristotle explains reality, his paradigm is the human being (the most complex of natural things), not the atom (the simplest). The most real thing is the human being.[32] Modern science, on the contrary, tends to say something is better explained the more it is reduced to its parts. Thus plants and animals are better explained as organs, tissues, and genes, better still as chemicals, and best as atoms. The idea of "thing" is reduced to the atom (and, today, to subatomic particles). All other "things" are explained in terms of these. Against this, Aristotle claims that the human being is one in a more primary sense than the atom (or the proton or the quark), for the rational soul, which is the form of the human being, unifies the most complex of matters.

The Enlightenment philosopher David Hume accuses Aristotle and his medieval disciples of anthropomorphizing reality. Hume asks why the human being should have a privileged place in our account of the

31. Aristotle, *On Parts of Animals* 1.640b30–36, in *Selected Works*, trans. Hippocrates G. Apostle and Lloyd P. Gerson (Grinnell, IA: Peripatetic Press, 1982), p. 313.

32. That is, the human being is the most real of the things whose essence we know. Aristotle argues for the existence of an ultimate explanation of all reality—God. Such a principle would have to be more real, since all reality comes from it, but we cannot use it as a paradigm since we do not know its essence (we cannot place it in genus and species so as to distinguish it from other things).

world.[33] Aristotle would respond with a "what else?" What would one take as the paradigm case of the real if not the human being? Anything less would not account for the accounting itself; that is, the very fact that we are thinking about and trying to explain reality is itself part of reality. Hence, if we mean to give a full account of the way things are, we need principles that can handle the characteristic activities of human beings: thought, free choice, and creativity.

Theories of physics, whether mathematical or empirical, cannot give such an account.[34] Mathematics provides formal structures but does not provide any principle of act. Thus it cannot explain the origin of motion, to say nothing of growth, sensation, and self-motivated activity. Although empirical theories of matter in motion fare better on the lower levels of motion (assuming, of course, that there is some initial input of energy—the Big Bang), they quite obviously fail to explain the higher, distinctively human activities such as thought, free choice, and creativity.

That these activities are part of our world is perfectly obvious, for we are aware of ourselves doing them. A theory of reality that cannot handle such activities is flawed. A mathematical paradigm, however sophisticated, must fail to capture the essence of these activities, and likewise a matter-in-motion paradigm. Put the two together in classical scientific method, and one fares no better.

These distinctively human activities reveal the three areas of human reason that form the focus of this book. In order for one to know something is true, one must think; one must know that one knows; one must be self-aware. Although a computer can mimic human thought in some of its activities, it is not self-aware: it does not know that it knows.[35] In order for one to be responsive to the good on the level of moral choice, one must have freedom of choice. Although Aristotle will admit that all things can be said, by analogy, to desire the good and that the higher animals' desire approaches human prudence, the unique sense of responsibility attributable to human beings—our ability to know and choose the good—involves a kind of freedom not found among the other things

33. "What peculiar privilege has this little agitation of the brain which we call 'thought,' that we must thus make it the model of the whole universe? Our partiality in our own favor does indeed present it on all occasions, but sound philosophy ought carefully to guard against so natural an illusion." David Hume, *Dialogues Concerning Natural Religion*, pt. 2, ed. Henry D. Aiken (New York: Hafner, 1951), p. 22.

34. There are philosophers who put the principles of thought and intention (those most human characteristics) in the very rudiments of physics, such as Leibniz and Whitehead, whom we shall discuss later (chapters 5 and 7, respectively). This is, perhaps, a plausible explanation, and it is, like Aristotle, making the human being (a microcosm, according to Aristotle) the main principle of explanation.

35. Descartes makes this point in part 5 of the *Discourse on Method*.

of the world. Finally, to appreciate something as beautiful, one must know it as an integrated whole; and to create something beautiful, one must bring such knowledge to bear in free acts of creativity whose end is the beautiful thing itself.

There is a fair amount of overlap in these activities, and indeed the three realms of reason—the true, the good, and the beautiful—are interrelated, as we shall see in chapter 9. For example, self-awareness or thought is not just a feature of knowing what is true, but also of acting freely and being creative. So also, creativity presupposes the freedom of choosing which materials to use and in what ways one will use them. And since every moral act is something new and unique (something that may not have been), moral choices involve a kind of creativity.

The crucial point is that these three activities inform our relations with the world and cannot be accounted for by the elements of scientific method (mathematics and sense verification). Any theory that excludes the meaningfulness of such activities is self-refuting since it cannot account for its own meaningfulness.[36]

Not only does Aristotle differ from all three of our moderns in his ideas about the kinds of explanations and their relative importance; he also differs dramatically from them in how he sees the human being in relation to the world. Bacon and Descartes start with doubt. Although it is not their intention to remain skeptics, they think that they have to answer the skeptics' objections before they can move on. This is the reason for the method: it provides the proper way out of doubt. Aristotle, on the contrary, begins with affirmation. The question is not whether or not we are in touch with other things through the senses or in any other way; rather, given that we are in touch with other things, how do we explain this? While the modern way of thinking considers the sense and the intellect (if they are judged to be distinct) as instruments, Aristotle understands them as ways of being other things.

> We may now sum up the main points concerning the soul under one heading and state once more that the soul is all things, but in a certain sense; for things are either sensible or intelligible, and in a certain sense, knowledge is the objects known while sensation is the sensible objects.[37]

Two important distinctions must be made concerning Aristotle's qualification "in a certain sense." In the first place, Aristotle is not saying that the

---

36. The distinctiveness of these three realms of human reason will be the topic of chapter 8. How such flawed theories are self-refuting will be explained differently according to whether one is addressing issues of the true, or the good, or the beautiful (metaphysics, ethics, or aesthetics).

37. Aristotle, *On the Soul* 3.8.431b20–23, in *Selected Works*, p. 293.

soul actually is all things, but only that it is able to be all things; for Aristotle held that knowledge is not innate but begins in sensation. Second, the soul in sensing or knowing is not other things in the full existential sense, for when a stone is seen, one does not become a stone or have a stone in one's head. Rather it is the sensible form without the matter with which one identifies when sensing. The same is true of knowing, except that, in addition to leaving out the matter, one also leaves out the particularity of the thing. To know the difference between a peach and an anteater is to have universal knowledge of some sort.

Both Bacon and Descartes are concerned with the unreliability of the senses. This goes back to Plato who thought of the body as the instrument of the soul, whose function, at best, was to reawaken the knowledge already contained in the soul. Although this Platonic model does not fit as well for Bacon as for Descartes, it is still true that Bacon thinks the senses are in need of aids (experiments) if they are to be made trustworthy. Perhaps the discovery of the telescope and other means of verifying data that go beyond the natural limitations of the senses also contributed to this notion of the senses as instruments, and untrustworthy ones at that. One might say that, since the telescope shows craters and mountains on the moon that the naked eye cannot see, the sense of sight is defective. But this would clearly be a false inference. The unaided sense of sight reports accurately what it sees: a round shape lit up with a kind of face on it. Then again the sense of sight reports accurately what it sees when looking through the telescope: craters and mountains. If one were to take seriously the doubt of the sense of sight, then one should no more trust the report of the craters and mountains than of the face. In short, if one doubts the senses in general, there is no way to verify their correct behavior.

In addition to doubting the senses, Bacon and Descartes are concerned about the unreliability of the intellect. The intellect is intrinsically defective and therefore cannot be trusted unless it is made to follow a corrective method. However, if the intellect is defective, why have confidence in one's method, since the method itself is an invention of the intellect?

While Bacon and Descartes begin with a doubt that stops the activity of sensing or thinking until the question of their reliability can been established (which of course can never be done without using them), Aristotle begins with the activity (whether it be sensing or thinking) and then goes on to explain it. The infallibility of sense and intellect in their proper spheres is taken as a first principle. There can be no proof that sense or intellect is infallible, for the activity of each is prerequisite to any proof. But, of course, any attempt at showing either to be intrinsically fallible must also fail; in fact, it must be self-refuting since the intellect or sense would have to be used in the attempt.

Thus the only way of showing the infallibility of sense and intellect (their privileged position as first principles) is to show the absurdity of denying them. This is perhaps more obvious in the case of the intellect. The first principle of theoretical reason is the so-called principle of noncontradiction: something cannot be and not be at the same time and in the same respect. To deny it (and mean what one says) is to use it, for one presumably does not also, at the same time and in the same respect, affirm it. Since sensation is not a power of logical reasoning, one cannot formulate a similar law of noncontradiction about sensation. However, one can answer the arguments against sense being reliable; that is, one can show that the doubts are not well founded. All doubts are built on apparent discrepancies between sense experiences (recall the basis for Descartes' doubts), but if the senses are not to be trusted at all, what reason is there to believe that the discrepancies are real? If the discrepancies are claimed to be real, some sense experience must be invoked as a criterion for establishing the real difference between the two discrepant sense experiences.

We are in communion with a world of things both sensible and intelligible, and there are no universal, intrinsic restrictions (due to defect) to the scope of sensation and intellect. There are, as we have seen, no good reasons to doubt this communion. Doubts that are intrinsically closed to solution (like the doubts about the trustworthiness of the senses and the intellect) are not worth entertaining. We have already seen three attempts to entertain and resolve these doubts about the senses and the intellect through the introduction of a new method. Insofar as a method takes us to certain ends that we desire, Aristotle would not be against using it. What he would be against is restricting reason to any one method. It does not make any sense to claim to restore reason by restricting it. The intellect is open to all being. Method is a limited use of intellect. As valuable as any method is (even the scientific method), since it is designed for a certain limited end and since the range of being to which intellect is open is infinite, the exclusive use of the method must always do damage to the intellect and, consequently, to the intelligibility of reality.

This affirmation of sense and intellect does not mean that we know all being, or even that given infinite time we shall know all being (or even any being) completely.[38] It is merely to insist that there are no intrinsic restrictions to what we can know. Through body and intellect, the human being can be, in a way, all things. "The intellect is the form of forms and the faculty of sensation is the form of sensible objects."[39]

---

38. This is because knowledge is always to some degree universal while individual things actually exist only as particular individuals. See Thomas Aquinas, *ST* 1.84.7.

39. Aristotle, *On the Soul* 3.8.432a2–3, in *Selected Works*, p. 294.

The horizon of human knowing is open to all that can be sensed or can be known, that is, to everything physical and intelligible.

Beauty

In addition to moral and metaphysical reasons, a high regard for beauty also tends to prevent the thinkers of the ancient and medieval tradition from adopting scientific method and technology as central to their intellectual efforts.[40] Although Plato (and Augustine following him) often speaks of beauty as a metaphysical principle (so that all the metaphysical reasons for not adopting science and technology as primary apply to his view of beauty), the tradition of Plato, Aristotle, Augustine, and Aquinas also holds beauty to be an intelligible object distinct from truth and goodness. Beauty is not primarily a vehicle for truth; rather, it is appreciated for its own sake. Beauty is an object of reason with its own first principles, and its appreciation and creation are fundamental human activities. Thus beauty is a basic good to be pursued and not violated. However, it is not essentially a moral principle any more than it is essentially a metaphysical principle. The recognition and creation of beauty are not essentially tied to morality, as if only a moral person could create or appreciate something beautiful, or as if the purpose of art were improvement of character. Unlike technology, appreciation of beauty is worthwhile in itself and not for what it brings. Hence it is a more fundamental end.

Although it is abundantly clear that there were many beautiful works of art created in the Renaissance, the philosophers of that period whom we have discussed show little or no interest in understanding what makes something beautiful. As we related in chapter 1, they view beauty as relative, subjective, and mostly a matter of feeling. This is quite unlike the view of Aristotle and the medievals, who understand that the appreciation of beauty involves the recognition of intelligible principles of order and relation within an integral whole, as well as delight of the senses. The acts of appreciating and creating beautiful things are held in high esteem, revealing more of the essence of humanity than the servile arts that promote the goods of the body. Indeed, the great works of art of the Renaissance owe more to this ancient and medieval understanding of beauty than to the modern view. But the philosophy of beauty (or lack of it) of our Renaissance philosophers will influence the aesthetics of future generations, much to their detriment. At least in literature, the quality

40. How beauty is regarded by this tradition will be discussed in more detail in chapter 8.

of the art erodes dramatically after this time. This is due, in large part, to the vacuum of intellectual content in aesthetics—one consequence of equating legitimate intellectual activity with scientific method.

Defending the Scientific Paradigm

Against the openness to being that is found in the ancient and medieval tradition (an openness that includes traditional morality, metaphysics, and a philosophy of the beautiful), our modern thinkers—Bacon, Descartes, and Hobbes—all argue for an ordering principle by which being could be restricted to fit what they hold to be the rather limited natural capacities of the human intellect. This done, they believe progress in the arts and sciences will follow and cooperation and unanimity be assured. Unfortunately, Bacon, Descartes, and Hobbes do not perfectly agree on the one method that will make this progress inevitable. Their disciples continue the experiment of making method the master of nature, variously defending and correcting their masters, but generally disagreeing with each other. The promised cooperation and unanimity were not so obviously forthcoming as the masters had supposed.

The implications of the move to make science the paradigm for all knowledge can be discerned in the developments of these disciples, which will be the topic of the next two chapters. In chapter 4, we shall examine the disciples of Bacon (aka the empiricists), and in chapter 5, we shall consider the thought of Descartes' disciples (aka the rationalists).

4

The Empiricist Quest;
or, From Matter to Meaning

Though Bacon and Descartes begin by attacking tradition, they soon spawn their own traditions—empiricism and rationalism, respectively. The key difference between these traditions is that empiricism takes sense experience as primary while rationalism gives primacy to ideas. That is, empiricism holds that all knowledge originates in the senses and must be verified by the senses; rationalism, on the contrary, holds that all knowledge is innate or is at least to be judged as correct or not by reference to ideas that are not learned from experience.

According to the empiricist, everything must be explained by reference to matter in motion (something that can be verified, at least in principle, by the senses). This creates an interesting challenge: how do we account for thought or freedom of choice? Hence one could characterize, in a general sense, the empirical quest as trying to explain meaning in terms of matter.

Recognizing the difficulty of explaining thought and free choice in terms of matter in motion, the rationalists begin at the opposite pole—with thought. Their quest is to explain the world in terms of the ideas we find in our minds, innate ideas that cannot have their origins in sense experience. Thus in a general sense, the rationalist quest could be characterized as one trying to explain things in terms of thought.

As antidotes to the skepticism of their day, Bacon and Descartes offered blueprints for progress in the sciences, technology, and human well-being as a whole. Many of the deficiencies in these blueprints, which we pointed out in the first chapter, were quickly recognized by their contemporaries, some of whom tried to correct them while honoring the spirit and key doctrines of the masters. To consider some of these refinements is to understand better the implications of the masters' projects. Let us see how well these projects succeed.

In this chapter, after a brief consideration of what the empiricist and rationalist projects have in common, we shall consider the implications of Bacon's method by examining the thought of three of his disciples—John Locke, George Berkeley, and David Hume. In the next chapter, we shall trace the implications of Descartes' project by considering a few of his followers.

Empiricism and Rationalism

There are three important similarities between the empiricist and rationalist traditions. First, both traditions begin with an attempt to overthrow skepticism: they try to show that some things can be known to be true. Skepticism presents two great challenges. One is the challenge of certainty: how can we be sure that we know anything about the world? From the vast amount of disagreement about important issues of metaphysics and morality, one might conclude that there is no right answer. The second and deeper challenge concerns the power of reason itself: how do we know that human reason is a reliable vehicle for pursuing the difficult task of discovering truth about anything? Perhaps the world is intelligible, but just not to us. Bacon and Descartes believe, against the skeptics, that reality is intelligible. However, they are not quite sure that the powers of the human being are up to the task, at least not if allowed to follow their natural tendencies. Both philosophers distrust the accuracy of the senses, and both have their doubts about the mind. Bacon warns against the inevitable idols of the mind, and Descartes is willing to doubt the principles of reason itself since it is logically possible that we are dreaming or systematically deceived by some higher power.

Hence we come to the second similarity between the two traditions: the introduction of a single method that will make knowledge of reality possible. Natural human reason is not able to arrive at the truth; only human reason restricted by method can do so. Recall that Bacon's method is basically inductive, focusing on the interpretation of data gleaned from nature according to very generalized laws. Descartes' method is taken from mathematics, which is particularly well suited for refuting skepticism because of the great clarity and distinctness of its objects and the complete certainty of its deductive method. We saw how this introduction of one method to cover all genuine knowledge leads to difficulties in dealing with the variety of objects of human reason (being as being, the good, the beautiful). The rigorous application of one method leads to the truncation of human reason in both Bacon and Descartes. We shall see in these next two chapters whether their disciples are successful in addressing the difficulties raised by adhering to these methods.

The third important similarity is a consequence of the second: if one begins with method, then one is beginning with the subject, not the object.[1] Both traditions hold that the only way to answer the twin challenges of skepticism is to move from subjective certainty to objective knowledge. This is very obvious in Descartes, who begins with the knowledge of his existence and of those ideas he finds in his mind. It is not as overt in Bacon, but it is implied. Although he intends to lead his disciples "to things themselves,"[2] the way to the things is through the filter of the correct method applied to the human knower. Knowledge is drawn from sensation, and sensation is subjective. "For the testimony and information of the sense has reference always to man, not to the universe; and it is a great error to assert that sense is the measure of things."[3]

Locke

Let us begin our examination of the empirical tradition, founded by Bacon and Hobbes, with John Locke. Like Hobbes before him, Locke is primarily a social and political thinker interested in applying the new method to questions of community and government. Both are well known for their theories of the social contract. Also like Hobbes, Locke thinks that one must have firm foundations if one is to settle political questions. He sees that Galileo's method, based as it is on mathematics, holds out the promise of supplying those foundations. Locke makes use of the geometrical model, not just for deducing implications from empirically derived truths, but also as a model for clarity. Here he takes a page from Descartes. In fact, he explicitly refers to clarity and distinctness when

1. It is, of course, possible to adapt the method to the object as does Aristotle. But this involves using different methods for different objects, and the moderns insist on one method for all.
2. Bacon, *Great Instauration*, p. 14.
3. Ibid., p. 21.

suggesting remedies for the abuse of words.[4] Unlike Descartes, however, his purpose is not to establish a metaphysics as the foundation for certainty in the sciences, but to solve the political and religious problems of his day. In order to accomplish this practical task, Locke has to be sure of the range and effectiveness of human understanding (just like his illustrious predecessors). Thus Locke writes his *Essay Concerning Human Understanding*, which becomes the most widely read philosophical work of his generation.[5]

The reasons for Locke's popularity are many. First, Locke makes every effort to keep his language nontechnical. "My appearing therefore in print, being on purpose to be as useful as I may, I think it necessary to make what I have to say, as easy and intelligible to all sorts of readers, as I can."[6] Second, Locke is something of a mediator; he is not adverse to drawing on the older tradition where it serves his purposes. Thus there are numerous places in his work where the influence of traditional metaphysics and ethical thought are to be found. He allows, for example, that we can know by natural reason the existence of God as well as the fundamental principles of ethics. These claims are in some tension with his theory of knowledge, as we shall see, but he does not begin with the virulent condemnation of tradition characteristic of Bacon and Hobbes. Third, in addition to following Bacon and Hobbes, Locke draws from Descartes directly, both as to the need for clarity and distinctness of ideas, and for knowledge of the self and the existence of God. Hence Locke's style, the accessibility of his thought, and his eclecticism lead to the enormous success of his writings and his influence on succeeding generations of philosophers and other thinkers.

All this being true, Locke still agrees with the moderns that it is essential to demarcate the limits of human reason by following the proper method. Not to do so is to risk wandering about in absurdity. His purpose is to establish the origin, the degree of certainty, and the extent of human knowledge. And indeed, he thinks the extent of reason is rather narrow, not extending very far into metaphysics (only the existence of God), nor indeed reaching certainty in physics.[7] The area where reason can be most successful, the one for which it is suited, is the moral sphere.

4. "It is not enough a man uses his words as signs of some ideas: those ideas he annexes them to, if they be simple, must be clear and distinct." John Locke, "Language and Its Proper Use," in *Selections*, ed. Sterling P. Lamprecht (New York: Scribner's, 1956), p. 40.

5. So claims Sterling P. Lamprecht in his introduction to *Selections*, p. xxxv.

6. John Locke, *An Essay Concerning Human Understanding*, ed. A. S. Pringle-Pattison (Oxford: Clarendon, 1969), p. 6.

7. Locke claims that we can know that God exists by demonstration (*Essay*, bk. 4, ch. 10), but that natural philosophy cannot be made a science (*Essay*, bk. 4, ch. 12).

For, though the comprehension of our understandings comes exceeding short of the vast extent of things, yet we shall have cause enough to magnify the bountiful author of our being, for that proportion and degree of knowledge he has bestowed on us, so far above all the rest of the inhabitants of this our mansion. Men have reason to be well satisfied with what God hath thought fit for them, since he hath given them whatsoever is necessary for the conveniences of life, and the information of virtue; and has put within the reach of their discovery the comfortable provisions for this life, and the way that leads to a better.[8]

The practical nature of his enterprise is here clearly indicated, both as to the technical benefits foreseen by Bacon and Descartes and as to moral and religious fulfillment.

Locke's range of reason is somewhat greater than that of Bacon or Descartes. In fact, Locke's position seems to be a cross between the two of them with the addition of a moral component. From Bacon, he inherits an empirical method that denies innate ideas: all ideas come from sense impressions. From Descartes, he imports into his empirical philosophy the knowledge of self and God.

In his treatment of ethical themes he distinguishes himself most clearly from his predecessors. He differs from Bacon and Descartes in his attempt to give a rational basis for ethics and politics rather than just accepting the status quo, and he differs from Hobbes in his answer to the question of the origin of our ethical ideas. For Locke includes in his state of nature not only Hobbes's natural motivation to care for one's own life and property, but also a natural motivation to care for others.[9] It is here that the evidence of his borrowing from the traditional notion of the common good is most evident.

Locke also recognizes that knowledge can be distorted by our misuse of words. This interest in language, in questioning the meaningfulness or ambiguity of words, is another part of the heritage that he receives from Bacon and Hobbes. According to Locke, there is a great danger that our words may lead us astray, either in the process of learning or in communicating our knowledge to others.

Thus at the end of the *Essay*, in summing up his analysis of human knowledge, he declares that there are "three great provinces of the intellectual world, wholly separate and distinct from each other."[10] These are physica or natural philosophy (this includes matters concerning self and God), practica or ethics (whose end is not truth but right conduct), and

8. *Essay*, bk. 1, ch. 1, p. 12.
9. John Locke, "Of the State of Nature," ch. 2 in *Second Treatise of Government*, ed. C. B. Macpherson (Indianapolis: Hackett, 1980), p. 9.
10. *Essay*, bk. 4, ch. 21, p. 371.

semiotica or the doctrine of signs (which is a kind of logic by which the ideas gained in the first two are related and communicated). In making this declaration, Locke seems to distinguish two of the three realms of reason that we also insist upon distinguishing: the realm of the true and the realm of the good. The question is: how does he do so, and is he successful?

Let us look more deeply into the range of reason, as Locke demonstrates it, to see how he differs from his predecessors. We shall consider first the origin of ideas in general and then turn to a discussion of two of Locke's "great provinces"—physica (the realm of the true) and practica (the realm of the good).

He takes as his point of departure Bacon's view of things: all ideas come from the senses. Their origins lie in some kind of external impulse from material reality, such as Hobbes mentions.[11] This means that Descartes is wrong: there are no innate ideas. Here Locke sounds a bit like Aristotle, who also claims that all knowledge comes through the senses. However, according to Locke, not only are there no innate ideas; there are also no innate principles, whether speculative or practical. Aristotle would clearly disagree, at least with the claim that principles originate in some external impulse. Although sense experience may be the occasion for our understanding first principles, these principles are not reducible to experience. The main issue for Aristotle is the self-evidence of these principles, not their origin. As self-evident, they are in need of no further explanation. Since they are prerequisite for all knowledge, first principles cannot be learned.

Defending his rejection of the innateness of first principles, Locke argues that these principles cannot be proven to be innate. This, I think, is true. However, their self-evidence and irrefutability argue against their being learned in the same way as ideas that are learned from an experience of individuals and a process of abstraction and generalization. For some principles are presupposed to the recognition of individuals. Thus that something cannot be and not be at the same time (the law of noncontradiction) is presupposed to recognizing that any particular thing exists (as distinct from other things). In support of his position, Locke argues that children are not explicitly aware of this principle when they begin to reason.[12] This is undoubtedly true; however, the child must be using the principle if he or she knows anything. Locke's problem is that he focuses on the question of a principle's innateness rather than its self-evidence. The only proof of a first principle is that one always uses it and cannot operate without using it. It is less important to first

11. Ibid., bk. 2, ch. 8, p. 68.
12. Ibid., bk. 2, ch. 1, p. 45.

principles that they be innate or learned: what is essential is their self-evidence. Whenever thinking occurs, they are being used.

The problem becomes clearer when Locke denies that practical principles are innate, thus supposing their being learned from experience. Like his treatment of speculative principles, Locke offers, as an argument against their innateness, the fact that not all people agree as to their nature. Thus he tries to give an empirical argument (from experience) against any moral principles being innate. However, once again, the issue is not whether the principles are innate, but whether they are self-evident and prerequisite for any moral judgment.

Locke wants to give practical reason its own sphere distinct from that of speculative reason, and in this he is correct. He also wants to maintain that there are universal and certain principles of right and wrong. Given these two points, it seems impossible that the origin of these ideas should be the same as those of speculative reason, i.e., "imprinted by external things."[13] Perhaps they are the result of cultural context, of receiving impressions of kinds of moral actions. This seems to be the direction in which Locke is headed (and must head if he is to claim the empirical origins of morality). However, if he goes in this direction he can no longer maintain certainty and universality of moral principles, since cultures may differ from each other and the same culture change over time. Although he does not directly say that all moral principles are based on custom (as his disciple Hume will do), Locke does maintain that custom is "a greater power than nature."[14]

Let us turn now to a more specific analysis of the two realms of reason that Locke seems to distinguish, and let us begin with the realm of the true or what Locke calls physica. Given that all knowledge arises from sensation, what do we know about the world of things? That is, what are the limits of our knowledge? According to Locke, all ideas come from sensation (external things) or reflection (internal sense). "We have nothing in our minds which did not come in one of these two ways."[15] Locke divides the qualities we ascribe to things into two categories—primary and secondary.[16] Primary qualities are solidity, extension, figure, motion or rest, and number. Here Locke follows the same mathematical understanding of material things as do Galileo, Descartes, and Hobbes. These qualities are in the things themselves. Secondary qualities are such characteristics as color, sound, and taste. These are caused by the primary qualities; however, they do not exist in things but only in the mind. As for the substance of things (which Aristotle stresses as so

13. Ibid., bk. 1, ch. 2, p. 22.
14. Ibid., bk. 1, ch. 3, p. 35.
15. Ibid., bk. 2, ch. 1, p. 44.
16. Ibid., bk. 2, ch. 8, pp. 66–67.

important), Locke considers this idea to be vague and inadequate, merely something to account for the coexistence of primary qualities.[17]

This distinction, however, between primary qualities in the things and secondary qualities in the mind is ultimately not to the point, for according to Locke, we have no direct access to external things at all. "Since the mind, in all its thoughts and reasonings, hath no other immediate object but its own ideas, which it alone does or can contemplate, it is evident that our knowledge is only conversant about them."[18] Thus knowledge is merely the correspondence of our ideas with each other, not the correspondence of our ideas with reality. This presents a problem for Locke's empiricism, for how can one know that knowledge arises out of sensation if all one knows are one's ideas? Perhaps because of this difficulty, Locke expanded the range of theoretical reason (reason concerned with the truth about things) beyond that of his empirical predecessors Bacon and Hobbes.

Locke indicates that there are three kinds of theoretical knowledge: intuitive, demonstrative, and sensitive.[19] They are ordered by degrees of clarity and certainty. Here the influence of Descartes on Locke's thought is most obvious. The prime example of an instance of intuitive knowledge is the knowledge of the self (Descartes' *cogito*). The prime example of an instance of demonstrative knowledge is mathematical knowledge, whose method and certainty can be extended to other areas including knowledge of God's existence (the second stage of Descartes' knowledge). Sensitive knowledge is, of course, dependent on sensation (as Descartes allows after he has proved his own existence and the existence of a perfect God).

Although Locke could, perhaps, argue for knowledge of self from internal sensation (consistent with empirical principles), he goes beyond this, invoking the same kinds of arguments that Descartes uses. "If I doubt of all other things, that very doubt makes me perceive my own existence, and will not suffer me to doubt of that."[20] Such knowledge of self is the most certain kind of knowledge.

Locke's application of the method of mathematical demonstration to proving the existence of God is somewhat like Descartes' second proof in his third meditation in that it is based on one's awareness of dependence. Locke argues from the existence of an imperfect thinking being to the necessity of a cause that is also intelligent, a cause that is eternal.[21]

17. Ibid., bk. 2, ch. 23, pp. 154–56.
18. Ibid., bk. 4, ch. 1, p. 255. This is very similar to what Bacon says about the testimony of the senses being merely about the subject.
19. Ibid., bk. 4, ch. 9, pp. 309–10.
20. Ibid., bk. 4, ch. 9, p. 309.
21. Ibid., bk. 4, ch. 10. This is a fairly traditional argument similar to Aquinas's third way of proving the existence of God. See *ST* 1.2.3.c.

Like Descartes, Locke thinks that the existence of God is more certain than the existence of material things.[22] There is one large problem with the proof. Since all knowledge is based on the relation between ideas within the mind, the proof is about Locke's idea of God and not necessarily about an extramental God. This is the same problem Descartes faces in his proof from the idea of God, and it seems to presage Kant's relegation of the idea of God to the role of completing the scope of reason and grounding moral obligation.[23] Locke uses the idea of God in similar ways—arguing from within reason that the idea of God is necessary and making use of God to guarantee the natural law.[24]

Sensitive knowledge is weakest in clarity and distinctness. Although it represents our access to other things, it does so in only an obscure and confused way. The certainty of the existence of these things is not as great as either of the other kinds of knowledge, but it is certain enough for our practical purposes. "For our faculties being suited not to the full extent of being, nor to a perfect, clear, and comprehensive knowledge of things free from all doubt and scruple; but to the preservation of us, in whom they are; and accommodated to the use of life: they serve to our purpose well enough, if they will but give us certain notice of those things which are convenient or inconvenient for us."[25]

Oddly enough, Locke most doubts this third kind of reason, reason as scientific method able to come to the truth (so basic for Bacon and Hobbes). In fact, Locke is not really very interested in physics. "Natural philosophy is not capable of being made a science."[26] Although scientific knowledge can provide some advantages of ease and health, and thus is useful, the prospects for real advances look bleak. Nor does Locke think that any certainty is possible in natural philosophy. The greatest stumbling block to certainty (insurmountable in principle) is the fact that we do not know whether our ideas about material things are accurate or not, since we have no direct access to those things.

Let us turn now to the realm of the good, what Locke calls *practica*. In the end, Locke's is a practical philosophy. *"Morality* is *the proper science and business of mankind in general."*[27] Locke clearly thinks that

---

22. *Essay*, bk. 4, ch. 10, p. 313.

23. We shall discuss Kant more fully in chapter 6. Here, let me just say that Kant does not think that one can argue demonstratively for the existence of God, only that the human mind is such that it cannot help but think about an ultimate cause of everything and that the mind requires this idea of God to guarantee the moral law.

24. In his *Essay*, Locke shows that we can know that God exists by natural reason (*Essay*, bk. 4, ch. 10); in *The Second Treatise*, Locke makes use of God often as a foundation for rights; see, in particular, ch. 5, "Of Property."

25. *Essay*, bk. 4, ch. 11, p. 325.

26. Ibid., bk. 4, ch. 12, p. 331.

27. Ibid., bk. 4, ch. 12, p. 332.

we can know with certainty the principles of ethics. There is, however, a problem here, for such certainty cannot be guaranteed by empirical method. Such a method gives only relative certainty. If moral principles are absolutely certain, they must not depend on sense experience. Yet Locke has denied that they could come from anywhere else.

Can Locke's other two areas of knowledge, which do provide certainty (the intuitive and demonstrative), help here? Moral principles are not known by intuitive knowledge, for that applies only to knowledge of self. If morality is certain and unchanging, it seems that morality must be a species of demonstrative knowledge like our knowledge of mathematics. This is indeed where Locke places it. And like our knowledge of mathematics, moral knowledge is really only about the relations among our ideas.

> And hence it follows that moral knowledge is as capable of real certainty as mathematics. All the discourses of the mathematicians concern not the existence of those figures. In the same manner, the truth and certainty of moral discourses abstracts from the lives of men, and the existence of those virtues in the world whereof they treat: nor are Tully's [Cicero's] Offices less true, because there is nobody in the world that exactly practices his rules, and lives up to that pattern of a virtuous man which he has given us, and which existed nowhere when he writ but in idea.[28]

In some ways this analysis of the principles of morality is correct, and it certainly shows the difference between Locke and Hobbes. Locke's ethics accepts the teaching of the tradition on natural law. These laws are not a mere statistical abstraction from experience, nor mere convention. However, if they are not based in experience of either the sensation of external things or of the inner sense, then what is their basis? Here Locke does not seem to have an answer. He continues to hold that moral precepts are known by reason, but it seems impossible to get the first principles of natural law from empirical experience or, as he says, custom. Locke can argue for the certainty of ethics only by straddling the issue by borrowing principles from Descartes.

Besides this inconsistency of principles, there is a problem with invoking mathematics as a model for ethics, for the distinctive and essential element in ethics—obligation—is nowhere in mathematics. Thus Locke has failed to really differentiate practica from physica, the realm of the good from the realm of the true. According to Locke, knowledge of the existence of God and moral knowledge are both examples of demonstrative knowledge arrived at according to Descartes' paradigm of geometrical deduction. Since neither mathematics nor metaphysics presents us with

28. Ibid., bk. 4, ch. 4, pp. 289–90.

obligations, why should a mathematical ethics? A unique kind of reason (obligation) requires unique principles.

A more general problem for truth of any sort arises here as well. Locke holds that morality is as certain as mathematics because they are both about ideas found in the mind. Unlike empirical knowledge, neither mathematics nor ethics depends on any extramental reality. Although this may be acceptable in terms of mathematics,[29] it can hardly work for ethics. If ethics is a practical science, as Locke says it is, then it is about acting for some end or purpose. It is not mere matter in motion, but neither is it mere formal relations: ethics is primarily concerned with final cause, not material, moving, or formal causes. But if there are no goods to be chosen except for ideas in one's mind, then acting for the sake of goods would make no sense. Ethics would be, like mathematics, a purely theoretical, contemplative activity, or if it were to be applied in action, it would have to be in a technical vein, rather as mathematics issues in technology. As such, its intelligibility or moral worth would be judged by its fruits. But this kind of ethics (basically a form of utilitarianism) is very unlike the absolutist position of Cicero and the certain, unchanging ethics that Locke espouses.

If such basic goods as life, knowledge, friendship, and beauty were merely ideas in our minds and not to be ascribed independent intelligibility, then they would not be worth pursuing, and further, it would make no sense to say that we ought to pursue them. Locke's disciple Hume (whom we shall discuss later in this chapter), seeing this difficulty, abandons reason as the origin of morality and turns to the moral sense, a kind of instinctual sentiment or feeling.

There is a famous passage in Locke that sets this problem of objective knowledge (whether theoretical or practical) in a bold light.

> I must here in the entrance beg pardon of my reader for the frequent use of the word "idea," which he will find in the following treatise. It being that term, which, I think, serves best to stand for whatsoever is the object of the understanding when a man thinks; I have used it to express whatever is meant by phantasm, notion, species, or whatever it is which the mind can be employed about in thinking; and I could not avoid frequently using it.[30]

My interest in quoting this passage is not to get a fix on how Locke means to use terms but rather to call attention to a point of doctrine that may

29. It would not be acceptable for Aristotle, who considered mathematics to be abstracted from sense experience of extramental things. This point will be discussed more fully in chapter 8.

30. *Essay*, bk. 1, ch. 1, pp. 15–16.

seem innocuous enough but is critical for understanding Locke and the entire modern movement. The point concerns the object of human knowledge. For Aristotle and Aquinas, the object of knowledge is anything that is ("the soul is in a way all things"); thus the human being is open to the entire world of being. For Locke, as for Descartes before him and others after him, the object of knowledge is the impression or idea in the mind.

Thus the question arises: how do I know if my idea corresponds to reality? The question is a good one, given Locke's unequivocal declaration that the object of human knowledge is our ideas. In principle the question can never be answered. If all one knows are one's ideas, then one cannot know whether they correspond to the things they represent, for we have no access to the things so as to make the comparison. This is the so-called problem of the bridge, and almost all the moderns develop their particular systems as attempts to get around it.[31]

Oddly enough, although the empirical method begins with the ideal of explaining everything (including thought) by material and moving causes (matter in motion), it ends up, quite like the rationalist project introduced by Descartes, trying to explain the reality of matter in motion through an examination of ideas. Since both Bacon and Descartes begin with method, they both end up trying to explain reality by thought. What fits the method (the proper structure of the mind) is counted as real. The difference, of course, is that the empiricists claim that the first of all "ideas" are sense impressions, while the idealists hold that the first of all ideas are innate and prior to experience.

The alternative position, which has been called realism and is most authentically presented in Aristotle and Aquinas, holds that ideas or impressions or species are not "what is known" but "that by which" real things are known.[32] The human being, through the senses and the intellect, *is*, in a way, other things: this is knowledge. This is where we must begin, with the activity of which we are aware. We must not instrumentalize the powers of intellect and sense; for if we do, they will always stand as an unbridgeable gap between us and the really objective world to be known. All the talk of species or impressions or ideas is secondary, words to indicate what must be the case if there is knowledge.

31. This problem was recognized by Montaigne, who gives it expression in his *Apology for Raymond Sebond*: "If you say that these sense-impressions convey the quality of outside objects to our souls by means of resemblances, how can our rational soul make sure that they are resemblances, since it has no direct contact of its own with the outside objects?" (*An Apology for Raymond Sebond*, trans. M. A. Screech [London: Penguin, 1993], p. 186). Montaigne sees this problem as one more nail in the coffin of reason, whose death is the birth of skepticism.

32. Thomas Aquinas, *ST* 1.85.2.

One begins in knowledge; only in knowledge can self-consciousness arise. One begins by assuming that knowledge (however rudimentary and incomplete) is occurring, and then goes on to say what must be the case if knowledge is occurring.

To begin with the question of whether knowledge is possible is to set oneself on the road to skepticism. Like Bacon and Descartes, Locke is no skeptic.[33] Skepticism would obviously be antithetical to his purpose of securing some certainty concerning the moral and political life. However, his way of establishing the certainty places his whole project in danger. According to Locke, the answer to the problem of moral skepticism is to be found in the certain knowledge of the mind. Like the other moderns, Locke begins with the subject. The immediate objects of our understanding are the ideas that we find in our minds. Locke hopes that his restraining of reason from wandering in the "vast ocean of being"[34] will cure us of our skepticism. In fact, the restriction of reason to the method of examining our ideas (Montaigne's new method as well) seals the fate of his project: it must lead, if followed logically, to skepticism.

Of course, the question can still be asked of the realist how well ideas reflect reality, and indeed Aristotle and Aquinas never claim that ideas contain a perfect representation of reality. However, this imperfection does not refute realism; quite the contrary, the affirmation that the mind knows things through ideas makes such a judgment of inadequacy plausible. Something about the real thing known raises a question that goes beyond the formulated idea, and thus moves the serious pursuer of truth to formulate a new and more comprehensive or accurate idea, which may in turn need to be revised if new data is discovered that does not fit the old structure.[35] The possibility of advances in science (as well as metaphysics and ethics) depends on such a realism. From the moment one is cut off from contact with things other than oneself, legitimate scientific inquiry is impossible, for the verification stage is in principle impossible.

This "problem of the bridge" is most concretely exemplified when considering knowledge of the physical world, for if all one knows is the idea of a rose and not somehow the rose itself, then how can one know whether the idea of the rose is correct? But the problem is also one for ethics. Given that one has some idea of how one should act, how can one find out whether this idea is correct? Unless there is some objective good, one can never, in principle, settle the question. Since this objective good is not a physical thing "out there" apart from my physical being,

33. See *Essay*, bk. 1, ch. 1, p. 13.
34. Ibid., bk. 1, ch. 1, p. 14.
35. For an excellent account of this theory of knowledge, see Bernard Lonergan, *Verbum: Word and Idea in Aquinas* (Notre Dame, IN: University of Notre Dame Press, 1967).

one may be tempted to deny that it is extramental. But of course, any reality that is not material is not literally "inside" or "outside" anything since these spatial terms are only appropriate for describing material things. Whether we speak of universal truths or moral ideals, these realities are immaterial but real. To deny their reality is to deny that there is any truth to our thoughts or goodness to our intentions.

In practice, Locke has a good deal to say about how we should live our lives and the foundations for such obligations. Given the absence of distinct principles of morality, how does he justify his position? It is clear that he cannot do so empirically; for empirical knowledge does not reach certainty, but Locke insists that morality is as certain as mathematics. The answer comes by way of Descartes' method. From the intuition of our existence, and the proof of the existence of God from this intuition, we can deduce our obligation to others. That is, God saves the day. Although his presentation speaks of the law of nature, this law is not known through self-evident first principles (as it is for Aquinas); rather it is known because we know the nature of God as creator.

> The state of nature has a law of nature to govern it, which obliges every one: and reason, which is that law, teaches all mankind, who will but consult it, that being all equal and independent, no one ought to harm another in his life, health, liberty, or possessions.[36]

So far this sounds just like Aquinas: it is the natural law given us in reason that tells us what we ought to do. However, the explanation is not complete. Locke continues:

> for men being all the servants of one omnipotent, and infinitely wise maker; all the servants of one sovereign master, sent into the world by his order, and about his business; they are his property, whose workmanship they are, made to last during his, not one another's pleasure: and being furnished with like faculties, sharing all in one community of nature, there cannot be supposed any such subordination among us, that may authorize us to destroy one another, as if we were made for one another's uses, as the inferior ranks of creatures are for ours.[37]

Because of God we should treat each other equally; we all have the same creator and the same faculties; therefore, we should not mistreat each other.[38]

36. Locke, *Second Treatise*, ch. 2, p. 9.
37. Ibid.
38. This point is underlined by what Locke says in his essay on toleration: atheists should not be tolerated, for without a belief in God, there can be no ethics. "Those are not at all to be tolerated who deny the being of God. Promises, covenants, and oaths, which are the

However, even if it is true that we are all created by God (though Locke's metaphysics, like Descartes', cannot really succeed in proving God's existence), it does not follow that we are obliged to act in one way or another. Hume will be quick to point out that premises of fact, whether scientific, mathematical, or metaphysical, do not logically imply conclusions of obligation: one cannot derive "ought" (the realm of the moral good) from "is" (the realm of the true). We already discussed this in chapter 1, but let me quote Hume here since the point pertains to this passage in Locke and since Hume will be discussed in this chapter as one of the disciples of the empirical tradition begun by Bacon and Hobbes.

> In every system of morality, which I have hitherto met with, I have always remark'd, that the author proceeds for some time in the ordinary way of reasoning, and establishes the being of God, or makes observations concerning human affairs; when all of a sudden I am surpriz'd to find, that instead of the usual copulations of propositions, *is* and *is not*, I meet with no proposition that is not connected with an *ought*, or an *ought not*. This change is imperceptible; but is, however, of the last consequence. For as this *ought*, or *ought not*, expresses some new relation or affirmation, 'tis necessary that it shou'd be observ'd and explain'd; and at the same time that a reason should be given, for what seems altogether inconceivable, how this new relation can be a deduction from others, which are entirely different from it.[39]

One cannot derive morality from metaphysics. If morality does not have its own first principles, it is not a matter of reason, for the first principles of morality cannot be deduced from theoretical truths (whether the intuition that one exists, or the existence of God, or facts about equal faculties in human beings). Thus Locke does not really distinguish between the realms of the true and the good, for he tries (unsuccessfully) to derive the realm of the good from the realm of the true.

Nor does Locke succeed in distinguishing the realm of the beautiful from the realms of the good and true. Given the practical nature of his enterprise, Locke shows very little interest in the realm of the beautiful. In fact, he is rather hostile towards it. In an essay considering the proper education for youth, Locke discourages any attention to poetry.

> If he have a poetic vein, it is to me the strangest thing in the world that the father should desire or suffer it to be cherished or improved. Methinks

bonds of human society, can have no hold upon an atheist. The taking away of God, though but even in thought, dissolves all" ("The Spirit of Toleration," in *Selections*, p. 50).

39. David Hume, *A Treatise of Human Nature*, bk. 3, pt. 1, sec. 1, ed. L. A. Selby-Bigge, 2nd ed., rev. by P. H. Nidditch (Oxford: Clarendon, 1978), pp. 468–69.

the parents should labor to have it stifled and suppressed as much as may
be. . . . For it is seldom seen that any one discovers mines of gold and silver
in Parnassus. It is a pleasant air, but a barren soil.[40]

Here, Locke sounds a good deal like Bacon; since poetry is not useful, it
is not worth pursuing. Worse than this, the pursuit of poetry is likely to
lead to the keeping of bad company and even to gambling.[41] The idea of
beauty as something with its own intrinsic value is completely foreign
to Locke's thought.

Since for Locke an idea is one thing (existing in the mind) and the
thing it represents is another thing (existing outside of the mind), and
since there is no bridge between these two things, attaining verified
certainty about reality is impossible. Even the existence of a world outside the mind is called into question. Thus when Locke says explicitly
that ideas are what we know, the return to skepticism is assured. With
Locke we see the fruit of Bacon's *Great Instauration*, and far from being
the restoration of the precious "commerce between the mind of man
and the nature of things" that Bacon had envisioned, it is just the opposite—the impossibility of any commerce between mind and nature,
or at least our knowledge of such a commerce. This is skepticism. Let
us trace briefly its progress in the empirical tradition as it develops in
Berkeley and Hume.

Berkeley

Bishop George Berkeley begins with the same practical concern as his
predecessors: fight skepticism and advance the sciences. The titles of his
major works make this clear. The subtitle of his *A Treatise Concerning the
Principles of Human Knowledge* runs as follows: *Wherein the Chief Causes
of Error and Difficulty in the Sciences, with the Grounds of Skepticism,
Atheism, and Irreligion Are Inquired into*. Consider also the full title of
his *Dialogues*, which is *Three Dialogues between Hylas and Philonous the
Design of Which Is Plainly to Demonstrate the Reality and Perfection of
Human Knowledge, the Incorporeal Nature of the Soul, and the Immediate
Providence of a Deity in Opposition to Sceptics and Atheists, also to Open a
Method for Rendering the Sciences More Easy, Useful, and Compendious*.
All the elements of the modern tradition are here: the practical nature of
the enterprise, the interest in establishing human knowledge on a solid
footing against the skeptics, and the introduction of a new method by
which the sciences can be advanced.

40. John Locke, "Some Thoughts Concerning Education," in *Selections*, p. 9.
41. Ibid.

The method is a rigorous application of Locke's claim that the object of our understanding is our ideas. Berkeley is quick to see that if all we know are our ideas, we cannot know external reality directly. Hence, authentic metaphysics equates perception with reality.

> Some truths are so near and obvious to the mind that a man need only open his eyes to see them. Such I take to be this important one, to wit, that all the choir of heaven and furniture of the earth, in a word all those bodies which compose the mighty frame of the world, have not any subsistence without a mind—that their *being* is to be perceived or known.[42]

While Locke rules out innate ideas but allows knowledge of sensible things through abstraction of many experiences, Berkeley rules out abstraction, for he sees that it is incompatible with Locke's first principle. If all we know are our ideas, then we do not derive these ideas from experiences of external things, for then we would know or perceive external things, which knowledge has been denied. Thus primary qualities, such as extension and motion, are no different from secondary qualities, such as color or sound. All qualities are nothing but perceptions in the mind. Hence we have no reason to believe that there is a world of things with its own independent existence.

Berkeley sees the full implications of the "problem of the bridge," and his solution is simply to deny the need for a bridge: all reality is perception.[43] The assumption of the existence of extramental reality is simply incompatible with making the study of mind primary. "It is very obvious, upon the least inquiry into our thoughts, to know whether it is possible for us to understand what is meant by the *absolute existence of sensible objects in themselves, or without the mind*. To me it is evident those words mark out either a direct contradiction, or else nothing at all."[44] Given Locke's starting place, any claim to extramental existence is absurd.

Does this mean that the world is dependent on me? Is this radical subjectivism? No, for there are other minds, and there is God. All Berkeley is claiming is that things must be perceived to exist, not that *I* have to perceive them. Hence his position is not solipsism. And although

---

42. George Berkeley, *A Treatise Concerning the Principles of Human Knowledge*, § 6, ed. Colin M. Turbayne (Indianapolis: Bobbs-Merrill, 1979), pp. 25–26.

43. Although this sounds a bit like the realist position in its identity of knowing and being, there is a significant difference. The realist position holds that to know something is somehow to be that thing. Berkeley, however, is saying that to be something is to be known. Aquinas would say that this is true for God, whose knowledge is the measure of things, but it is not true for us for whom things are the measure of the accuracy and fullness of our knowing. See Aquinas, *ST* 1.14.8.

44. *Treatise*, § 24, p. 34.

science would be threatened if reality depended on human minds (since it is conceivable that there was a time when no human being existed), the world studied by science (at least as to its intelligibility) is saved by Berkeley's claim that God perceives all things. "So long as they are not actually perceived by me, or do not exist in my mind or that of any other created spirit, they must either have no existence at all, or else subsist in the mind of some Eternal Spirit—it being perfectly unintelligible, and involving all the absurdity of abstraction, to attribute to any single part of them an existence independent of a spirit."[45]

How do we know that there is a God and not just me perceiving the world? Berkeley's answer, following Descartes, is that some of the ideas I perceive come to me without or against my will. If I open my eyes, it is not in my power to change what I see; if I step outside, it is not in my power to change what I hear. Hence there is some other will or spirit that produces these perceptions. Some of these perceptions follow so regularly that Berkeley calls them laws of nature. Such laws are obviously not the product of other human beings, but of a being that transcends this world in power and wisdom. "This insistent uniform working . . . so evidently displays the goodness and wisdom of that governing Spirit whose will constitutes the laws of nature."[46]

This argument is fairly traditional in one way: it argues from the regularity or order in nature to the origin of that order and regularity in an intelligent governing being.[47] What is different about it is its lack of reference to a world of extramental things. Berkeley's empiricism is restricted to our experience of the ideas we find in our minds. His conclusion from experience to God is not through the things of this world. This is typical of modern metaphysics and is consistent with the metaphysics of Descartes. One begins with ideas and traces out their implications.

From the material mechanism of Hobbes as one extreme of rational explanation, we have arrived at the other extreme—the immaterial mentalism of Berkeley, and Locke has been our transition. The empirical assumption of Bacon and Hobbes is from its inception a threat to the legitimacy of thought; for if thought is conceived as merely matter in motion, it is hard to see how it could reasonably be trusted. Locke is uneasy with this model and carves out a place for intuitive knowledge of self, demonstrative knowledge of God, scientific knowledge (though weak) of the sensible world through some kind of abstraction, and also a place for ethical knowledge (perhaps also by abstraction, but less clearly

45. Ibid., § 6, p. 26.
46. Ibid., § 32, p. 37.
47. See, for example, Thomas Aquinas's fifth way, *ST* 1.2.3.c.

so). Having denied innate knowledge, abstraction seems the only way to have knowledge of extramental realities, whether physical or moral.

Berkeley, however, sees immediately that abstraction of universal knowledge is not compatible with radical empiricism or with Locke's statement that all we know are our ideas. Since sense perceptions are more real than thoughts, yet these perceptions cannot give us certain knowledge, evidently thoughts cannot be trusted to give us certain knowledge, unless they can be said to originate otherwise than from perceptions. Berkeley solves the problem of the bridge (how we can know reality if all we know are our ideas) by equating reality with perception, and he solves the problem of how to get universal ideas from perception by saying that all perception comes to us from God, not material things.[48] Hence, ideas such as the laws of nature or moral rules can be real because their origin is not in the weakness of the human intellect, which must work from empirical beginnings, but from the mind of God.

Yet Berkeley cannot succeed in having it both ways, that is, in having certain knowledge and empirical foundations. In keeping with empirical foundations, he holds that sense ideas received from God are more real than those we call thoughts.

> The ideas imprinted on the senses by the Author of nature are called *real things*; and those excited in the imagination, being less regular, vivid, constant, are more properly termed *ideas*, or *images of things*, which they copy and represent. But then our sensations, be they never so vivid and distinct, are nevertheless ideas, that is, they exist in the mind, or are perceived by it, as truly as the ideas of its own framing. The ideas of sense are allowed to have more reality in them, that is to be more strong, orderly, and coherent than the creatures of the mind; but this is no argument that they exist without the mind.[49]

Two problems arise here. The first is the problem of representation; the second is the problem of overall intelligibility.

First consider the problem of representation. Although Berkeley is keen to point out that the problem of the bridge is insurmountable on Locke's terms (that is, Locke cannot know that his ideas represent external things), Berkeley is not as quick to see the same difficulty in his philosophy. How can Berkeley claim that ideas or images of things represent real things (that is, sense impressions)? He has merely shifted the problem from a comparison of ideas and things to one of different

---

48. Here Berkeley sounds very much like Malebranche, a disciple of Descartes whom we shall discuss in the next chapter. Indeed, Berkeley knew and was influenced by the work of Malebranche.

49. *Treatise*, § 33, p. 38.

kinds of ideas. How does he know they are representative? Does he have a criterion by which to judge which are and which are not? He might point to God as the guarantor of one's knowledge of the difference, but how does that suffice, since it could be that God as first principle might reverse the order of precedence if he so chose?

Even if the representational connection between sense impressions and ideas could be maintained, the precedence of sense impressions in terms of reality (his pure empiricism) threatens the legitimacy of his conclusions. For what kind of status does reason have in a system where sense impressions are said to be more real than ideas that are derived from them? Reason clearly must take a back seat to sensation, and if it does, we are back to the fundamental problem of empiricism—its unintelligibility. A theory of knowledge in which sensation has precedence over thought (not only in time, but in reality) is one in which mind is effectively lost.

To save the mind, Berkeley has recourse to God. But this will not serve any more than Descartes' reliance on God to guarantee the validity of his knowledge of extramental reality. For it is the mind operating according to its natural powers, apparently, which is able to know that God exists. But if the whole issue of universal ideas is called into question (since they are less real than impressions, and impressions carry no universality), and if the only way to know that God exists is to believe that the universal ideas that one has are valid (since they call for a universal cause), then it is illegitimate (begging the question) to introduce God as the origin of the universal ideas that show one that God exists.

Given his understanding of the relationship between intelligibility and God, it is not surprising to find that Berkeley grounds both his ethics and aesthetics in God. Like Locke, the support for moral obligation comes from knowing that God exists as creator, although for Berkeley, the dependence of creatures on God is even more pronounced. At the end of the *Treatise*, Berkeley encourages his reader to be good by invoking the knowledge of God's omnipotence and omnipresence.

> He is present and conscious to our innermost thoughts; and we have a most absolute and immediate dependence on him. A clear view of which great truths cannot choose but fill our hearts with an awful circumspection and holy fear, which is the strongest incentive to *virtue* and the best guard against *vice*.[50]

Again, Hume would point out that, even if the absolute dependence of everything on God can be proven by Berkeley (which Hume will deny), such a truth does not and cannot imply the obligation to be virtuous.

50. Ibid., § 155, p. 104.

Not only does Berkeley call on God to establish why we should be virtuous; he also argues that knowing that all intelligibility comes from God solves the problem of evil. Since we know that God exists as the perfect being, we know that what appears to be evil to us really is not evil. Here we have the same metaphysical method of arguing from God to the world that we found in Descartes and Locke. And again, the problem with this argument is that we cannot deduce truths about the world from the essence of God, for we do not and cannot know that essence. Such an argument, while invoking the faith of the reader in the mystery of God's providence, does nothing to show the reader that it is rational to consider evil as good. And, in fact, such a consideration would seem to be highly dangerous from the perspective of morality.[51]

Unlike Locke, Berkeley does recognize beauty as worthy of appreciation for its own sake. Perhaps this is because of Berkeley's primary interest in metaphysics. The ultimate object of metaphysics—God—is an object of contemplation, infinitely worthy of appreciation though not useful in any practical sense. Since beauty is also to be appreciated in itself, it is rather like an object of contemplation. And when Berkeley speaks of the beautiful, he does so in ways consonant with the tradition I shall discuss in chapter 8. That is, he considers the integrated order and proportion to be key elements in the beautiful. "We should further consider that the very blemishes and defects of nature are not without their use, in that they make an agreeable sort of variety and augment the beauty of the rest of creation, as shades in a picture serve to set off the brighter and more enlightened parts."[52]

However, although beauty is not dismissed out of practical concerns as it was for Locke, it is ultimately absorbed by metaphysics. Just as metaphysics is invoked as a principle of moral order, so it is invoked as a principle of aesthetic order. Because God exists we know that the relationships between things must be beautiful. We do not begin with our experience of beautiful things that have their own principles of beauty, since all we know are our perceptions. Just as all intelligibility is to be found in God, so all the intelligibility of beauty is to be found in God. There is no room in Berkeley's system for an analysis of the beauty of natural things such as flowers, mountain vistas, or human faces, or of beautiful works of art, for these things have no objective being of their

51. Hume will also complain about such ungrounded arguments being used to reconcile us to the evil in the world (see *Dialogues Concerning Natural Religion*, pt. 10). In the *Dialogues Concerning Natural Religion*, Hume's target is Leibniz, whom we shall discuss in the next chapter. However, since Berkeley's position is very like Leibniz's here, Hume's complaint would stand against Berkeley, as well.

52. *Treatise*, § 152, p. 101. This is very much like Augustine's treatment of the issue in *Of True Religion* 40.76.

own that warrants our appreciation. "It is indeed an opinion strangely prevailing amongst men that houses, mountains, rivers, and, in a word, all sensible objects, have an existence, natural or real, distinct from their being perceived by the understanding."[53] Their beauty is not in them but in the perceiver. Although Berkeley does not go with aesthetic subjectivism (for the being of things is independent of our perceiving since God perceives them), he avoids it only by claiming that things subsist in God. If Berkeley's metaphysics fails to prove that God exits (and it does), then the foundations for his aesthetics are taken way.

More generally, since Berkeley's metaphysics fails to prove God's existence, the guarantee of any objective knowing, whether of the true, the good, or the beautiful, is taken away. Insoluble on empirical grounds, the problems in Berkeley's metaphysics, ethics, and aesthetics lead inevitably to skepticism. It did not take long for someone to see the implications of Berkeley's thought. Hume takes up the banner of empiricism only to find that empiricism's fight against skepticism has ended in skepticism's camp.

Hume

Hume shares the basic tenets of the moderns: concern over philosophical disagreement and obscure metaphysical debates, a practical desire to overcome these, and the conviction that to do so one must study the self. Only by discovering the proper method can we overcome the natural defects of the mind. He adopts the basic empiricist principles of Locke and Berkeley. With them he claims that all we know are our perceptions[54] and that sense impressions are more real ("forceful" and "vivacious" are his terms)[55] than thoughts, which are faint copies of them. If we are ever in doubt as to the meaningfulness of an idea, all we have to do is ask whether or not it is derived from a sense impression. If it is, then it is legitimate although weak and obscure; if it is not, then it is meaningless.

However, while adopting their principles, Hume is critical of both Locke and Berkeley for their conclusions. He thinks that Locke is too influenced by the scholastics. We mentioned that Locke is a moderate in his attitude toward the ancient and medieval tradition, adopting (perhaps uncritically) numerous points that he thought were helpful in establishing his position. Hume is not a moderate. He shares the

53. *Treatise*, § 4, p. 24.
54. David Hume, *An Enquiry Concerning Human Understanding*, sec. 12, pt. 1, ed. Eric Steinberg (Indianapolis: Hackett, 1980), pp. 104–5.
55. *Enquiry*, sec. 2, p. 10.

attitude of Bacon and Hobbes: all things scholastic are suspect, both philosophically and religiously, tainted as they are by the superstition of Roman Catholicism. Hume agrees with Berkeley's criticism of Locke's abstraction, and he rejects Locke's claim that morality is a relation of ideas as clear and certain as mathematics. In Hume's two categories of human understanding—relations of ideas and matters of fact—he places morality in the second category, reserving relations of ideas for mathematics and logic.[56]

However, Hume is also critical of Berkeley. Having rightly seen the problem with Locke's representational theory of knowledge (that if all we know is our ideas, then we cannot know whether they represent reality), Berkeley makes the more outrageous claim that we know God to be the eternal perceiver and hence the guarantor of the reality of external things. Hume does not think that Berkeley has any grounds for making this move. Given that our powers are suitable only for making probable statements about what we experience, discussions of an infinite immaterial being (which we obviously have not experienced) are highly suspect. "However we may flatter ourselves, that we are guided, in every step that we take, by a kind of verisimilitude and experience; we may be assured, that this fancied experience has no authority, when we thus apply it to subjects, that lie entirely out of the sphere of experience."[57] If ideas are copies of sense experiences, as Berkeley asserts, then there must be a sense experience that is the basis of our idea of God. Since there is none, the idea of God is meaningless. Also, if we are ignorant of the forces acting between bodies (so much so that we deny that they are real), how much more must we be ignorant of forces acting between minds and bodies, or between minds.

> We have no idea of the Supreme Being, but what we learn from reflection on our own faculties. Were our ignorance, therefore, a good reason for rejecting any thing, we should be led into that principle of denying all energy in the Supreme Being as much as in the grossest matter. We surely comprehend as little the operations of one as of the other. Is it more difficult to conceive, that motion may arise from impulse, than that it may arise from volition? All we know is our profound ignorance in both cases."[58]

If we cannot understand either the interactions of material things or acts of volition, then we can understand nothing of the real world in

---

56. Ultimately, Hume says that morality is not a matter of fact to be studied by reason, but a fact of our passional nature to be felt. See *A Treatise of Human Nature*, bk. 2, pt. 1, sec. 1, pp. 468–69.

57. *Enquiry*, sec. 7, pt. 1, p. 48.

58. Ibid.

which we exist. This, of course, is skepticism—the logical end of a philosophy that begins with doubt about the possibility of any knowledge
and turns to the self as the way out. Hume sees the inevitability of this
conclusion in the very principles of Descartes. Methodic doubt must end
in skepticism. If one begins by doubting not only the accuracy of one's
knowledge but the very knowing power itself, then there is no way to
reason to certainty, for the validity of reasoning is called into question.
"The CARTESIAN doubt, therefore, were it possible to be attained by
any human creature (as it plainly is not) would be entirely incurable; and
no reasoning could ever bring us to a state of assurance and conviction
upon any subject."[59]

However, not only does Cartesian doubt, prior to philosophizing, lead
to skepticism; so also does the empirical method. Once one affirms that all
we know are our own perceptions, the road is blocked to any knowledge
of reality. According to Hume, the most sophisticated of the empirical
systems (Berkeley's) itself ends in skepticism, for his introduction of
God as explanatory cause is inconsistent with his empirical foundations.
"That all his arguments, though otherwise intended, are, in reality, merely
skeptical, appears from this, *that they admit of no answer and produce
no conviction*. Their only effect is to cause that momentary amazement
and irresolution and confusion, which is the result of skepticism."[60]

Does Hume have an answer to this skepticism? Yes, but it does not
lie within reason's power. It is custom and ultimately instinct that guide
us in our thoughts and actions. Hume arrives at this conclusion rather
early in his work and remarks that this is the conclusion to which all
our reasonings will bring us.

> All these operations are a species of natural instincts, which no reasoning
> or process of the thought and understanding is able, either to produce,
> or prevent. At this point, it would be very allowable for us to stop our
> philosophical researches. In most questions, we can never make a single
> step farther; and in all questions, we must terminate here at last, after our
> most restless and curious enquiries.[61]

This passage is found about one third of the way through the *Enquiry*.
Why Hume continues to explore ideas and argue for or against them is
a question that his principles cannot explain. But then again, perhaps
he is being consistent with his vision of the "whimsical condition of
mankind, who must act and reason and believe; though they are not
able, by their most diligent inquiry, to satisfy themselves concerning

59. Ibid., sec. 12, pt. 1, p. 103.
60. Ibid., sec. 12, pt. 1, p. 107, fn. 64.
61. Ibid., sec. 5, pt. 1, p. 30.

the foundation of these operations, or to remove the objections, which may be raised against them."[62] Thus we carry on, although we cannot say how it is we know anything or why it is we act. The picture is pretty bleak, but that is to be expected if one chooses the empirical route. We are essentially no different from the beasts; all our actions (speculative, moral, aesthetic) depend on experimental reasoning, and this reasoning is a mysterious activity. "The experimental reasoning itself, which we possess in common with beasts, and on which the whole conduct of life depends, is nothing but a species of instinct or mechanical power, that acts in us unknown to ourselves."[63]

At this point Hume makes a very interesting move. With the foundations of theoretical reason destroyed, and with them the foundations of moral reason, Hume looks around for some other mode of explanation. This, as we have noted, is instinct. But how does he conceive this instinct? Apparently he does so through reference to what we have called the third area of human reason: beauty. It is taste and sentiment that guide us in our moral lives, most obviously, but also in our speculative and scientific endeavors. Hume rejects the idea of Locke that morality is a matter of abstract rules as clear and certain as mathematics (an object of reason), and instead follows Francis Hutcheson in making morality a matter of feelings of internal taste and sentiments.[64] "The case is the same as in our judgments concerning all kinds of beauty, and tastes, and sensations. Our approbation is imply'd in the immediate pleasure they convey to us."[65] However, Hutcheson's and Hume's idea of beauty does not focus on beauty's intelligible components but rather emphasizes the subjective and affective aspects. In fact, given Hume's reduction of reason to affection, the association of instinct and beauty is clearly not to be understood as intelligible but is an association to be felt.

> Morals and criticism are not so properly objects of the understanding as of taste and sentiment. Beauty, whether moral or natural, is felt, more properly than perceived. Or if we reason concerning it, and endeavor to fix

62. Ibid., sec. 12, pt. 2, p. 111. His position is very like that of Montaigne two hundred years earlier. Montaigne writes extensively, giving many reasons and examples, to show that reason is entirely incapable of establishing any truth about reality or morality.

63. Ibid., sec. 9, p. 72.

64. Hume, "Letter from a Gentleman to His Friend in Edinburgh," in *Enquiry*, p. 122. This theory originated in the work of Shaftesbury (Anthony Ashley Cooper) a generation earlier. Shaftesbury does not distinguish the three realms of reason (the true, the good, the beautiful) but collapses truth and virtue into beauty and equates beauty with taste. Newman quotes him in his *Idea of a University* (p. 150): "The most natural beauty in the world is honesty and moral truth; for all beauty is truth." Like Hutcheson and Hume, Shaftesbury means by beauty a kind of feeling or taste, not in any sense an intellectual insight.

65. Hume, *Treatise*, bk. 3, pt. 1, sec. 2, p. 471.

its standard, we regard a new fact, to wit, the general taste of mankind, or some such fact, which may be the object of reasoning and inquiry.[66]

Although it may not be clear (and perhaps by the nature of the case cannot be clear) exactly how Hume is going to use this principle of beauty in his philosophy, what is clear is his severe limitation of reason. Metaphysics and normative ethics are out. So is science taken as a study yielding truth and not just probability. Mathematics and logic he retains as having certainty, but they are irrelevant to human action. And while he seems to want to preserve beauty (perhaps even as a kind of first principle), it is not beauty known, but beauty felt.[67]

Note that the senses that he emphasizes (taste and touch) are precisely those said to be farthest from a participation in beauty in the ancient and medieval tradition. According to this tradition, sight and hearing, as the most intellectual of the senses, most participate in beauty. Even today our language (if not our theory of beauty) tends to support the ancient and medieval view. We speak regularly of beautiful sights and sounds, but almost never do we call a taste or a smell beautiful; and except for the innocuous and nearly completely empty notion of a "beautiful feeling," we do not tend to speak of touch as appreciating beauty. Thus to say that Hume slides from the true and the good, as criteria for judgment, into beauty is only partially accurate, for beauty is not an intelligible term for Hume, but a word to indicate an irrational source of our preferences.

For Hume, reason has a very limited role. It does not understand first principles, whether of physics, metaphysics, morality, or aesthetics: custom and instinct provide for these. Reason is merely a logical process, either deductive (concerning relations of ideas) or inductive (concerning matters of fact). All speculation that is not either relations of ideas (mathematics and logic) or matters of fact (able to be resolved back to sense impressions) is illegitimate. This point he makes dramatically in the last words of his *Enquiry*:

> When we run over libraries, persuaded of these principles, what havoc must we make? If we take in our hand any volume; of divinity or school metaphysics, for instance; let us ask, *Does it contain any abstract reasoning concerning quantity or number?* No. *Does it contain any experimental reasoning concerning matter of fact and existence?* No. Commit it then to the flames: For it can contain nothing but sophistry and illusion.

66. *Essay*, bk. 12, ch. 3, p. 114.
67. Beauty clearly does involve an element of feeling. However, in judging one thing more beautiful than another, we also make use of intelligible characteristics such as unity, integrity, and proportion.

Hume, of course, has a problem. If reason is some kind of unknown mechanical power, then it is unintelligible. But if reason is unintelligible, then everything for which Hume has argued in this book is unintelligible—nothing more than matter in random motion. If this is true, then there is clearly no reason to believe what Hume tells us.

The Fruit of Empiricism

The ultimate implications of empiricist principles seem to be well borne out in Hume: we return to a skepticism much like Montaigne's. Not only is reason incapable of pronouncing on metaphysics, ethics, or aesthetics; it is incapable of pronouncing even on science. The ideal of explaining everything by reference to matter in motion (scientific method) proves to be unable to explain anything. For thought itself and freedom of choice cannot be verified by such a method and hence are unintelligible to the empirical scientist. Matter in motion is always changing and hence can provide no intelligibility over time or space, and if we act mechanically according to the dictates of matter in motion, then we are not free. If thought is unintelligible, then so are all the pronouncements of thought.

Thus, the experiment of getting matter to explain meaning fails, so much so that it turns into its opposite—the attempt to get meaning to explain matter—only meaning has now been transformed from ideas and sense impressions to taste and instinct. Taste and sentiment reign supreme over all areas that had once been held to be the provenance of reason. Nothing is known, not even science. This is skepticism, the inevitable end of making a subrational principle the principle of all explanation.

Perhaps Descartes' disciples, beginning as they do with thought, will be more successful in preserving intelligibility. Let us see.

5

The Rationalist Quest;
or, From Thought to Thing

Although the empiricist wing of the scientific tradition, which collapses human nature into animal nature, leads logically to the skepticism of Hume, perhaps the rationalist wing fares better. After all, it takes as its point of departure the insight that reason is what distinguishes us from the beasts and that intelligibility is not reducible to matter in motion. Not being tied to the verification principle, the rationalist tradition can better account for the universality of ideas as well as the transcendence of freedom of choice over material conditions. The challenge for rationalism is to account for the world that science understands (the physical world) from the content of innate ideas. Admittedly, Descartes runs into some problems relating ideas to external reality and mind to body; however, it might be that with minor corrections, Descartes' scheme can be made to work. Let us take a look at some of these corrected versions of Descartes' thought presented by his disciples.

Three of his immediate disciples—Baruch Spinoza, Nicolas Malebranche, and Gottfried Wilhelm von Leibniz—we ought to consider, both for the kinds of solutions they offer to Descartes' problems and for the ways in which they influence future thinkers. From the paradigm science of mathematics, Descartes takes clarity and distinctness as primary for his method and reasons to the radical distinction and separateness of thinking substances from extended or corporeal substances. This creates

113

two related problems. First and foremost, how can a thinking substance know corporeal substance? Second, if corporeal substance can be known, how are thinking substances and corporeal substances related? In particular, how are mind and body related in the human being?

Descartes' answers are familiar. God is the mediating principle between knowing that we exist as thinking beings and knowing that there is a corporeal world. We have a clear and distinct idea of something other than thinking substance—a world of extension defined by mathematics. God would be a deceiver if he were to allow judgments based on such a clear and distinct idea of corporeal substance to be false. However, since God is perfect, he cannot be a deceiver. Hence, there is a world of extension distinct from thought. As for how a thinking substance (mind) and a corporeal substance (body) can be related, Descartes answers this question by bringing them together in the pineal gland though the agency of very fine animal spirits. Each of these answers has its problems, which Descartes' disciples point out and try to correct.

Spinoza and Malebranche were almost exact contemporaries of Descartes, while Leibniz lived a generation later and commented on the works of his predecessors. Although Spinoza was born eight years prior to Malebranche, the latter's major work, *The Search after Truth,* appeared before Spinoza's *Ethics,* which was published posthumously.[1] Hence we shall treat Malebranche first, then Spinoza, and finally Leibniz.

Malebranche

Reading Malebranche, the influence of Descartes is immediately apparent. From Descartes' "I think, therefore I am" to the proof for the existence of God to the existence of matter as extension, Malebranche is true to his master. However, when it comes to explaining how mind and matter are related, Malebranche shows his independence. Beginning with the premise of God's absolute power, Malebranche deduces the absolute weakness of created things—material things first, but also thinking things. Power is seen as divided between God and creature: the more the creature has, the less God has; the more God has, the less the creature has.[2] Since God as perfect must be all-powerful, creatures must have no power. Following the medieval identification of creation with conservation (sustaining things in being), Malebranche maintains that God's will is the cause of anything's existing at any particular time

---

1. Spinoza died in 1677.
2. In this Malebranche continues the trend in late medieval theology, which we discussed in chapter 2, toward minimizing the reality of creatures in the face of the omnipotence of the Creator.

and place. Since God's will is all-powerful, it is impossible that any created power could move something against God's will. Hence, nothing is moved *except* by God. From this Malebranche deduces the conclusion that things are moved *only* by God.

> Hence, it is a contradiction that one body be able to move another. I say further: it is a contradiction that you should be able to move your chair. Even that is not enough. It is a contradiction that all the Angels and Demons joined together should be able to move a wisp of straw.[3]

This doctrine is known as occasionalism. On the occasion of the wind blowing, God moves the leaves on the tree. On the occasion of my hand touching the chair, God moves the chair. Malebranche extends this teaching of occasionalism to all creatures. All depend directly on God for existence and for activity. Causal relations between creatures (secondary causes) are mere figments of our imagination. "Creatures are united by an immediate union to God alone. They depend essentially and directly only on Him. As they are all equally powerless, they do not mutually depend on one another."[4] This is true of human beings as well as other creatures. "I get nothing from my nature, nothing from that imaginary nature of the philosophers; everything is from God and his decrees."[5] Thus God is not only the guarantor of the legitimacy of one's ideas of material substances; God, and not the substances, is the cause of one's knowing them.

This doctrine is at once ancient and progressive: a tradition among the Muslim theologians of the tenth century accorded all power to God and none to creatures,[6] and this doctrine is very influential on the thought of Berkeley and Hume. Berkeley follows Malebranche in holding that all is done by God, and Hume uses Malebranche's model to show how it is impossible for us to know with certainty what effect will follow any particular cause. In the cases of both Malebranche and Berkeley, God saves the day by providing power and intelligibility to the created world. Hume, realizing that it is illegitimate to argue from God to the world, drops God out of the picture, and we are left with skepticism.

3. Nicolas Malebranche, *Dialogues on Metaphysics*, seventh dialogue, sec. 10, trans. Willis Doney (New York: Abaris Books, 1980), p. 157. The position of Aquinas is that in natural activity both God and creature are causes of the act, God being the cause of the creature. In other words, God's activity in creatures is to make them what they are, not to interfere with their natural activities. See Aquinas, *ST* 1.105.

4. *Dialogues*, seventh dialogue, sec. 13, p. 163.

5. Ibid.

6. These were the Ash'arites, followers of Al Ash'ari (873–935). One finds the same tendency among the late medieval Christian theologians, especially William of Ockham.

Here, I am afraid, Hume is right. Hume had a very keen mind, and he was quick to point out the limits of legitimate implication. If we do not, and cannot, know the nature of God by natural reason, then we cannot deduce conclusions about the world from the definition of God. We have again lost the world of things. If no distinctions are natural to things, then the created world has no intrinsic intelligibility. In itself, therefore, it is unknowable. Saving the day by bringing in God may be a theological possibility (though, perhaps, with unacceptable implications), but it is not a philosophical option.[7]

While traditional metaphysics argues from the intrinsic intelligibility of things to the existence of a cause of all intelligibility, the metaphysics of Descartes and Malebranche begins with a supposedly self-evident (intrinsically intelligible) idea of perfection and tries to deduce things from this idea. But this is impossible, first because our notion of perfection is not self-evident but based on our recognition of a hierarchy of limited perfection among things, and second because we do not know what absolute perfection is, only that there must be an explanatory cause for the degrees of perfection we find among creatures, a cause that transcends in perfection the limits of those things.

Besides the metaphysical difficulties Malebranche faces, there are also problems for moral philosophy. Like Descartes, he does not apply his method to ethical matters in any systematic way. However, there would appear to be some insurmountable barriers to his doing so. If all of our actions are really God's and not our own, two things follow: one, God is directly responsible for our evil deeds, and two, we are not really free. The first conclusion implies that God is not good since he intentionally causes evil. The second undercuts moral responsibility, for such responsibility extends as far as freedom of the will. If we are not free, then we cannot reasonably be blamed for our bad deeds (or praised for our good ones).

Malebranche does argue that his theory of occasionalism supports ethics since it means that God is present to us at all times and places. Knowing this, we should not "impose upon His power."[8] But how can we abuse God's power if we have no power of our own? Malebranche continues:

7. We have seen how Hume is equally sharp in moral matters. If we allow only theoretical premises ("is" propositions based on scientific analysis of the way the world is or on metaphysical statements about the nature of God), we cannot legitimately conclude to practical premises of obligation ("ought" propositions). Although Hume arbitrarily limits reason, denying that reason can legitimately claim metaphysical or moral knowledge (and here he is wrong), one should give credit where credit is due, and Hume is right in his criticism of the rationalist claim that knowledge about the world can be deduced from our knowledge of God.

8. *Dialogues*, seventh dialogue, sec. 14, p. 165.

Nothing is more sacred than power, nothing is more divine. It is a kind of sacrilege to put it to profane uses. I now understand, this would be to make the just avenger of crimes serve iniquity. By ourselves we can do nothing. Hence, by ourselves we should not will anything. We can act only through the efficacy of divine power. Hence, we should will nothing other than what agrees with divine law. Nothing is more evident than these truths.[9]

There is no reason to doubt Malebranche's sincerity here; as a good Christian, he certainly believed that one ought to do good and avoid evil. However, according to the principles of his metaphysics, these truths are far from evident. For if none of our activities can be really attributed to us, then how could it be possible that we ought to do anything? To insist on the obligation not to implicate God in our crimes is pious, but it is not a reason to accept Malebranche's occasionalism. Indeed, as noted above, it is a reason to reject it. Clearly one does not want to attribute evil to God, but if all our actions are really God's and not ours, the attribution of evil to God seems inevitable.[10]

Of course, one could always point to the inscrutability of the divine plan, claiming that God will bring good out of evil (as Leibniz will do). However, this is a theological answer, not a philosophical one, for we do not know naturally what God's plan is and so cannot understand how evils (particularly moral evils—the acts of Hitler, for example) are part of the good. Thus, despite the declaration that this account provides "marvelous principles for Morality,"[11] the account offers no moral principles at all.

Nor does Malebranche offer any rational principles for an aesthetics. In fact, he says very little about beauty at all. The possibility of his doing so would seem to be severely limited, for if things have no intrinsic intelligibility, they can have no intrinsic beauty. What makes something beautiful is some kind of unique order, some particular instance of proportionally integrated elements. But if all order and unity are in God alone, then there cannot be a human appreciation or creation of beauty. The word beauty becomes another term for speaking of the only reality, as it sometimes gets used by Plato to refer to the One or the Good. As such, it is vacuous when applied to things.

Thus it is not very surprising to find that Malebranche denies that reason has anything to do with beauty and art.[12] Beauty is a matter of imagination and taste, and imagination is a word we use without any

9. Ibid.
10. Also, remember Hume: there is no implication from "can" to "ought."
11. *Dialogues*, seventh dialogue, sec. 14, p. 165.
12. *The Search after Truth*, bk. 2, pt. 2, par. 3.

clear meaning.[13] And, as rooted in imagination, beauty is subjective rather than objective. "You ought to know that the various kinds of beauty that you detect in the world are actually located in your soul. That harmony, those boundless delights, all are within your soul."[14]

Although metaphysics cannot make a physics or an ethics or an aesthetics (since the objects of these fields of study are distinct), a bad metaphysics can distort or even preclude these other fields of study. This is what happens to Malebranche and what we have seen happening in all the modern thinkers. Their theories of what is real distort their views of the good and the beautiful.

These problems might be avoided by a proper metaphysics. According to Aquinas, God's activity and any creature's activity are not two kinds of activity. If they were, then there would have to be some more fundamental explanation for what they share in common (why one calls them both activities) and that more fundamental explanation would be what we mean by God. As Aquinas says, both God and human beings are total causes of free actions.[15] There is no division of power so that the more the human being has, the less God has and vice versa. God's activity is the creating and sustaining cause of human activity, including free choices.

What God's activity would be like one cannot say. In one way this admission is, of course, very unsatisfactory, for once we know the existence of something, we want to know its essence. However, one must admit this lack of knowledge about the nature and activity of God. This is the major parting of the ways in metaphysics between the tradition handed down from Aristotle through Aquinas and that of Descartes and his disciples (including Locke and Berkeley in the empiricist tradition, as well as Malebranche, Spinoza, and Leibniz). Descartes and his disciples begin with the assumption that we know what God is and what his activity is like. With this assumption as a first principle, Descartes and his followers claim to deduce true statements about the world. But this deduction must always be illegitimate, for we do not know what God is, only *that* God is (and what God is not).[16] Legitimate statements about God either must be negative—God is not moved, not caused, not contingent, not limited in perfection, not guided by another (the insights of Aquinas's famous five ways)—or they must be analogical—whatever reality exists in creation preexists in God, only in a more perfect way.

13. Malebranche, *Treatise on Morality*, ch. 12.
14. Malebranche, *Christian Meditations*, quoted in Tatarkiewicz, *History of Aesthetics*, vol. 3, pp. 368–69.
15. See *ST* 1.105.2.
16. *ST* 1, prologue to Q. 2.

The entire content of natural theology (there is always, of course, the possibility of revealed knowledge of God) is taken from creatures—e.g., the need for a first cause, the need for a standard of perfection. Hence if we have any notion of perfection, it must be derived from creatures, from recognizing a hierarchy of perfection among creatures and understanding that such a hierarchy implies perfection without limit (whatever that is).[17] Since the natural objects of human knowledge are the natures of material things,[18] we can have no natural knowledge of God. We have no direct access to the divine nature. Those who assume that our knowledge of God is essential (that we know what God is) and go on to deduce further truths about the world from this primary essential knowledge are on the wrong track from the beginning.[19]

Malebranche adopts the basic principles of Descartes' metaphysics, and his thought suffers accordingly. Not only do thinking substances and extended substances have no interaction; there are also no interactions among any created things, bodies or minds. If there are no creaturely actions of any kind, then clearly there cannot be any moral actions (free choices about what ought or ought not be done), nor are there any objects to appreciate for their beauty (trees, human faces, paintings, music, etc.). Descartes' principles as followed out by Malebranche have led to a perfectly unintelligible world, a far cry from the certainty and clarity that Descartes envisioned.

Spinoza

It is, of course, possible that Malebranche just went about solving Descartes' problems the wrong way, that occasionalism is the wrong model for explaining the relations of things in the world to each other and to God. Let us consider the solution offered by Spinoza. Like Malebranche, he accepts Descartes' starting point—that only what is clearly and distinctly conceived can be considered true. And like Descartes'

17. Because of this need for hierarchy in order to affirm that there must be a source of all perfection (even though we do not know the nature of that source), it is not possible to begin with the self alone and there find, prior to experience, a notion of perfection.

18. Thomas Aquinas, *ST* 1.84.7.c.

19. Hume and Kant dismantle such a metaphysics, but it is the false metaphysics of Descartes, not the metaphysics of Aquinas. Thus when Hume and Kant declare metaphysics to be dead, their declaration applies to this deductive metaphysics that claims to deduce truths about the world from our knowledge of absolute perfection (God). It is obvious that such a deduction is impossible, since we have no conception (no definition) of God as perfect being. Therefore its demise is to be expected and says nothing about the health of legitimate metaphysics, which argues to the existence of God from the existence of material things and the questions raised by those things.

method, that of Spinoza in his *Ethics* is strictly geometrical. Indeed, in this he outdoes his master, beginning with definitions and axioms from which he deduces various propositions about God, the human mind, and the emotional and ethical life of the human being. However, seeing Descartes' problems in trying to explain the relations between the absolutely distinct and separate thinking and extended substances (in particular the mind and the body), Spinoza claims that there is only one substance; all those things that we call thinking or corporeal substances are merely modes of that one substance. Thus instead of beginning with the *cogito*, Spinoza begins with the concept of God.

With Descartes and Malebranche, Spinoza understands that God is the infinitely perfect being. Unlike them, he does not think of God as creator, for if substance is what stands alone, clearly and distinctly separate from all other things, then it has nothing in common with other things, not even "thinginess." Now, according to Spinoza, the only way to understand that which does not have anything in common with any other things is to affirm that there is only one substance. This substance he calls God or Nature (the two words are synonymous).[20] In some ways this is a continuation of the idea in Malebranche of emphasizing God's power. Malebranche does this by saying that no created thing really exercises any power, that all activity is the activity of God. All Spinoza does is rid Malebranche's system of the inconsistency of saying that there are any created things. All is one. While thinking things and extended things are really distinct, they are distinct as attributes of the one substance, not as distinct things. Now it should be apparent why Spinoza begins with God, not thinking. If one is to embody accurately the deductive style of geometry, one must begin with that which is first absolutely—that which is substance, not what is mode or attribute.

Consider Spinoza'a argument, which begins with his definition of substance. "By substance, I mean that which is in itself and is conceived through itself: that is, that the conception of which does not require the conception of another thing from which it has to be formed."[21] Given this definition, the outcome of any discussion of things is clear: it will lead to the affirmation of one thing. Thus when Spinoza states his first axiom—"everything which exists, exists either in itself or in something else"—one already knows which side of the disjunction will be considered true. If substance is to be understood in complete separation from any other thing, then no thing can exist because of another, for then it

20. Here Spinoza picks up on something that Descartes says in the sixth meditation, where he explains nature as being either God himself or all the things created by God (*Meditations*, sixth meditation, p. 50).

21. Baruch Spinoza, *The Ethics*, pt. 1, definitions, trans. Samuel Shirley (Indianapolis: Hackett, 1982), p. 31.

would involve the concept of the other thing in its definition. This being in itself is the being whose essence involves existence: God.

Aquinas would, of course, agree that God's essence involves existence, but he would say that the only way one knows this is by recognizing that no essence of anything we experience involves existence (what the thing is is not identical with existence, for then no other thing would exist). It is only by recognizing that the things we experience do not explain their existence that we understand that there must be a cause of their existence. What for Aquinas is a knowledge of cause from its effects Spinoza reverses. While Aquinas says that we know the existence of God (cause) only from his effects, Spinoza says (axioms 2 and 4) that we know the nature of an effect only by knowing the nature of its cause. In short, inductive knowledge of any sort is invalid; the only legitimate knowledge is deductive (like geometry).

There is a small problem with this tidy package: it is unable to explain how we have the concept of a self-caused being whose essence involves existence. Presumably (it is not clear in Spinoza's writings), we come across this notion in somewhat the way Descartes claims we do—by understanding some limitation in us (for Descartes it is that he is imperfect, since he doubts). And like Descartes, Spinoza is also concerned with overcoming doubt, which is why he insists on clear and distinct ideas. However, although Descartes does offer a kind of argument from effect (imperfect Descartes) to cause (perfect God), such an ordering is not quite in accord with the geometrical method. It implies some distinction between Descartes and God. Since, according to Spinoza's principles, there can be no distinction between created substance and creating substance, Spinoza cannot make use of such an argument. He must deduce everything (including the existence of thinking things like himself) from the one substance.

The rest of the *Ethics* is an exercise in doing so, but how this can work is a real question. For how does one deduce particular attributes from a single undifferentiated substance? Presumably God can do it, knowing his own nature. But how can Spinoza—unless he were God? In some sense, of course, Spinoza would say that he is God, since what we call things are merely attributes or modes of the divine being.[22]

In the second book of the *Ethics*, Spinoza lays down as axioms the differences between thought and extension as attributes of God. Axioms are typically propositions for which one does not argue, but given what Spinoza says about the absolute simplicity of substance, these attributes must be deduced from substance. If they are not, then they cannot be

---

22. This point reaches its most clear implication in the absolute idealism of Hegel, which owes much to Spinoza. Hegel's thought will be discussed in chapter 6.

known, for they can have no other cause. Thus, either Spinoza's claim that all things are caused by God (proposition 4) is irrelevant because it tells us nothing significant about things, or if (what seems more to his purpose) the essence of God or Nature is supposed to explain the various things we experience, it is unclear how this can happen.

Spinoza tries to do what Bacon and Descartes fail to do, which is to show how his method can be applied successfully to ethics. Indeed, the purpose of the initial metaphysics seems to be to establish an ethics. After declaring that he is going into territory where Descartes did not tread, Spinoza reiterates his absolute commitment to geometrical method. "[Critics] will doubtless find it surprising that I should attempt to treat of the faults and follies of mankind in the geometric manner, and that I should propose to bring logical reasoning to bear on what they proclaim is opposed to reason, and is vain, absurd and horrifying."[23]

Unlike Bacon and Descartes, Spinoza does not think that there is a defect anywhere in nature, whether in the mind or in the order of things. How could there be, if all derives by necessity from the infinitely perfect substance? "In Nature [which, for Spinoza, is another word for God] nothing happens which can be attributed to its defectiveness, for Nature is always the same, and its force and power of acting is everywhere and always one and the same."[24] According to Spinoza (here he follows Descartes), we are able to understand God and therefore have that first principle from which we can deduce all truth. "The human mind has an adequate knowledge of the eternal and infinite essence of God."[25] Thus things relating to human action, emotions, and choices happen of necessity and hence can be understood by reason. "I shall, then, treat of the nature and strength of the emotions, and the mind's power over them, by the same method as I have used in treating of God and the mind, and I shall consider human actions and appetites just as if it were an investigation into lines, planes, or bodies."[26]

Two problems immediately come to mind for such an enterprise: how to account for moral obligation through metaphysical deduction, and how to present a meaningful account of human freedom. As to the first problem, it is clear that Spinoza reduces moral matters to metaphysical (more precisely, mathematical) ones. The way things are dictates the way things ought to be. This can issue in one of two results: either the relation between the two spheres is unstable (as it is in Locke, where the empiricism does not sit well with obligation), or the idea of obligation is lost and one is left with a kind of description (rather than prescription)

23. *Ethics*, pt. 3, preface, p. 103.
24. Ibid.
25. Ibid., pt. 2, prop. 47, p. 94.
26. Ibid., pt. 3, preface, p. 104.

of human action.[27] The latter seems to be the case in Spinoza, for all things come from one first substance and hence cannot be in conflict. Thus good and evil are not objective, for all must be good, issuing as it does by necessity from God; rather good and evil are subjective and are to be explained in terms of our emotional reaction to pleasure and pain or in terms of what is useful to us. "Knowledge of good and evil is nothing other than the emotion of pleasure and pain insofar as we are conscious of it."[28] "By good I understand that which we certainly know to be useful to us."[29]

The idea of final cause as purpose is described as a species of appetite, by which we are moved. In other words, final cause is reduced to efficient cause. "What is termed a 'final cause' is nothing but human appetite in so far as it is considered the starting-point or primary cause of some thing."[30] Like Bacon and Descartes, Spinoza declares final cause—understood as some conscious and intelligible intention—to be unreal. This clearly follows from his first principle, for if there are no substances or things but only one substance, there can be no final cause. The one substance can have nothing toward which it is oriented in seeking its perfection for the obvious reasons that there are no other things and it is already perfect. With the destruction of the distinction between things, and the attendant rejection of the doctrine of creation with its radical distinction between creatures and creator, there is no place for final cause.

But with the loss of final cause goes the loss of meaningful ethics. Without the idea of basic goods, which invite us (as final causes) to a participation in which we may or may not choose to engage, there can be no moral responsibility. Such motivation by intelligible good is replaced by emotional drives that move us by necessity as natural deductions from the one substance, and virtue is considered what is to one's advantage (much like Hobbes). "By virtue and power I mean the same thing; that is, virtue, in so far as it is related to man, is man's very essence, or nature, in so far as he has power to bring about that which can be understood solely through the laws of his own nature."[31] Humility and repentance are not considered virtues, because they exhibit weakness and pain.[32]

27. If, as Hume points out, one begins with theoretical principles, one can conclude only to theoretical implications. Thus only description of moral action (and not prescription) can be implied by theoretical premises.

28. *Ethics*, pt. 4, prop. 8, pp. 159–60.

29. Ibid., pt. 4, definitions, p. 155.

30. Ibid., pt. 4, preface, p. 154.

31. Ibid., pt. 4, definitions, p. 156.

32. Ibid., pt. 4, prop. 53 and 54, pp. 184–85.

Besides the problem of trying to deduce morality from metaphysics (an impossible undertaking), there is also the problem of giving an intelligible account of freedom. The two problems are obviously related, for freedom as anything more than a description of behavior cannot be deduced from theoretical principles. But freedom in its essential moral role (freedom of choice) is a first principle of practical reason and refers to our ability to respond to good. It is freedom to pursue what ought to be done.

Spinoza defines freedom as follows: "That thing is said to be free [*liber*] which exists solely by the necessity of its own nature, and is determined to action by itself alone."[33] It follows that only God is free, since only God exists on its own. Human freedom, then, is a figment of our imagination, just like the idea of final cause or purpose. This implies that there is no personal responsibility for our actions, for how can one be blamed for doing what is natural and, in fact, necessitated? "If men were born free, they would form no conception of good and evil so long as they were free."[34] To be free is to be independent. If we wish to attach the notion of freedom to human beings, we must do so by removing from them obligation to anyone or anything, thus making them like God. These principles point to the position of Nietzsche, which we shall discuss later in this chapter.[35]

Spinoza criticizes Descartes for the obscurity and occult nature of the latter's explanation of motivation, both mechanically (in locating the relation between body and mind in a gland at the center of the brain) and morally (in explaining how sin is possible—the will extending beyond the clearly understood ideas).[36] However, Spinoza's explanation, although clear in form (geometric deduction), is not at all clear in content. Spinoza thinks that somehow knowledge of God or Nature will make us good—much like Plato's idea that knowledge is virtue. There is no such thing as the will understood as a faculty that may or may not (according to freedom of choice) make the emotions follow reason. Rather, there are just understanding and emotional urges. Spinoza holds that there is an isomorphism between the mind and the body (rather like Leibniz's preestablished harmony, which we shall discuss shortly). If, therefore, the mind gets itself in order, the body will fall into order too. Proper understanding will dispel improper urges. "Therefore, since the power of

33. Ibid., pt. 1, definitions, p. 31.
34. Ibid., pt. 4, prop. 68, p. 193.
35. Indeed, there are numerous similarities between Spinoza and Nietzsche, e.g., the reduction of purpose to appetite, the emphasis on virtue as power, and the focus on courage and nobility as primary virtues.
36. For Descartes' explanation of the connection of mind and body in the brain, see *Meditations*, sixth meditation, p. 54 and also *The Passions of the Soul*, art. 31; for the will extending beyond the understanding in sin, see *Meditations*, fourth meditation, p. 38.

the mind is defined solely by the understanding . . . , we shall determine solely by the knowledge of the mind the remedies for the emotions."[37]

Spinoza's account of freedom leaves him with a number of problems. Why, for instance, include some urges as improper and others as proper if all are necessitated by the laws of nature? Further, why is Spinoza so forceful in his criticism of religion for being violent if all people are acting under necessity?[38] And again, although it may be true that a proper understanding will dissipate the emotions, why (or even how) should one try to dissipate the emotions? Why should we try to be good? Given Spinoza's descriptive account of human action, there are no grounds to affirm any prescription (to say nothing of how the necessitarianism of Spinoza's account logically precludes meaningful freedom). Nietzsche sees this problem in Spinoza's thought. His move will be to keep all the material on emotions and power, and to forget all the talk about reason.

A philosophy of beauty is also reductionistic in Spinoza's thought. Judgments about what is beautiful or ugly are merely "modes of imagining," and imagining is merely a state of our nerves. The ideal of explanation, though deduced from one substance, is to explain all in terms of the mechanics of matter in motion. "For instance, if the motion which objects we see communicate to our nervous system by objects presented through our eyes is conducive to our feeling of well-being, the objects which are its cause are said to be beautiful, while the objects which provoke a contrary motion are called ugly."[39] Since all intelligibility is to be found in one substance from which everything is deduced in mathematical order, all that is real must be found in that one substance. The possibility of beauty as some kind of harmony or unity of diversity is thus denied, for pure, undifferentiated unity cannot be a harmony. The notion of harmony "has driven men to such madness that they used to believe that even God delights in harmony."[40]

There is really no such thing as harmony or beauty of any sort, no more than there is really hot or cold or good or evil. All these categories are figments of human imagination.

> We see therefore that all the notions whereby the common people are wont to explain Nature are merely modes of imagining, and denote not the nature of any thing but only the constitution of the imagination. And because these notions have names as if they were the names of

37. *Ethics*, pt. 5, preface, p. 205.
38. See Benedict de Spinoza, *Theologico-Political Treatise*, preface, in *Chief Works of Benedict de Spinoza*, trans. R. H. M. Elwes (New York: Dover, 1951), pp. 3–7.
39. *Ethics*, pt. 1, appendix, p. 61. This sounds a good deal like Hobbes's mechanism.
40. Ibid.

entities existing independently of the imagination I call them 'entities of imagination' (*entia imaginationis*) rather than 'entities of reason' (*entia rationis*). So all arguments drawn from such notions against me can be easily refuted.[41]

What cannot be logically deduced from the single substance is not at all real, and even what can be deduced finds its reality ultimately in the one substance rather than its own integral existence. Thus not only are good and evil, beauty and ugliness, figments of the imagination, but so also are all other notions that cannot be directly deduced from the one real substance. Like Malebranche, Spinoza considers beauty to be a subjective phenomenon, not objectively derivable from the one substance. "Beauty, Esteemed Sir, is less a quality of the object studied than the effect arising in the man studying that object."[42]

Basically, in Spinoza's thought, ethics is reduced to metaphysics and metaphysics to mathematics. As geometry begins with the definition of a point, so Spinoza's system begins with the definition of a metaphysical point, i.e., self-caused cause or substance. As all knowledge is knowledge of cause, so all our knowledge of the world and ethics is a deduction from this metaphysical point. But how things in all their diversity can be deduced from a single substance is not at all clear.

In one way, Spinoza's quest for a unified explanation is natural and commendable: the traditional metaphysics of Aristotle and Aquinas pursues this as well. However, while traditional metaphysics says that there is a first cause of all things, such a claim is based on an analysis of the things themselves and concludes only that there is such a first cause, not that we know the nature of that cause. When Spinoza turns this procedure around and claims that one must start with knowledge of the nature of the first cause and then deduce the world of things from it, he ends up unable to say *what* things are or even (oddly enough) *that* they are. If all our knowledge of things comes from knowing the metaphysical point in which there are no distinctions (and not from knowing the plurality of things themselves), then there is no good reason to believe that there are diverse things. One point, at least, is apparent: how things can come from undifferentiated unity is far from clear and distinct. What *is* clear is the narrowness of such an explanation. Ethics and aesthetics are reduced to metaphysics, and metaphysics to deductions from unity. In attempting to explain everything in terms of undifferentiated unity, Spinoza narrows human reason to a point.

41. Ibid., pt. 1, appendix, p. 62.
42. Spinoza, epistola 58 (to H. Boxel, 1674), in Tatarkiewicz, *History of Aesthetics*, vol. 3, p. 380.

Leibniz

Leibniz belonged to the generation following Malebranche and Spinoza. He was raised in an intellectual family; his father was a professor and his mother the daughter of a professor. Leibniz was very widely read, and his interests ranged across nearly all aspects of intellectual life, from mathematics (he discovered the infinitesimal calculus independently of Newton) to physics, to politics, history, and theology. Philosophically and theologically, he had a good grounding in the scholastic tradition, from which he drew heavily in natural theology. Not only was he familiar with the writings of Descartes, Malebranche, and Spinoza, but he also knew the works of the empirical philosophers Bacon, Hobbes, and Locke.

Like Locke, Leibniz is a consensus builder. He does not reject the tradition of the schools entirely, though he does favor the modern methods of inquiry. Theologically, he seeks common ground between Catholics and Protestants. The only work published in his lifetime, the *Theodicy*, makes extensive use of traditional arguments drawn from Aquinas, among others, to defend what he sees as core Christian belief. His wide-ranging abilities and moderate positions give to his work a certain added credibility.

Leibniz's system does not rely on one method, but makes use of several. Although he is intrigued by the mathematical method because of its clarity and order, he is grounded in the experimental method of Bacon.[43] But most important for Leibniz is theology. Without this, there can be no morality, nor ultimate happiness. Since Descartes' mathematical method alone cannot tell us about these things, it is insufficient for philosophy and theology.[44] Because of this interest in morality, Leibniz never abandons the idea of final cause as did Bacon, Descartes, and their followers. In fact, Leibniz takes as a first principle the harmony of the universe with the well-being of mankind as its end.[45] Thus he holds mathematics and experimental method to be second to theology. For this reason, he never denigrates absolutely the medieval tradition culminating in the thought of Aquinas; in fact he even acknowledges his gratefulness for his training in this philosophical and theological tradition.

43. "Bacon and Gassendi were the first [of the modern philosophers] to fall into my hands. Their familiar and easy style was better adapted to a man who wanted to read everything." Gottfried Wilhelm von Leibniz, "Letter to Simon Foucher," trans. Leroy E. Loemker, Philip P. Wiener, and Austin Farrar, in *The Philosophy of the Sixteenth and Seventeenth Centuries*, ed. Richard H. Popkin (New York: Free Press, 1966), p. 307.

44. Leibniz complains about the weakness of Descartes' mathematically ordered proofs for God's existence (*On True Method in Philosophy and Theology*, in Popkin, *Philosophy*, p. 312).

45. See *On True Method in Philosophy and Theology*, in Popkin, *Philosophy*, p. 315; and *New System of Nature and of the Communication of Substance, as Well as of the Union of Soul and Body*, § 5 and 8, in Popkin, *Philosophy*, pp. 325 and 327.

The value of a religious philosophy will be recognized by those who return to it, and mathematical studies will be used partly as an example of more rigorous judgment, partly for the knowledge of harmony and the idea of beauty, experiments on nature will lead to admiration for the author of nature, who has expressed an image of the ideal world in the sensible one, so that all studies finally will lead to happiness.[46]

Although he never severs his roots in the tradition, Leibniz does jump into the problematic raised by Descartes concerning how to explain the relations between bodies (science) and the relations between minds and bodies. He thinks that the traditional explanations of reality and the human being by Aristotle and Aquinas fail and that new ones are needed.[47] Leibniz begins by accepting Descartes' absolute distinction between mind and body and the metaphysical difficulties it raises.[48] "In strict metaphysical language, there is very truly no real influence of one created substance on another."[49] However, he does not think that Descartes succeeded in explaining the interactions of bodies or the relations between mind and body, nor does he agree with the solutions of either Malebranche or Spinoza.

Descartes had explained bodies mathematically, in mechanical terms; that is, every physical thing is to be conceived on the order of a machine working according to fixed laws. Leibniz is unhappy with this explanation and considers it degrading to animals (to say nothing of human beings) to be considered as purely mechanical beings.[50]

Physical nature requires some principle of activity, some force, in addition to mechanics. Otherwise it is hard to see how substances can interact, and in particular, how soul could influence body or vice versa. Leibniz comments on the lack of clarity on this point in the thought of Descartes: "I found no way of explaining how the body causes something to happen in the soul, or vice versa; nor how substance can communicate with another created substance."[51]

Since Leibniz's solution to the mind/body problem is the same as for the interaction of material things, let us turn to his mind/body solution. Leibniz says that there are three models for considering how the mind and the body are related. The first is the idea of mutual influence, what

46. *On True Method*, in Popkin, *Philosophy*, p. 313.
47. Leibniz speaks of freeing himself from the yoke of Aristotle (*New System of Nature*, in Popkin, *Philosophy*, § 3, p. 324).
48. "And this confirms M. Descartes' excellent thought concerning the proof of the difference between body and soul, since one can doubt the one without being able to question the other" (Leibniz, "Letter to Simon Foucher," in Popkin, *Philosophy*, p. 310).
49. *New System of Nature*, § 3, in Popkin, *Philosophy*, p. 329.
50. Ibid., p. 324.
51. Ibid., p. 328.

he calls popular philosophy. It seems that Descartes' explanation falls under this category: fine animal spirits move between mind and body in the pineal gland. "But as we cannot conceive of material particles which can pass from one of these substances to another, we must abandon this idea."[52]

The second is the way of continual assistance of the creator—basically Malebranche's occasionalism. Since there can be no communication between substances, Leibniz thinks that Malebranche is on to something here. However, the invocation of God as a general cause is unsatisfactory, for it is a *deus ex machina* and has no reference to any intrinsic property in things.[53] Since this introduces a supernatural explanation for a natural occurrence, it is inadequate as a philosophical explanation.

The third is Leibniz's position: the way of harmony. "From the beginning God has made each of these two Substances of such a nature that each by following its own laws, given to it with its being, still agrees with the other, just as though there were a mutual influence or as though God always took a hand in it beyond his general supervision of things."[54] All things exist in preestablished harmony from the first moment of creation and are never destroyed.[55]

Leibniz agrees in some way with Spinoza's definition of substance as something that stands alone in complete independence from other things. However, while Spinoza interprets this as implying that there is only one substance from which all other things proceed by necessity, Leibniz introduces his monad. This theory of the monad is a kind of atomism, but with a difference. Although Leibniz respects Bacon and his predecessors in the Greek tradition (Democritus in particular) for their theory of atoms, he thinks that they were wrong to make the atoms material unities; for material unities are divisible (hence not ultimate), and because they are inert, they cannot explain anything. Thus Leibniz brings back the idea of substantial form although in a very different way from either the traditional view of Aristotle or that of Spinoza.[56] These forms are his monads; they are metaphysical points rather like points in mathematics.[57] They have no size, and they cannot influence or be

52. *Second Explanation of the System of the Communication of Substances*, in Popkin, *Philosophy*, p. 332.

53. *New System of Nature*, § 13, in Popkin, *Philosophy*, p. 329.

54. *Second Explanation*, in Popkin, *Philosophy*, p. 332.

55. *The Principles of Philosophy, or the Monadology*, § 78, in *Discourse on Metaphysics and Other Essays*, trans. Daniel Garber and Roger Ariew (Indianapolis: Hackett, 1991), p. 79. This theory is rather like Augustine's theory of "seminal reasons," which he inherits from the Stoics. See Augustine, *Literal Commentary on Genesis* 9.17.32.

56. See *New System of Nature*, § 3, in Popkin, *Philosophy*, pp. 324–25.

57. *New System of Nature*, § 11, in Popkin, *Philosophy*, p. 328. Alfred North Whitehead will develop this idea. We shall discuss his thought in chapter 7.

influenced by any other monad: "the monads have no windows."[58] Nevertheless, they are intrinsically intelligible; in fact, they are microcosms, programmed in a sense with the whole rest of creation. And because they cannot be influenced by any other thing, they are indestructible.

If they are windowless, how are they related to other things? Here is where the doctrine of preestablished harmony comes in. The relations between things are fixed by their creator at creation. Although still requiring God as a cause, preestablished harmony avoids the *deus ex machina* criticism by ascribing to each monad its own intrinsic mode of activity. "We must say that God has from the first created the soul or any other real unity in such a way that everything arises in it from its own internal nature through a perfect *spontaneity* relatively to itself, and yet with a perfect *conformity* to external things."[59]

Because it cannot be affected by any other piece of the universe, each monad is free.[60] This preserves the freedom that Hobbes's mechanism and Spinoza's geometrical deduction from one substance deny.[61] The freedom that Spinoza applies to the one substance, Leibniz extends to all the monads (his idea of substance). Thus Leibniz's world is full of freedom. Instead of limiting freedom to one substance as Spinoza does (and hence effectively denying freedom to human beings), Leibniz extends freedom to all things, for all things are made up of intelligible monads. As intelligence and freedom go hand in hand (we, for example, have both), and as the monads are intelligent, the monads are free.

It is interesting to note how Leibniz has brought Aristotle's paradigm example of substance back into his philosophy. Like Aristotle's notion of the human being, the monad is, in a way, all things.[62] As Aristotle's notion of the human being is a kind of microcosm, so is Leibniz's monad. There is, of course, a significant difference in what each means by his microcosm. Aristotle means that the human being is potentially all things—able to be, in a way, material things through sensing them, and all things by knowing them. The communion is effected by the human being interacting with the world. Leibniz's monad, however, is windowless: it cannot be affected by any other thing. Thus it is not actualized by interacting with other things, but from within, according to God's plan of preestablished harmony.

Thus Leibniz's solution to the mind/body problem is just the opposite of Hobbes's. Both agree that there cannot be two independent substances,

58. *Monadology*, § 7, in *Discourse on Metaphysics*, p. 68.
59. *New System of Nature*, § 14, in Popkin, *Philosophy*, p. 329.
60. This is basically the same definition of freedom as Spinoza's: to be free is not to be affected by another, a freedom from interference.
61. See *New System of Nature*, § 16, in Popkin, *Philosophy*, pp. 330–31.
62. See Aristotle, *On the Soul* 3.8.

mind and body, acting in wholly different ways. But while Hobbes reduces mind to body, Leibniz reduces body to mind. If the building blocks for all reality are these immaterial, intrinsically intelligible monads, then the basis for all reality—immaterial and material—is immaterial. Hence just as material atomism was Hobbes's solution to both the relationship between physical things and that between mind and body, so immaterial or intelligible atomism is Leibniz's solution to both problems. Yet Leibniz holds that there are no immaterial creatures. Every being but God has a body.[63] How immaterial monads make up material bodies is a problem that Leibniz does not seem to solve.

As for how this system affects morality, Leibniz claims that it avoids the necessitarianism of Hobbes and Spinoza.[64] Since the unit of reality is the monad, which is independent of every other bit of the universe, reality is intrinsically free. God causes us to act, but that does not take away our freedom. Monads act according to a preestablished harmony (established at the first moment of the universe) based on the perfect goodness of God. To understand Leibniz's ethics, one must take a look at his natural theology since it is the basis of all the rest of his philosophy. It is here, at the roots of his system, that serious questions of coherence arise.

Let us begin with Leibniz's proofs for the existence of God. One is *a priori*, or based on ideas that do not depend on experience; the other is *a posteriori*, or drawn from experience. These two proofs follow the two kinds of truth available to the human mind: truths of reasoning and truths of facts.[65] Each has its first principle: that of reasoning he calls the principle of contradiction; that of facts he calls the principle of sufficient reason. In other words, the proof for the existence of God can begin either with innate ideas or with empirical evidence. Here we find Leibniz trying to mediate between the rationalist and empiricist positions.

The *a priori* proof begins with the idea of the necessary or perfect being and argues to its existence. This is like the ontological proof of Descartes. Leibniz says that for God alone, if he is possible, he must necessarily exist.

> Thus God alone (or the necessary being) has this privilege, that he must exist if he is possible. And since nothing can prevent the possibility of what is without limits, without negation, and consequently without contradiction, this by itself is sufficient for us to know the existence of God *a priori*. We have also proved this by the reality of the eternal truths.[66]

63. *Monadology*, § 72, in *Discourse on Metaphysics*, p. 78.
64. *Theodicy*, in Popkin, *Philosophy*, pp. 333–34.
65. Compare with Hume's relations of ideas and matters of fact.
66. *Monadology*, § 45, in *Discourse on Metaphysics*, p. 74.

The proof from experience is rather different from those of Aquinas. Where Aquinas begins with things in motion or things in a hierarchy of perfection or the contingency of things, Leibniz begins with figures and motions, following Descartes' idea of what bodies are.[67] Or, Leibniz says, one can begin with tendencies or dispositions of the soul. Both sets of contingencies are infinitely divisible, since the universe is infinite in variety so that relations can be multiplied forever. These infinite contingent causal chains cannot explain why things are the way they are. Therefore, there must be a substance outside the infinite series that is the sufficient reason for the way things are, down to the last detail. This being we call God, who is the most real or most perfect being; all the details of the related beings of the universe are present in him potentially.

Even though Leibniz claims to prove God's existence in two ways, the *a posteriori* proof seems to be in tension with his theory of monads, for if the monads are windowless and none can affect any other, then the chains of contingent relations (efficient causal chains for bodies, final causal chains for souls) on which the proof is based are really illusory. We are left then with the rather unhelpful argument that illusory activities prove the real existence of God. Thus the *a priori* proof that he inherits from Descartes and Spinoza best fits his system.

However, there are a couple of serious problems with the system. For it seems that either God is a means for allowing interactions between things or the interaction between things is somehow deduced from God. In either case God is, so to say, being misused. If, as may be the case, Leibniz develops his system of monadology to solve the problems introduced by Descartes' mind/body dualism, then God is made to serve as the guarantor of a physics. This places God in a kind of subservient role that is incompatible with God being the first and perfect creating cause. Leibniz, sounding quite like Spinoza, says: "Thus God alone is the primitive unity or the first [originaire] simple substance; all created or derivative monads are products, and are generated, so to speak, by continual fulgurations of the divinity from moment to moment."[68] However, further on he speaks as if creatures had a hold over God.

> But in simple substances the influence of one monad over another can only be ideal, and can only produce its effect through God's intervention, when in the ideas of God a monad rightly demands that God take it into account in regulating the others from the beginning of things.[69]

67. See ibid., p. 73.
68. Ibid., pp. 74–75.
69. Ibid., p. 75.

The other possible scheme is that the monadology is deduced from God. Because God is infinite and perfect, monads must all operate in just the proper ways. This is troubling in several respects. First, there seem to be exceptions to this conclusion: freaks of nature and, more seriously, moral evil. Second, however one may try to explain the evidence in terms of its goodness or fulfillment of design, the whole project of judging the state of the world by our concept of God is wrongheaded. Although deducing things about the world in the light of God's revelation is appropriate procedure in theology, it is illegitimate in philosophy for the simple reason that we do not know the nature of God. Leibniz admits this when he says that God is infinite and without limit. If this is true, then we cannot conceive of God as he is. If we proceed to use our concept of God—as imperfect as it is—in order to prove things about creatures, then we are bound to falsify the world. The only way to know the world created by God is to study that world. By trying to deduce conclusions about the world from our concept of God, we succeed only in making God in our own image, and so also the world he creates. This narrows the way the world can be for us, prior to our experiencing it.

Leibniz's famous doctrine about this being "the best of all possible worlds" is an example of this bad metaphysics. It assumes that we have some notion of what God's unlimited reality is like. What could it mean to say that "there is an infinity of possible universes in God's ideas"[70] and that, because God is perfectly good, he chose the best of all possible worlds? There is no positive reason to think that there are different possible worlds: it is merely a logical possibility. This, coupled with an illusory concept of God (produced perhaps with the intention of increasing God's power), has yielded the idea of other possible worlds. It is not the world that raises this question for us. If it were, then this world and the others would be related and therefore there would not be two or more possible worlds, but one multidimensional world.

Returning to the issue of morality, the *sine qua non* for moral responsibility is freedom. Leibniz provides for this by stating that each monad is free from every other monad. But how is this freedom defined with regard to granite monads and to human monads? All monads have perception, which is a kind of knowledge. However, human monads have self-consciousness, too. Why do we have this when other things do not? The answer cannot really be empirical since we cannot know any other monad, not even that of granite. Thus it must be based on ideas, in this case the idea of God granting us a special place in his creation. There is nothing wrong with this theologically, but philosophically it does

70. Ibid.

sound like a bit of a *deus ex machina*, for which Leibniz has criticized Malebranche roundly.[71]

Thus either we have an insufficient philosophical idea of freedom as freedom *from* interference by other monads rather than a freedom *for* choosing to interrelate well or poorly with other human beings in a shared world of basic goods, or we have a moral theology. What we cannot have, based on Leibniz's metaphysics, is conscious interactions between people. For example, there could be no such thing as friendship in the sense of caring for the other person for that person's own sake (as in Aristotle), for there are no interactions between monads. "The perceptions or expressions of external things occur in the soul at a fixed moment by virtue of its own laws, as in a world apart and as if there existed nothing but God and itself."[72] Given this picture of monads in relation to God, it is possible that there could be special moral relations imprinted on the monad as well, which would raise it above the perceptions or consciousness of all other things, but this would seem to involve the miraculous just as much as Malebranche's occasionalism.

This issue of the reality of freedom and the responsibility that goes with it is even more apparent when we turn to the problem of moral evil. Why would a God who makes the best of all possible worlds allow moral evil? Since moral evil seems to depend on the freedom which is unique to human beings, it is unlike the other kinds of evil that we meet in the world. The idea that God permits moral evil only under the condition that he will bring good out of it is a tenet of faith, but it is not something we comprehend philosophically. If we claim to do so, then we have skewed the notion of good. This happens in the thought of Leibniz. Good and evil are defined in terms of consequences rather than in terms of intentions. The harmony of the physical world is designed to provide for the reward or punishment of moral agents.[73] "It is again well to consider that moral evil is an evil so great only because it is a source of physical evils, a source existing in one of the most powerful of creatures, who is also most capable of causing those evils. . . . One single Caligula, one Nero, has caused more evil than an earthquake."[74]

This account leaves completely out of the picture the essence of moral evil that lies in intention, not consequences. An evil act is wrong in itself by reason of the object intended, not because of the pain the act causes. Even if it caused no pain, it would still be evil. There is indeed

71. Leibniz recognizes the need to distinguish between "the physical kingdom of nature and the moral kingdom of grace" (*Monadology*, § 87, in *Discourse on Metaphysics*, p. 81).

72. *New System of Nature*, § 14, in Popkin, *Philosophy*, p. 329.

73. *Monadology*, §§ 89–90, in *Discourse on Metaphysics*, p. 81.

74. *Theodicy*, sec. 26, in Popkin, *Philosophy*, p. 339.

damage that always attends moral evil, but it is the damage done to the immoral agent. Moral evil destroys the integrity and character of the agent.[75] Perhaps Leibniz neglects this point because of his assumption that each human monad has been programmed from creation to do all the things that fit God's plan. But if this is so, then what happens to responsibility? Consider the last lines of the *Theodicy*: "But God being inclined to produce as much good as possible, and having all the knowledge and all the power necessary for that, it is impossible that in him there be fault, or guilt, or sin; and when he permits sin, it is wisdom, it is virtue."[76] How can one say that permitting a Nero or a Hitler to carry on is wise or virtuous? If we knew how good could be brought out of moral evil, then maybe we could make such a claim, but we do not know this. What is morally clear is that for us to permit such evil, if we could easily prevent it without ourselves doing evil, would not be wise or virtuous. Leibniz's metaphysics gravely skews his ethics here. Hume recognized this, and was appalled at Leibniz's claim that this is the best of all possible worlds.[77]

Leibniz says little about beauty and art. What he does say is generally in line with the other rationalists in that he relegates the recognition of beauty more to taste than to reason.[78] Unlike Descartes, Malebranche, and Spinoza, however, Leibniz does not relegate beauty merely to subjectivity. He holds that artists do recognize when some work of art has been well-executed,[79] and that we do appreciate music.[80] However, we are not able to explain why this is so. Making use of Descartes' criteria for an acceptable idea, Leibniz says that beauty is clear but not distinct.[81] That is, beauty is recognized but cannot be explained.

Leibniz does not consider the appreciation of beauty to be a distinct realm of reason, with its own principles and method. Rather, our appreciation of beauty is only partly rational in that it meets one criterion (clarity) but not the other (distinctness). *That* there is beauty to be appreciated is clear, but *what* beauty is cannot be understood.

75. This is a fundamental idea of traditional natural law ethics passed on from Plato through Aristotle, Augustine, and Aquinas.

76. *Theodicy*, sec. 26, in Popkin, *Philosophy*, p. 339.

77. See Hume, *Dialogues Concerning Natural Religion*, pt. 10. Again, Hume is correct in his criticism, for one cannot deduce conclusions about the state of the world (metaphysically or morally) from our knowledge of God, for we do not know God's nature or plan.

78. Leibniz, *Meditationes de cognitione, veritate et ideis*, 1684, in Tatarkiewicz, *History of Aesthetics*, vol. 3, pp. 381–82.

79. Ibid., p. 382.

80. Leibniz, *Principes de la nature et de la grace* 17, in Tatarkiewicz, *History of Aesthetics*, vol. 3, p. 382.

81. Leibniz, *Meditationes de cognitione*, in Tatarkiewicz, *History of Aesthetics*, pp. 381–82.

Thus while Leibniz tries to integrate Bacon's empiricism with Descartes' rationalism in order to save intelligibility from empirical reductionism and the physical world from a reduction to ideas, he does not quite succeed on either score. Perhaps the reason for this is his assumption, along with both the empiricists and the rationalists, that one must begin one's philosophy with the self and what one finds in the self. If all we know are our impressions and ideas, as Locke said, then we cannot know whether or not these ideas conform to reality. We can try to build a system in which they do, and perhaps this system will not involve a contradiction and so be possible, but confidence that we know reality cannot begin anywhere but in the affirmation of our immediate contact with reality—our being, in some sense, other things, as Aristotle held. It may be *possible* that Leibniz's scheme is correct: this is one of its strengths according to him. "This hypothesis is at least possible."[82] The question is: why would one hold it to be true?

There is a constant in the rationalist tradition: the system is guaranteed by the nature of God. God as perfect being guarantees that Descartes' clear and distinct ideas really do conform to reality. God as perfect being guarantees the relationships between things by being the only cause of these relationships, according to Malebranche. God as the perfect and only substance guarantees the necessary deduction of all things along the lines of clarity and distinctness, according to Spinoza. And now God as perfect being harmonizes all the windowless monads in the universe and guarantees that this is the best of all possible worlds. However, as we have mentioned often, the problem is that we do not have an idea of God, nor does it seem possible, given the accepted starting point of these philosophers, that we could have one. If God is defined as perfection without limit, and all concepts involve some kind of limit (in that they are clear and distinct from other concepts), then we can have no concept of God. If we have no concept of God, we cannot deduce anything from God. Hence all the efforts of the rationalists to get at the nature of the world from God are in vain. At best we have a series of explanations that are logically possible.

Nor does it seem that any notion of God (even to know *that* God exists) is possible according to the rationalist approach. How is it possible to have an understanding of perfection, or a most perfect being, without some kind of comparison? If all one has is oneself, how can one conclude to God? If one claims to find all manner of degrees of perfection in the ideas one has in mind, how did one get these ideas? If we get them from extramental reality, then we must have some recourse to a theory of abstraction such as Aristotle's. If these ideas are

82. *New System of Nature*, § 15, in Popkin, *Philosophy*, p. 330.

innate (as the rationalists tend to say), why are there many when the self is one?

Of course, the rationalist solution is to say that the ideas of God and of the world are simply innate. If so, one cannot know whether these ideas correspond to reality. Thus one is left with oneself, a false concept of God (any concept must be limited, but God is said to be unlimited), and a world to which our only access is through our concept of God. Science and morality are guaranteed by God. Interactions between things or people are really just God acting. All secondary causality has been denied. God guarantees the intelligibility of physical interactions and the intelligibility of moral interactions. Thus all intelligibility has been rolled back into God.

Nietzsche

Take this world of the rationalists and eliminate God's role in it, and you have the philosophy of the nineteenth-century thinker Friedrich Nietzsche. Nietzsche gives us a vision of a skeptic who is not bothered at all that he cannot know. Why not untruth rather than truth?[83] We sail right over morality, beyond good and evil.[84] In Nietzsche one finds a skeptic with a physiopsychological explanation of human activity rejoicing in his isolation from community and meaning. This seems the logical ending for a tradition that begins with the self, for to begin there is to end there—in solipsism (literally, "the self alone"). Nietzsche debunks philosophers for producing systems according to their individual foibles.[85] Beginning with the self and without the ability to

83. Friedrich Nietzsche *Beyond Good and Evil*, pt. 1, sec. 1, trans. Walter Kaufmann (New York: Random House, 1966), p. 9. Nietzsche has influenced a whole contemporary tradition of removing the truth claim from philosophy. "Truth" is reduced to useful language games. Disciples include Jacques Derrida, Richard Rorty, and Thomas Kuhn. "What people like Kuhn, Derrida and I believe is that it is pointless to ask whether there really are mountains or whether it is merely convenient for us to talk about mountains. . . . Given that it pays to talk about mountains, as it certainly does, one of the obvious truths about mountains is that they were here before we talked about them. If you do not believe that, you probably do not know how to play the usual language-games which employ the word 'mountain.' But the utility of those language-games has nothing to do with the questions of whether Reality as It Is In Itself, apart from the way it is handy for human beings to describe it, has mountains in it" (Richard Rorty, "Does Academic Freedom Have Philosophical Presuppositions?" *Academe*, November–December 1994, pp. 56–57).

84. *Beyond Good and Evil*, pt. 1, sec. 23, p. 31.

85. This sounds very much like Bacon's idols of the theater. Indeed, Bacon's notion, taken up by Nietzsche, grounds the postmodern, deconstructionist movement in philosophy and literature. According to this view, there is always more on the agenda than the search for truth, and this "more" is ultimately reducible to some kind of search for power.

verify the correspondence between one's ideas and extramental reality, the philosophers' positions end up appearing subjective. In some sense Nietzsche is right. If philosophical systems rely on God to bail them out of absurdity, they are absurd.[86]

Since reason (as defined by the enlightenment) has proved unable to prove anything, Nietzsche turns to the will, understood basically as Hobbes and Spinoza understand it—not as a mode of reason, but of desire. And like Hobbes and Spinoza, Nietzsche holds that the will is not moved by good as final cause, but by physiological drives for preservation or power. Ultimately, everything is to be understood as will to power. "The world viewed from inside, the world defined and determined according to its 'intelligible character'—it would be 'will to power' and nothing else."[87] It is this subrational force that determines all we do.

How does Nietzsche's philosophy relate to the three realms of reason—the true, the good, and the beautiful—that we have distinguished? If Nietzsche were consistent, he would not have written anything, for if untruth is as valuable as truth, then what is the point of saying what one thinks is true? However, Nietzsche is not consistent. He cannot refrain from thinking, from trying to understand the world, how it came to be, and our place in it. Thus he too has a kind of metaphysics or first philosophy. However, instead of giving physics or mathematics the status of queen of the sciences, Nietzsche chooses psychology. "Psychology shall be recognized again as the queen of the sciences, for whose service and preparation the other sciences exist. For psychology is now again the path to the fundamental problems."[88] By psychology, Nietzsche means physiopsychology, not at all the study of the soul found in Aristotle or Aquinas. It is a psychology of forces and drives, rather like that of Freud. Thus Nietzsche returns to the materialism of the early empiricists and ancient Greek philosophers. Such a psychology sails right over morality.

Nietzsche picks up a number of ideas from Spinoza and Leibniz. His idea of freedom is like theirs in that it is defined in terms of independence—freedom *from*. His theory of the life force in everything owes a

86. The metaphysics of Aristotle and Aquinas, on the contrary, begins with a world of diverse things that raise questions for us. Pursuing answers, we are led to affirm the existence of what Leibniz would have called the sufficient reason for things. What Aristotle and Aquinas would never have done is call upon God to make the world intelligible. Whatever intelligibility there is in our philosophical notion of God (which is affirmation of existence, not definition of essence) is taken from the intelligibility we find in the world. Thus if the world is intrinsically unintelligible, it cannot lead to an intelligible account of God; it is illegitimate to bring God in, *deus ex machina*, to bail out the unintelligibility of the world.

87. Nietzsche, *Beyond Good and Evil*, pt. 2, sec. 36, p. 48.

88. Ibid., pt. 1, sec. 23, p. 32.

good deal to Leibniz's theory of the monad. The difference is that, while for Leibniz this life force is intrinsically intelligible (a perception that is in the order of knowledge), for Nietzsche this life force is irrational—a physiological drive like the instincts of Hume. Given that each person is a monad with a drive or will to power that is untrammeled by moral restraints, it is a short step to Nietzsche's notion of the superman who stands outside the constraints of common morality.[89]

Just as Nietzsche cannot avoid a kind of metaphysics, so he cannot avoid a kind of ethics, even though any ethical precepts are incompatible with his principles. Thus, according to Nietzsche, it is bad (ugly, tasteless) to live according to herd morality, and it is good to be courageous and noble.[90]

> And to remain master of one's four virtues: of courage, insight, sympathy, and solitude. For solitude is a virtue for us, a sublime bent and urge for cleanliness which guesses how all contact between man and man—"in society"—involves inevitable uncleanliness.[91]

Of course, Nietzsche would want to say that he does not mean good in the old way. However, either Nietzsche recommends his positions as preferable to the old morality or not. If he does, then he admits some objective criteria of moral goodness. If he does not, then his writings are interesting specimens of rhetoric and style (and they are), but cannot be taken seriously as presenting intelligible recommendations. Like Hume, Nietzsche's principles do not allow him to make general statements about reality or about ethics.

And like Hume, Nietzsche's philosophy seems to be dominated by a kind of aesthetics. Taste is critical in all kinds of judgment. But again, like Hume, aesthetics is not a matter of reason in any way, but is a physiological response to experience, or even the creation of experience according to feelings and imagination. This basic view of the nature of beauty is prepared by Nietzsche's predecessors: Descartes, Malebranche, and Spinoza. All three deny that beauty is an object of reason. Beauty is subjective, a matter of feeling, imagination, emotion, or instinct.[92]

In some ways it is not surprising that Hume and Nietzsche should turn to the aesthetic to fill the void left by reason, for of the three realms of reason that we have distinguished, the realm of the beautiful has the

89. On the new man or superman, see *Beyond Good and Evil*, pt. 2, sec. 44, and *The Will to Power*, aphorisms 960 and 1001.

90. Notice the connection to Spinoza's ethics.

91. *Beyond Good and Evil*, pt. 9, sec. 284, p. 226.

92. Leibniz basically concurs in denying that beauty is an object of reason, but not in making beauty merely subjective.

most obvious connection to sensation and feelings. People in general are more apt to consider aesthetic than moral judgments to be based on personal feelings or taste, and least likely to speak of judgments about how things are (mathematical, scientific, metaphysical) as a matter of feeling or taste. And they are correct to the extent that, of the three realms, the aesthetic does involve sense experience most intimately. In fact, sense experience is an essential element in the appreciation of beauty.

Nietzsche takes this idea of beauty and moves it into the central place for all explanation. Thus explanation becomes a function of some instinctual taste or feeling. The one thing that Nietzsche wants to avoid is system. In this he tries to overturn the rationalist tradition of deductive truth, returning to the tradition of Bacon.

It is interesting to note that both Bacon and Nietzsche prefer the aphoristic style. It avoids overcommitment to preconceptions and allows for insights without having to back them up by relating them to other insights and principles within a consistent view of reality. Indeed, Nietzsche is a master of the aphorism, and many of them are very telling. What he does not do (and likely does not want to do) is to give a justification for his position. Thus his philosophy becomes a form of play, guided by taste and instinct. As such, it is not intelligible in itself: it does not give coherent accounts of the way things are, or the way they should be, or why they are beautiful.

With Nietzsche we come around again to the exhaustion of reason, or perhaps the perfection of reason as conceived by Descartes and Bacon—reason as critique. If one begins with doubt about the ability of reason to know the truth without some method of correction, then one will be left with the method of correction. Each method of correction will, however, be its own personal take on how to solve the problems of philosophy. Nietzsche is devastating in his critique of these critical methods. None of them, he claims, can rise above the personality of its inventor.[93] Hence there is no way that the critical project can reach universality. All truth is subjective and as variable as personalities. Thus Nietzsche abandons reason as truth-discovering, and has recourse to reason as play. We are at the beck and call of physiological drives that are, after all, the real sources of our choices.

Philosophies of the Self

As the empirical tradition ends in the skepticism of Hume, so the rationalist tradition ends in the irrationalism of Nietzsche. Of course,

93. *Beyond Good and Evil*, pt. 1, sec. 6, pp. 13–14.

Hume and Nietzsche begin their own traditions. Thus the Humean ideal of explaining everything in terms of what can be known empirically is carried on by Jeremy Bentham and Auguste Comte in the nineteenth century and Bertrand Russell and A. J. Ayer in the twentieth. Although these disciples do not end with a profession of skepticism in all areas, they do follow principles that rule out traditional morality, metaphysics, and an aesthetics that is more than mere feeling. As Nietzsche died in 1900, his influence is on twentieth-century thought. He is clearly influential in the existentialist movement of Sartre and Camus, as well as on the postmodernism of Heidegger, Lacan, Derrida, and Rorty. Thus the two traditions are still alive and well in the contemporary world through the disciples of Hume and Nietzsche. Perhaps one should not say "well" since, as philosophical positions, they are self-defeating; that is, they lead to the abandonment of reason and hence of philosophy (love of wisdom) in any meaningful sense.

Paradoxically, it could be said that both Hume and Nietzsche are masters of a kind of reason, for they show with clarity and style the implications of beginning philosophy with the self. If that is done, regardless of pretensions, one cannot arrive at an objectively defensible position—whether that position be based on empiricist or rationalist foundations. Hume and Nietzsche are rigorously consistent in sticking to the principles of their traditions. That they have nothing new to offer as a solution to the problems posed by those traditions is in some ways a testament to their rigor and consistency. If one begins with the self (for whatever reason), then one ends with the self. Given the rules of the game established by their predecessors, Hume and Nietzsche could be said to be the best players. That their games are absurd merely follows from the absurdity of the first principles. Only by accepting other first principles could the outcomes of the games have been different. Such a move they were either unable or unwilling to make. That is their tragedy and the tragedy of modern thought in general.

Gains and Losses

Having traced the implications of the revolution in philosophy based on method, let us recall what has been gained and lost. Without a doubt, the new method has brought success in the sciences and particularly in technological progress. To treat the world as matter in motion according to general mathematical laws, without concern for things with distinct formal and final causes, does prove fruitful in terms of improving the material condition of mankind. However, treating things as merely matter in motion gives one a false understanding of them, precludes a genuine ethics of responsibility, and reduces beauty to mere feeling and imagination.

Hence there is a loss of truth. Without an understanding of things (as opposed to undifferentiated stuff in different accidental shapes and sizes), there is no possibility of metaphysical knowledge, which leads (when it is authentic, as in Aristotle and Aquinas) not to a concept of a first principle from which all truth can be deduced, but to the frontier of understanding, to the edge of knowledge, and to wonder. Ironically, it is precisely this wonder that is the impetus of genuine science. Without it there would be no reason to probe further and hence no progress.

Not only is a good deal of truth about the world arbitrarily denied and wonder curtailed by making scientific method paradigmatic; the foundations of moral obligation are also destroyed. For if all is matter in motion (with the empiricists) or all is deduced from one theoretical principle (with the rationalists), then the traditional basis of moral obligation in something like natural law must be rejected. This normativity obviously cannot be derived from random motion, for normativity is not random. True, there can still be various kinds of descriptive sciences of human action, whether anthropological, psychological, sociological, biological, chemical, or physical. However, these sciences are accidental to ethics, for ethics is centrally concerned with how we *ought* to act, not with a description of how we *do* act. Nor can ethics be derived from any other theoretical principle at all, whether empirical, mathematical, or metaphysical. As Hume points out so well, moral obligation (ought) cannot be logically derived from amoral premises (is). In other words, the first principles of moral obligation must be first principles of reason, not corollaries of theoretical judgments about the nature of God, or the way the world is, or the way we are.

Finally, delight in beauty is lost. With the rejection of the ideal of contemplation as an end worthy in itself (the wonder to which metaphysics leads), the capacity to contemplate things for their own sake is also lost. On either the empirical or the rationalist view, the reality of things is in doubt. For the empiricists, matter in motion, guided by universal laws, is primary: there is no place for things of beauty, for intermediate formal unities. For the rationalists, reality is to be found only in one first principle: all other things are necessary deductions from such a principle. Things do not exist in any sense for their own sake; they exist merely as necessary deductions from a first, undifferentiated principle. And both empiricists and rationalists begin with the self and its ideas or perceptions. On this model, judgments of beauty are subjective, just a matter of either the structure of ideas or of feelings. The appreciation and celebration of beautiful things has been transformed into a logical or psychological analysis of the human being.

Beauty and art suffer also from the paradigm of progress so central to the modern revolution in philosophy. Whereas the traditional philosophy of beauty and art judges according to principles of the intellect that transcend space and time, the modern criterion for judging good art is often novelty. For art to be good, it must be new. Sometimes mere novelty (as opposed to beauty) is enough to qualify it as good art.

How do benefits and costs balance out? Was the change in the ideal of reason worth it? Unfortunately, such a weighing and measuring cannot be done, for there is no common standard by which to measure the value of distinct objects of human reason. Happily, however, there is no reason to try to sum up the various gains and losses, nor indeed to give up any of these goods—not science and technology, not metaphysics, not ethics, not delight in beauty. The moderns were wrong: it is not necessary to conform all areas of human knowledge to one method, as if science and technology could thrive only if metaphysical speculation, moral obligation, and aesthetic appreciation were put aside. In fact, science (and technology insofar as it follows science) suffers if the other aspects of reason are curtailed. Science dies if frontier questions are rejected because they do not fit the current system; science dies if the moral absolute of seeking and honoring the truth is denied; science dies if the mind is not allowed to wonder at the beauty of the universe.[94]

The last four chapters of the book will focus on the restoration of reason to its place of wide-ranging and prosperous activity. In chapters 6 and 7, we shall consider a number of philosophers who recognized that undue restrictions had been placed on reason and who sought to reinvigorate the life of the intellect. Unfortunately, these thinkers still more or less adhered, if not to scientific method as formulated by Bacon, at least to the idea that a general method is suitable for all spheres of knowledge. Hence, their restoration of reason remained incomplete.

Following these discussions, we shall dive into the systematic heart of the book. In chapter 8, we shall discuss the three distinct areas of reason—the true, the good, and the beautiful—each having its own first principles and method. Finally, we shall return in chapter 9 to the issue of reason's unity (so important to the moderns), examining the ways in which the distinct areas of reason are one.

---

94. Consider the advance of Copernicus over Ptolemy, or Einstein over Newton: if the old system had been honored as inviolable, the new would never have come about. Moreover, Copernicus and Einstein are explicit about the role of beauty in their discoveries.

6

The Road to Recovery

Not all the thinkers of the modern era agreed with the severe limitation of reason that we have witnessed in the preceding chapters. Many scholars (mostly in the religious orders) continued working in the scholastic tradition. As such, they were more or less in tune with the distinction between the fundamental objects of human reason—the true, the good, and the beautiful. Even in the mainstream of modern philosophy, some argued for a broader scope for reason than that outlined by Bacon or Descartes. Chief among these were Immanuel Kant and Friedrich Gottfried Hegel. In this chapter we shall examine the thought of these two great thinkers with an eye to their understanding of the range of reason. Following this analysis, we shall take a look in chapter 7 at two twentieth-century thinkers, Alfred North Whitehead and Bernard Lonergan, who in many ways built on the work of Kant and Hegel and continued the recovery of reason.

Kant and Hegel recognize that scientific method, whether steered toward hypothesis (rationalism) or verification (empiricism), is insufficient to account for the full range of intelligibility. To limit reason to such a method is to prevent an account not just of other aspects of reality within the realm of the true but also of the distinctiveness of obligation (the realm of the good) and aesthetic delight and creation (the realm of the beautiful). However, although these thinkers clearly do consider distinct realms of reason, they are still bound by the project set up by Bacon and Descartes, in which method is prior to content and subject to object. To this extent, they fall short of a full recovery of reason.

Kant

Immanuel Kant is in a curious position in that he seems to be at once the culmination of the modern movement and its critical opponent. One finds in the prefaces of Kant's famous *Critique of Pure Reason* the same issues voiced by Bacon and Descartes: concern for progress, criticism of scholasticism for its endless controversies, and confidence that he has the true method, which will sort out these difficulties. Just as Bacon and Descartes want to justify the new science of Copernicus and Galileo and place it on a road serviceable to mankind, so Kant wants to do the same with Newtonian physics. Neither rationalism, with its reduction of the material world to the world of ideas, nor empiricism, with its reduction of thought to subrational principles of matter in motion, has been able to validate scientific knowledge.

Kant is surely aware of the intellectual tradition in which he is working. He commends Bacon for bringing scientific method to its true form, and also Locke for his work on human understanding (which has replaced traditional metaphysics as the queen of the sciences and will continue to do so in Kant).[1] And he credits Hume with waking him from his "dogmatic slumber."[2] Following Hume, Kant rejects the metaphysics of Descartes, arguing that the mere idea of an absolutely necessary being in no way proves that such a being actually exists.[3] If the argument for the existence of God fails, then the various projects for saving science by the guarantee of God also fail. However, on Hume's account, all knowledge seems to be impossible. The conclusions of Hume prove that pure empiricism leads to skepticism. One could say that as Bacon and Descartes are to the skepticism of Montaigne, so Kant is to the skepticism of Hume. Kant believes that the problems that bedeviled the empirical tradition and led to the skepticism of Hume could be corrected by one major move—again, a new method of approaching reality.

Specifically, two grave difficulties arise from the adoption of empirical method as the sole means of verifying truth claims. The first is the apparent impossibility of any certain knowledge about the world. The second is the apparent impossibility of normative ethics. David Hume had given both problems their full expression. If all our knowledge of the physical world is taken from experience, and if experience is by definition limited to certain times and places, then science can at best give

---

1. Kant commends Bacon in the preface to the second edition of *The Critique of Pure Reason* and commends Locke in the preface to the first edition.

2. Immanuel Kant, "Preface," in *Prolegomena to Any Future Metaphysics*, trans. James W. Ellington (Indianapolis: Hackett, 1977), p. 5.

3. Immanuel Kant, "Transcendental Dialectic," bk. 2, ch. 3, sec. 4, in *Critique of Pure Reason*, trans. Werner S. Pluhar (Indianapolis: Hackett, 1996), pp. 578–86.

us probable knowledge of the world of physical things. One must always admit that the causal connections could change completely in one's next experience since such a change would not involve a contradiction. As for morality, if all real existences must be verifiable by sense experience and if morality deals with real actions in the real world, then morality must be concerned with verifiable aspects of our actions. Since universal moral norms such as justice and honesty cannot be verified by sense experience, empirical philosophy counts them as meaningless. It must be that we are guided by passions or emotions or habits and not by moral ideals given by reason. But if this is so, then we have no natural universal moral laws. For passions, like every other kind of physical occurrence, are unique and notoriously changeable, or in the event that there is a universal passion that moves us (e.g., Hume's moral sense), it does so beneath the level of reason and hence of choice and responsibility.

Facing this exhaustion of reason, where certain knowledge of the world and our obligations are apparently ruled out, Kant makes his move. It is a revolutionary one that will come with a price (as we shall see), but it does seem to meet these two challenges of Hume's skepticism. The move is, of course, Kant's "Copernican revolution."[4] Just as Copernicus revolutionized our thinking about the solar system by placing the sun at the center instead of the earth and, by so doing, cleared up the growing number of anomalies discovered in the old Ptolemaic system, so Kant wants to revolutionize our way of thinking in general. Instead of assuming that the mind conforms to reality, we should assume that reality conforms to the mind. If we do so, the twin problems of scientific uncertainty and moral relativism can be solved, for then certainty can be established without having to consult our experience of a changing world.[5]

Kant's notion of mind, here, is not the patchwork of sense impressions and their faint copies that the empiricism of Locke and Hume professed, but the storehouse of *a priori* certainties found in the thought of the rationalists from Descartes to Leibniz. Just as the rationalists claim that their ideas are universal and certain because they are not based on experience, so Kant claims that his *a priori* forms of intuition and his categories of the understanding are universal and certain.[6] Kant, however, does not hold

4. See *Critique of Pure Reason*, preface to second edition, pp. 21–23.
5. Notice that this is an assumption, not something proved to be true. Just as Copernicus claimed his new model saved the appearances better than the Ptolemaic model, so Kant's new way of looking at things is presented as a more efficient way of saving the appearances. Kant's is a possible position on first principles, to be understood as likely or not by its consequences for helping us understand reality and moral obligation.
6. See the introduction to second edition, sec. 2, in *Critique of Pure Reason*, pp. 46–48.

that all reality is deduced from the ideas in our minds but that only the forms of things come from the mind; their matter comes from experience. Kant tries to mediate between rationalism and empiricism, admitting the empirical claims of Hume but relegating them to the matter or data of knowledge.[7] Kant's position, with its distinction of form and matter, also looks a bit like a return to the hylomorphism of Aristotle and Aquinas. This synthesis of both the experiential and the innate elements of knowledge and its expression in terms of matter and form make Kant's thought subtle and powerful and support the credibility of his claim to express the truths of all previous philosophy in a new revolutionary formulation.

However, although this insistence on the complementarity of empirical and rational elements holds for knowledge of the world, Kant argues that moral knowledge is strictly *a priori*. Since morality is about how we ought to act, it is not concerned with knowing how things are. Unlike physics, ethics does not require data drawn from experience. Kant sees clearly that reliance on scientific method for all knowledge would rule out the possibility of normative ethics. In fact, Kant's desire to provide foundations for morality leads the way in his revolution. Reason must be restricted to its merely formal role, or else we are back to Hume's moral skepticism. For let reason operate empirically, and we shall have only probable guides, which are no guides at all when it comes to knowing what we ought to do.

One might argue that Hume is not a moral skeptic, for he declares that we have a moral sense that directs us to act in benevolent ways toward others. Hume's account of a universal guide for morality, however, is strictly descriptive or psychological, not prescriptive. Since, as Hume stresses so forcefully, one cannot derive obligation from facts alone, the fact that there is a universal moral sense in no way implies that we ought to follow it. Kant understood that, unless there are first principles of moral obligation, there can be no conclusions of obligation—i.e., no prescriptive ethics. The idea of duty implies moral absolutes and freedom, but neither a moral absolute nor freedom is empirically verifiable.

It appears that reason's role is not the same in science as in morality, for in one case it is linked with data from experience to give us knowledge of nature, and in the other it is purely *a priori*. Unlike his modern predecessors, Kant explicitly distinguishes between theoretical reason and practical reason, insisting that the principles and methods that lead to the truth are distinct from those that direct us in pursuit of the good.[8]

7. "There can be no doubt that all our cognition begins with experience" (*Critique of Pure Reason*, introduction to second edition, sec. 1, p. 43).

8. One might object that such a distinction had already been made by Locke, but it sits very uncomfortably with Locke's denial of all innate ideas and with his insistence that the origin of all knowledge is in sense experience.

In addition to distinguishing between reason's relation to the true in his *Critique of Pure Reason* and its relation to the good in his *Critique of Practical Reason*, Kant writes a third critique, the *Critique of Judgment*, in which he considers beauty. Hence, Kant seems to be doing what we have been recommending: giving to each of the areas of human reason its own distinctive realm. The thoroughness of his treatments is remarkable, and his insight into the foundations of ethics seems to be on target.

However, this revolution comes with a price: the association of the mind and the world of things that Bacon and Descartes had tried so hard, but unsuccessfully, to establish through empirical and rationalist methods is, by Kant, excluded on principle. If we insist on the role of reason in providing merely the formal dimension of scientific knowledge, then we must limit our knowledge to things as they appear to us, as opposed to things as they are in themselves.[9] We have no access to the thing-in-itself, since the latter is not an object of possible experience. Having witnessed the skepticism that results from making knowledge either innate or empirical, Kant insists that the *a priori* structures of the mind are only one ingredient in our understanding; the other is sense experience. Hence human understanding of reality is limited to objects of possible experience. Whereas Aristotle and Aquinas keep the world of things and knowledge related through the doctrine of abstraction (which assumes the objective existence of things and our ability to know them), Kant's revolution rules out this relation. Knowledge is not about the adequation of our concept to the thing (since we have no access to the thing). Rather knowledge is in our image, and hence not in the image of the thing as it is in itself but only as it appears to us. Thus the world of things and the metaphysics arising out of the questions such a world raises for us (Aristotelian/Thomistic metaphysics) are destroyed.

Metaphysics is now to be the study of pure reason. Given this new meaning of metaphysics, we can have a metaphysics of nature and a metaphysics of morals.[10] Although this renaming of metaphysics may seem a radical departure from the rationalist tradition, it actually is not. From the moment Descartes (without reference to our experience of the world) goes to work on his idea of perfection, metaphysics in the traditional sense is dead. From then on it becomes a study of the human mind.[11] Kant sees his explication as the fruition of the movement begun by Bacon and Descartes (and expressed earlier by Montaigne) of considering the self. Since all we can know are our thoughts and sensations,

9. See *Critique of Pure Reason*, preface to second edition, pp. 23–25.

10. Immanuel Kant, *Groundwork of the Metaphysics of Morals*, preface, trans. H. J. Patton (New York: Harper & Row, 1964), p. 56.

11. This is true for the empirical tradition as well. The major works of Locke, Berkeley, and Hume are all studies of human understanding.

reality is, for us, just these thoughts and sensations. Since metaphysics is the study of the principles of reality, metaphysics must be the study of mind, for that is reality.[12]

I have said that Kant's thought is dominated by a moral concern: the realm of the true is arbitrarily restricted in order to make room for the realm of the good. Etienne Gilson goes so far as to say that metaphysics has been replaced with ethics as first philosophy in Kant's thought.[13] Let us begin by examining Kant's conception of a "metaphysics of morals" and why he makes practical reason the paradigm for reason. Then we shall consider how this first philosophy affects the other aspects of his thought.

In terms of essential morality, Kant's fundamental insight is basically right: the requirements of morality are not derived from theoretical reason, i.e., Hume's relations of ideas and matters of fact. That we are obliged in some ways and that we are free to honor or reject these obligations cannot be derived from mathematics (remember Spinoza's geometrical deduction) or physics (recall Hobbes's attempt to trace all choice and action to matter in motion). Kant's revolution is an attempt to save physics but also to show its limitation in order to make room for morality. Theoretical reason provides the categories for understanding the world of phenomena but is limited to objects that can be formed in intuition, that is, those that exist in time and space.[14] Such objects are necessarily particular and localized. Moral absolutes, such as "do not kill innocent people," however, are universal and timeless.

According to Kant, although theoretical reason can fully understand only what can be provided by intuition, it inevitably thinks beyond the sensible realm, inventing principles to fulfill its desire for complete knowledge—ideas such as God, the world, and the immortal soul.[15] However, since such ideas cannot possibly be verified by experience, such speculation is idle. When theoretical reason pursues questions that go beyond the possibility of verification by the senses (such as questions about God, creation, the immortal soul, and freedom), it finds itself embroiled in contradictions. These Kant calls the inevitable antinomies of

---

12. Kant is explicit about his understanding of metaphysics as post-Cartesian: "Since the Essays of Locke and Leibniz, or rather since the origin of metaphysics so far as we know its history, nothing has ever happened which could have been more decisive to its fate than the attack made upon it by David Hume." *Prolegomena*, preface, p. 3.

13. Gilson, *The Unity of Philosophical Experience*, pp. 234–36.

14. For Kant, these forms of intuition are *a priori*, that is, they are not objectively found in the world, but we bring them to our experience of the world. Were space and time not *a priori* constituents of ourselves, we could not even experience the world.

15. *Prolegomena*, pt. 3, § 44, pp. 72–73. Note that these are the three ideas of Descartes' metaphysics—metaphysics as Kant knows it.

pure reason.[16] Since contradictory statements nullify each other, reason's excursions into the world of traditional metaphysics are illusory.

Thus theoretical knowledge is, by dint of Kant's revolution, limited to sensible phenomena; but practical knowledge, as universal and certain, transcends the phenomena. It is not limited by sense experience, nor does it give rise to antinomies, since it is about what we ought to do, not the nature of a reality (things as they are in themselves) to which we have no direct access. Thus there is a legitimate act of reason that goes beyond the senses, but it is practical reason, not theoretical reason.

> Once we have denied that speculative reason can make any progress in that realm of the suprasensible, we still have an option available to us. We can try to discover whether perhaps in reason's practical cognition data can be found that would allow us to determine reason's transcendent concept of the unconditioned. Perhaps in this way our a priori cognition, though one that is possible only from a practical point of view, would still allow us to get beyond the boundary of all possible experience, as is the wish of metaphysics.[17]

Thus the paradigm for reason (the legitimate use of pure reason) is practical, not theoretical. By practical reason, Kant means the knowledge of the first principles of morality, not our ability to apply reason to make technological advances, or to become virtuous. Although the Copernican revolution and its limitation of reason is for the sake of saving science from skepticism, this saving of science is not ordered to technology for our material benefit, but to an even more important end—the saving of morality. "I therefore had to annul *knowledge* in order to make room for *faith*. And the true source of all the lack of faith which conflicts with morality—and is always highly dogmatic—is dogmatism in metaphysics, i.e., the prejudice according to which we can make progress in metaphysics without a [prior] critique of pure reason."[18] The unbelief Kant refers to here is skepticism, the doubt that there can be any certain knowledge.

Although Kant is right to give practical reason its own first principles, the priority of such principles over other aspects of human reason causes some problems. That is, Kant's Copernican revolution does indeed have a cost. Practical reason tends to usurp the appropriate authority of other aspects of human reason to their detriment, and ultimately to its own

16. For example, Kant claims that there is equal evidence that the world has a beginning in space and time and that it has not such a beginning, and also that there are causes acting from freedom and that there are not such causes (see *Prolegomena*, pt. 3, § 51, p. 80).

17. *Critique of Pure Reason*, preface to the second edition, p. 25.

18. Ibid., p. 31.

detriment as well. Let us consider how Kant's paradigm of reason affects his theoretical philosophy (the realm of the true), his aesthetics (the realm of the beautiful), and his practical philosophy itself (the realm of the good).

First of all, the revolution instituted to allow for the use of reason in its practical mode unduly restricts the operation of theoretical reason. Given the terms of the revolution, the Aristotelian definition of truth as the adequation of thought and thing must be rejected. Since knowledge of the world is only of the world as it appears to us, there can be no knowledge of the world as it is in itself. Of course, Kant is right here if one accepts the starting point of the modern tradition. If one starts with the self (whether as an empiricist or a rationalist), one cannot get to things. Kant just accepts this and limits the role of knowledge of the world to knowledge of phenomena—things as they appear. The only real alternative would be a return to some notion of Aristotelian abstraction, which Kant (because of his assumptions) is unable or unwilling to make.

Although Kant's theory in principle accommodates the elements of scientific method (hypothesis and verification), it is rather weak on verification: to check whether the world is really the way we suppose it to be is to assume some kind of contact with an intrinsically intelligible world. But this Kant denies. Kant's model fits the ideal of a completed science whose structures are already formulated in the mind. And indeed, Kant believed that Newton had brought science to such a state.[19]

Thus Kant's model cannot account for scientific exploration and discovery. The realist position of Aristotle, and the most commonsensical explanation of changes in science, is that our provisional understanding of the world changes when the world raises questions for us that our old formulations cannot handle. At that moment we reformulate our position to explain better the order that we find. Of course, Kant could say (as Hegel will) that all the advances of science are implicit in our minds. But then, what is the point of referring to the necessary ingredient of experience coming from the things-in-themselves? Why call the world of things-in-themselves the intelligible world, if such a world is not ordered by form?

Kant's revolution takes its toll on his aesthetics, too, denying it any conceptual justification. In his analysis of beauty in his *Critique of Judgment*, Kant carves out a unique place for the appreciation of beauty. The judgment in each realm of reason is distinct. Moral judgment is a purely *a priori* act of reason. Theoretical judgment is reason bound by the categories of the understanding and by sensation. Aesthetic judgment involves

19. Further developments in science since Newton show that Kant was wrong on this point.

neither cognition (reason) nor sensation. "For we may say universally, whether it concerns beauty in nature or in art: *beautiful is what we like in merely judging it* (rather than either in sensation proper or through a concept)."[20] Appreciating beauty is a matter of the imagination, not reason or understanding, and it is subjective, although it carries with it a conviction of universality. "If we wish to decide whether something is beautiful or not, we do not use understanding to refer the presentation to the object so as to give rise to cognition; rather, we use imagination (perhaps in connection with understanding) to refer the presentation to the subject and his feeling of pleasure or displeasure."[21]

Even though Kant denies that aesthetic judgments are acts of reason, he does express a number of keen insights into the nature of the beautiful. Given that beauty is merely a matter of aesthetic satisfaction, Kant distinguishes it from the satisfaction of pleasure and from moral satisfaction. Unlike the satisfaction of pleasure, the appreciation of beauty is not merely a response to stimulation. Unlike moral satisfaction, the satisfaction in the beautiful is not the result of some purpose achieved: the desire for the beautiful is disinterested and, as it were, contemplative. The object of beauty is appreciated for its own sake. This analysis has quite a lot in common with the traditional account of beauty, which we shall discuss in chapter 8.

In the end, however, Kant (like Leibniz) stops short of giving to beauty its own rational principles. Not being an object of theoretical reason or practical reason, Kant denies that the appreciation of beauty is an act of reason. Although he rejects feeling as a guide to ethics (the position presented by Shaftesbury, Hutcheson, and Hume), Kant seems to accept it as a guide to the appreciation of beauty. He adopts a basically Romantic interpretation of the beautiful in which rules play little or no part and taste dominates. Natural beauty is more perfect than art since it is less governed by rules. "Even bird song, which we cannot bring under any rule of music, seems to contain more freedom and hence to offer more to taste than human song, even when this human song is performed according to all the rules of the art of music."[22]

As for art, genius is the key. Rather than accounting for a beautiful work of art by reference to objective standards or rules being fulfilled in a unique way, Kant points to uniqueness itself as the explanation. Since beauty is not a matter of concept or sensation, beautiful art must be explained by reference to a judgment not guided by rules or standards—the unique judgment of genius.

20. Immanuel Kant, *Critique of Judgment*, pt. 1, div. 1, bk. 2, § 45, trans. Werner S. Pluhar (Indianapolis: Hackett, 1987), p. 174.
21. Ibid., bk. 1, § 1, p. 44.
22. Ibid., bk. 1, § 22, p. 94.

The concept of fine art does not permit a judgment about the beauty of its product to be derived from any rule whatsoever that has a *concept* as its determining basis, i.e., the judgment must not be based on a concept of the way in which the product is possible. Hence fine art cannot itself devise the rule by which it is to bring about the product. Since, however, a product can never be called art unless it is preceded by a rule, it must be nature in the subject (and through the attunement of his powers) that gives the rule to art; in other words, fine art is possible only as the product of genius.[23]

Here Kant reflects the Romantic notion of art as self-expression.

Although the appreciation of beauty is a matter of feeling and not rational judgment, it carries with it a kind of universality. *"Beauty* is what, without a concept, is liked universally."[24] We judge that something that seems beautiful to us should seem beautiful to others, as if the beauty were something objective in the thing.[25] But the universality is merely subjective; it is a matter of the imagination and taste, not of the understanding. When judging the beautiful, "the understanding serves the imagination and not vice versa."[26]

There are a number of problems here. Just as Hume's claim to a universal passion of concern for humanity is in doubt (since passions are notoriously changeable), and just as the mere fact of a feeling of any kind does not carry with it an obligation, so it is hard to substantiate the universality of aesthetic appreciation and hard to explain why others ought to honor it, too. According to Kant, there are not beautiful things, but beautiful feelings. Cut off from reference to objective criteria, Kant's theory cannot explain the essence of aesthetic appreciation. He can analyze its nature as feeling or satisfaction and how it differs from sensual gratification and moral interest (and he does this well), but this is more a theoretical account of beauty—psychological or perhaps physiological. He cannot account for its essential intelligibility. In fact, he denies that it has any, if one means by intelligibility something that can be understood.

A judgment of taste is merely *contemplative*, i.e., it is a judgment that is indifferent to the existence of the object: it [considers] the character of the object only by holding it up to our feelings of pleasure and displeasure. Nor is this contemplation, as such, directed to concepts, for a judgment of taste is not a cognitive judgment (whether theoretical or practical) and hence is neither *based* on concepts, nor directed to them as *purposes*.[27]

23. Ibid., bk. 2, § 46, p. 175.
24. Ibid., bk. 1, § 9, p. 64.
25. Ibid., § 7, pp. 55–56.
26. Ibid., § 22, p. 93.
27. Ibid., § 5, p. 51.

Aesthetic judgment is a fact, but unintelligible. Kant's position seems rather like Leibniz's claim that we recognize the beautiful but cannot explain it. Neither the concepts of rationalism nor the sense experience of empiricism will do. The judgment cannot be validated by either thought or sensation. It is a purely subjective act that nevertheless feels objective and therefore universal. That is, we feel that others should agree with our aesthetic judgments. This is rather meaningless conceptually (as Kant would admit); for since there are no intelligible criteria for explaining what makes something beautiful, it would be impossible to try to convince someone to agree with one's judgment. In such a case, why would others, or more importantly why should others, agree with one's judgment? Like Hume's account of the universal moral sense, Kant's account of the universal aesthetic feeling is unintelligible. Just as Kant argues that the universality of Hume's moral sense can be morally (as opposed to psychologically or physiologically) intelligible only as a principle of reason (practical reason), so I would argue that Kant's universal aesthetic judgment can be aesthetically intelligible only as a principle of reason (aesthetic reason).

Ultimately, just as Kant's treatment of theoretical reason is a means to the end of establishing morality, so too is his aesthetics. He suggests that the appreciation of beauty in the universality of its feeling is a symbol of and a means to the end of social harmony. In fact, this is the only way to justify the claim to universality. "Now I maintain that the beautiful is the symbol of the morally good; and only because we refer the beautiful to the morally good (we all do so naturally and require all others also to do so, as a duty) does our liking for it include a claim to everyone else's assent."[28]

Finally, let us consider how Kant's revolution affects his treatment of ethics itself, since practical reason seems to be the foundation for all his thought. As was said above, it seems that Kant is right in his insight that moral principles are not derived from metaphysics or aesthetics, and that they are first principles in their own right. However, his understanding of reason rules out the possibility of ethical virtue, that is, of reason's precepts living in the body in the development of character. Ethical virtue is possible for Aristotle and Aquinas because they recognize the priority of the human being over mind and body and because they have some idea of the cooperation of matter and intelligence in gaining knowledge (abstraction). Holding that anything relating to the body and experience is a threat to morality (since it could be traceable to self-interest or direct inclination), Kant's ethics is in danger of falling into a dualism, with the body being evil and the autonomous self being

28. Ibid., pt. 1, div. 2, § 59, p. 228.

good.[29] This allows him only the most general of moral principles (treat humanity, whether in oneself or another, always as an end and never merely as a means)[30] and no theory of the virtues and the unity of the human being—rationally, emotionally, and physically. Although Kant's categorical imperative is correct as far as it goes, the many goods that fulfill one's humanity (e.g., life, knowledge, friendship, beauty) remain unspecified or are to be understood only as they pertain to reason and autonomy, not as they contribute to integral human fulfillment.[31]

Kant's use of practical reason in place of theoretical reason to prove the existence of God, the immortal soul, and freedom[32] is also in tension with his central ethical insight. Kant is right in arguing that freedom is intimately tied to practical reason. Since acts of free choice occur in response to a recognition of good to be done, rather than being to be known, there can be no theoretical proof of freedom of choice. Kant's insight that the only proof of freedom is the practical proof based on the absurdity of denying that one's actions are really one's own is surely correct.[33] Freedom is a first principle of practical reason. However, the proof of the existence of an immortal soul and an unconditioned cause of everything (God) are irrelevant to morality, particularly as Kant understands it. The fact that one has an immortal soul that must abide by one's actions forever and receive rewards or punishments according to desert, and the fact that there is an ultimate judge to impose these rewards and punishments, are irrelevant to moral duty. They are consequentialist arguments that do not fit the character of Kant's moral absolutism. Kant himself stresses that one should do the right thing because it is known to be right, not because one seeks rewards or fears punishments. He insists that duty is the essence of morality, not self-interest or direct inclination.[34] Of course, promises or threats may be psychologically helpful in getting us to fulfill our duties, but they are accidental to moral

29. This is rather like Plato's position that the soul is the human being and the body a hindrance to the soul. In practice, however, Kant does not always so bifurcate the human being. See, for example, Immanuel Kant, "Duties Toward the Body in Respect of Sexual Impulse," in *Lectures on Ethics*, trans. Louis Infield (Indianapolis: Hackett, 1963), pp. 162–68, where he speaks of human love involving, not just good will, but also affection and happiness. He stresses, in this article, the unity of the human person. Although in practice Kant at times avoids the problem of dualism, this does not change the fact that his principles tend in that direction.

30. *Groundwork*, p. 96.

31. This is the term John Finnis uses to indicate what Aristotle and Aquinas meant by happiness. See John Finnis, *Moral Absolutes* (Washington, DC: Catholic University of America Press, 1991), pp. 11, 30, 45–46.

32. See *Critique of Pure Reason*, preface to the second edition, pp. 27–31.

33. *Groundwork*, p. 116.

34. Ibid., pp. 65–67.

obligation, which cannot be derived from psychology or anthropology or any theoretical science.

This is a little like Hume's no-ought-from-is argument, only here the absurdity is moral rather than logical. Just as it involves a theoretical absurdity to conclude to obligation from merely factual premises (since there would be something in the conclusion not found in the premises), so Kant's way of arguing for the existence of the immortal soul and God involves a moral absurdity. Unless morality can be reduced to consequences and thus to some theoretical science of motivation, Kant's argument fails. But we need go no further than Kant himself to know that morality cannot be reduced to such a theoretical science. This insight is central to his whole metaphysics of morals. Hence Kant refutes Kant.

Kant rightly notes that we cannot help but think about God as a principle of unity of all things. And he understands that the arguments for God's existence based on our concept of God fail for the simple reason that we cannot adequately conceive of an infinite being. However, he wrongly judges that moral obligation is the source of our knowledge of God, for moral obligation does not require God. An atheist has the same basic moral obligations as a believer. Thus Kant's practical proof fails.

In the end, Kant gives us a very sophisticated view of the world, but it is an "as if" world. The world of science is certain if we treat the phenomena *as if* they are real. We can make aesthetic judgments *as if* there were real objects of beauty that we judge by reason according to universal criteria. And we can know that the ideas of pure reason—God, the soul, and freedom—are genuine through practical reason, *as if* they had been proven by theoretical reason. This can only be an "as if" world since it is produced from human reason. It is a subjective world. True, Kant keeps one toe in objective reality in his claim that there is an intelligible world of things as they are in themselves and not as they appear to us, but we have no direct access to such a world.

Hegel

While Kant hesitates on the shore of reality, Hegel plunges right in, declaring all to be real and intelligible. What is this doubt about the adequacy of reason? Why distinguish between a sensible world of appearances that we know and an intelligible world of things as they are in themselves that we do not and cannot know? Overturning a tradition stemming from Bacon and Descartes to Kant, Hegel declares that there is no problem of the bridge: thought and thing are identical.

In a way, this is a return to the position of Aristotle. And indeed Hegel says that the metaphysics of Aristotle is superior to that of the moderns.[35] While the moderns' first step is to declare the clear and distinct separation of mind and body and so the impossibility of mind knowing physical reality, Aristotle affirms the unity of mind and body and insists that the human being not only knows other things but also is other things. Seizing upon this insight, Hegel announces the adequation of thought and thing by declaring that reason and reality are identical. After the endless doubts as to the health of reason and the numerous methods to correct the illness (none of which can legitimately do the job since it has been developed by the same reason), Hegel is a breath of fresh air. With Hegel we are back to a kind of realism. The mind not only can but *does* know reality.

Of course, Hegel's position is very unlike Aristotle's in a number of important respects. Most essentially, when Aristotle says that the mind is all things intelligible, he means the human mind, and he means that the mind is *able* to be all things by conforming to them, not that it is now or is necessarily ever going to be all things. When Hegel says the mind is all things, he means by mind Absolute Spirit, and the potentiality is merely one of time: inevitably, Absolute Spirit is coming to the knowledge of nature, which is ultimately knowledge of itself.

How can Hegel make this rather bold statement? He does so by claiming to have found a new method—the method of reason itself. This is rather like Bacon's claim. When Bacon presents his *New Organon*, he believes he has a logic to replace that of Aristotle. Believing all Aristotelian philosophy to be a deduction from Aristotle's logic, Bacon thinks that by changing the logic, he can correct the flaws of Aristotelian thought. It is, of course, untrue (as we have said before) that Aristotle thinks of his logic as the source of all the sciences. For Aristotle logic is the structure of thought; the content of thought is given by the object of a particular field of study and differs for ethics, physics, metaphysics, psychology, aesthetics, etc. Bacon, however, thinks that his new logic is appropriate for all areas of human thought: scientific method with its empirical approach to knowledge is the sole appropriate avenue to human knowledge.

Hegel agrees with Bacon that all forms of knowledge, indeed all aspects of reality, follow logic. However, Hegel's logic is revolutionary. Instead of logic being a tool that helps us know reality either by extending our knowledge through syllogistic deduction or by discovering knowledge through empirical induction, Hegel declares logic to be the very structure of reality. "In this way the Logic is the all-animating spirit of all the

---

35. Georg Wilhelm Friedrich Hegel, *The Science of Logic*, introduction, trans. W. H. Johnston and L. G. Struthers (London: George Allen & Unwin, 1966), vol. 1, p. 55. Of course, Hegel means by metaphysics what the moderns do: the study of reason.

sciences, and the thought-determinations contained in the Logic are the pure spirits; they are what is most inward, but, at the same time, they are always on our lips and consequently they seem to be something thoroughly well known."[36]

In a way this position is an extrapolation of Aristotle's notion of God as self-thinking thought. Aristotle is not really defining God here, but giving the best suggestion as to what God could be like. Since God, as ultimate final cause, is the perfection toward which all things tend and since thinking is the most perfect activity with which we are familiar, the best analogue for God's nature is thinking.[37] But if God is the most perfect of all beings, then he must be thinking about the most perfect of objects: himself. Hegel understands self-thinking thought as the identity of subject and object: the thinker (with all the structures of thought) is identical with reality (the object of thought). Logic is both the form and content of thought. It is reason and reality.

Thus Hegel identifies the God who is self-thinking thought and the world as two aspects of one Absolute Spirit that is coming to self-consciousness, to the stage of complete self-knowledge in which it thinks itself perfectly. World history is the development of this dialectic of spirit in time; nature is its development in space.[38]

Let us consider the main lines of Hegel's new logic and how he sees it as foundational to all thought and reality. Against Kant, Hegel holds that not only being but also nonbeing is a meaningful predicate, and that the antinomies Kant discovered in reason are not contradictions, which we would avoid if we could, but the very life of the mind and reality. The logic of dialectic is the inevitable unfolding of all thought and reality: every thesis carries with it its own contradiction or antithesis, which gives rise to an inevitable synthesis, which transcends the thesis and antithesis in a higher viewpoint.[39] This synthesis is itself a thesis that carries its own antithesis to be transcended in a further synthesis, and so on. This dialectic is the pattern for all areas of human thought and reality: physics, biology, psychology, art, ethics, metaphysics, politics, religion, and history.[40]

36. Hegel, *The Encyclopaedia Logic*, sec. 24, trans. T. F. Geraets, W. A. Suchting, and H. S. Harris (Indianapolis: Hackett, 1991), p. 59.

37. See *Metaphysics* 12.7.

38. Hegel, *Reason in History*, ch. 4, sec. 3b, trans. Robert S. Hartman (Indianapolis: Bobbs-Merrill, 1953), p. 87.

39. *Science of Logic*, introduction, vol. 1, pp. 64–65.

40. The introduction of history as an object of knowledge (and indeed of logic) is new with Hegel. That is, it is new among the moderns. Augustine in his *City of God* presents a theology of history. Of course, Hegel's theological perspective is quite different from Augustine's, as different as their notions of God and God's relation to the world. For Augustine,

The basic dialectic at the heart of logic itself and every discipline is that concerning being. If we begin with the most basic notion of the human mind, i.e., being, we find that it carries with it its own antithesis, i.e., nonbeing. Any concept, if it is to be intelligible, must be distinct, and what else is distinct from being but nonbeing? From the clash of these two ideas arises the notion of becoming. Becoming is the synthesis of the thesis "there is being" and the antithesis "there is nonbeing." Any becoming has a certain direction that carries with it its opposite, with the two generating a third direction that includes the other two but from a higher viewpoint.[41]

Although Hegel would note that this dialectic is found in the very heart of reason, where its moments are not temporal but logical, it is also a feature of reality that takes the form of changes through time. Thus the clash of ideas that arises in reason is also played out in history. Whether we speak of the history of metaphysics, or art, or philosophy of nature, or ethics, or politics, all these are expressed, not just in their logical relations, but also in time and space. Like Spinoza, Hegel identifies thought and thing not only in the realm of intelligibility but also in the realm of matter.

Overarching the whole movement is a kind of providence, not indeed of a Creator for his creation, but of the Absolute Idea coming to self-realization. That is, the whole dialectic and all its parts are unified in an ultimate end, which is the self-consciousness of Absolute Spirit, which Spirit is nature. Here Hegel is rather like Spinoza, except that, where Spinoza begins with God or nature as first principle and deduces all truths in the timeless manner of geometry, Hegel's God or nature acts more as a final cause toward which all things tend in a temporal dialectic. Perhaps it would be better to say that, in addition to Spinoza's deductive method, Hegel adds the temporal dimension. Hegel's thought is clearly influenced (as is Spinoza's) by the Neoplatonic notion of all reality coming forth and returning to the One.

This idea of final causality, banished from modern thought since Bacon,[42] is a second feature of Aristotle's thought that Hegel recovers. But whereas the ultimate final cause in Aristotle's thought, as the orderer of all things, is arguably distinct from nature (and certainly is so understood by Aquinas), in Hegel this final cause is intrinsic to Nature. Thus Hegel claims that in the beginning there is no clear direction to the becoming.[43]

God is Creator of the world, and it is a free creation; for Hegel, God is the world marching inevitably toward self-consciousness.

41. For Hegel's discussion of this most basic dialectic, see *Science of Logic*, bk. 1, ch. 1, vol. 1, pp. 94–120.

42. The notable exception is Leibniz, who makes use of final causality to explain the dynamism of the intelligent monad.

43. "World history does not begin with any conscious aim" (*Reason in History*, ch. 3, sec. 2a, p. 30).

The clarity of self-consciousness and the act of self-realization of the Spirit grow with time. There is something rather odd about what Hegel says here, for how is it possible for a process that has an inevitable outcome to begin without a direction? Such a notion seems absurd since it makes chance (disorder) a fundamental principle of necessity and order.

The difference between Aristotle and Hegel on this point is that, for Aristotle, final cause is clearly the first cause, with efficient cause responding, whereas in Hegel they are identical, or if there is a priority, it goes to efficient cause. Perhaps this is due to the influence of scientific method with its insistence on matter in motion as basic and its rejection of final causality, or perhaps it is due to the intervening Christian metaphysics of Aquinas and others in which God is identified as the final cause and the first efficient cause of all things. In any case, according to Aquinas, to be the first efficient cause is to be Creator, and there is an absolute distinction between creatures and Creator. When Hegel collapses the distinction between creatures and Creator, the first efficient cause takes on the role of temporal agent (like Bacon's matter-in-motion idea of science or Leibniz's efficient causality).[44]

Clearly Hegel is influenced by the idea of providence, the idea that everything happens according to one plan.[45] The difference between Hegel's thought and the thought of Aristotle and Aquinas is that Hegel thinks that he knows that plan. Aristotle does not mean his final cause to be the explanation of the intelligibility of things, as if we know about things because we know the essence of self-thinking thought, nor does Aquinas mean his first efficient cause (God as creator) to be an explanation for the intelligibility of things. Rather, the intelligibility of things raises questions for us that suggest the existence of an ultimate final cause and first efficient cause. We do not know what this ultimate cause is or how it acts, and therefore we cannot use it to explain other things. To claim to do so is to lose the intelligibility of things, as we argued often in the last chapter.

It is true that, if we knew what self-thinking thought or God is, then we would know the intelligibility of all things. But we do not and cannot

44. Leibniz had distinguished efficient cause as the cause of material things, and final cause as the cause of intellectual things.

45. We have noted the influence of Neoplatonism on Hegel. However, in some ways Hegel's idea is closer to the idea of providence, for he holds that Absolute Spirit is reason and reality, not beyond reason and reality as the Neoplatonists held. Of course, there are some very serious differences between Hegel's Absolute Spirit and God understood by Aquinas, even philosophically. First of all, God, for Aquinas, is not all things but the cause of all things—hence the absolute distinction between all creatures and God. Second, God, for Aquinas, is not changing or developing but, as lacking no perfection, is pure actuality. Of course, our idea of God might change, but this does not signify a change in the Creator, but a change in us.

know God's nature. If Hegel claims to, he is applying only a limited idea (not fully intelligible) to reality. He is clearly aware of this, for he speaks of Absolute Spirit as coming to know itself, i.e., not yet there. Hegel is stuck with the peculiar problem of trying to explain everything without knowing everything.

Thus Hegel is traditional in saying that all things come to be according to providence. However, Hegel (following the modern rationalists) thinks that he knows what the being and activity of that first cause is. This idea is supported to some degree by Hegel's choosing to do history, for what has happened is fixed and has contributed to the present: thus the providential pattern by which reality has arrived at the present could, theoretically, be traced. This Hegel tries to do with more or less success. Theoretically, we can play God as regards the past, for we have some necessary knowledge of it. However, we cannot do this for the present or the future, particularly if the God we play is unfolding and therefore not complete. Thus Hegel's dialectic can claim some limited necessity in its analysis of the past (although clearly much—indeed most—of history is not included in Hegel's analysis), but it cannot, in principle, accurately project the future. This is true not only because we do not know the nature of God but also because, on Hegel's terms, that future is not even known by God himself. Efficient cause has priority over final cause: God's purposes are not fully known even to God. Hegel's dialectic can tell of the future only by extrapolation, by application of a method to reality. Since any method is a limitation of reality, such an extrapolation must be false, or at least incomplete.

Hegel (like Kant) seems to distinguish the various realms of reason that we claim ought to be distinguished: truth, goodness, and beauty. Hegel's logic (like Aristotle's) is applicable to various fields. One can have a dialectic of art or morality as well as of metaphysics or history. However, for Hegel these fields themselves are in dialectical order: the realm of beauty and art seems to be prior to and generative of the realm of ethics and religion, which in turn is prior to and generative of the realm of philosophy, by which Hegel means the pure dialectic of ideas.[46] Thus theoretical reason is more perfect than practical reason, which is more perfect than aesthetic reason. Hence it could be objected that Hegel does not keep the distinction between the areas of reason clear. Indeed, this is to be expected if everything is ultimately caught up in the dialectic of Spirit coming to the absolute unity of self-consciousness.

46. In *Reason in History*, Hegel says that art feeds the senses, religion the feelings, and philosophy the thinking spirit (ch. 4, sec. 3d, p. 63). The priority of this order is in time, in history, and in efficient causality. However, there is some notion of final cause in Hegel (though apparently not foundational as for Aristotle) in which philosophy would be prior as the more important end.

It is instructive to consider the relationships between the realms of the true, the good, and the beautiful developed by the great German philosophers, Kant, Schelling, and Hegel. Although they all discuss these realms in some depth, each thinker ends up emphasizing one realm over the other two—a different realm in each case.

As we have said, for Kant, the realm of the good takes priority, so much so that the primary instance of reason is practical reason. Theoretical reason gives us only an "as if" world, and aesthetics' function is ultimately to recognize and produce symbols of the good.

Friedrich Wilhelm Joseph von Schelling (1775–1854), who was a disciple of Kant and precursor of Hegel, holds that the realm of the beautiful takes precedence. Aesthetics is primary. Schelling's system of transcendental idealism has three stages: theoretical, practical, and aesthetic (ordered from lowest to highest stage).[47] All begins with intuition, and, in fact, all is intuition. By intuition we know that we exist and that there is an objective world outside ourselves; by intuition we know that we can act freely in that world; and by intuition we reach full objectivity in art. "The whole continuity of transcendental philosophy rests merely on a continuous potentiation of self-intuition, from the first, simplest stage in self-consciousness to the highest stage, the aesthetic."[48] Like Kant, Schelling's philosophy of art is strongly Romantic. Genius is the guiding principle in art, and hence in all philosophy. In fact, philosophy becomes objective—fully real—only in art. "The objective world is only the primitive, as yet unconscious, poetry of the spirit; the general organon of philosophy—and the keystone of the whole arch—is the *philosophy of art*."[49]

In Hegel, as we have noted, the dialectic of the three realms is the beautiful, the good, and the true. That is, the realm of the beautiful (aesthetics) is sublated by the realm of the good (ethics), which in turn is sublated by the realm of the true (philosophy). While for Kant reason is most itself in ethics, and for Schelling in art, the reality of Absolute Spirit transcends these two realms for Hegel. Self-consciousness of Absolute Spirit is attained, beyond the realms of the beautiful and the good, in the realm of the true. Thus Hegel considers the lower realms as symbolic of the realm of philosophy. "Although the endowment by art of sensuous shape is not in this respect accidental, yet on the other hand, it is not the highest mode of grasping the spiritually concrete. Thought is a higher

47. See sec. 3 of the introduction to Schelling, *System of Transcendental Idealism*, trans. Albert Hofstadter, in *Philosophies of Art and Beauty*, ed. Albert Hofstadter and Richard Kuhns (Chicago: University of Chicago Press, 1976), pp. 352–55.

48. Ibid., sec. 6, § 3, p. 375.

49. Ibid., introduction, § 3, p. 355.

mode of presentment than that of the sensuous concrete."[50] The idea
comes to self-consciousness in stages: the idea as fine art, the idea as
morality/religion, and the idea as philosophy. The lower stages are real,
but they are transcended. Thus the realms of the beautiful and the good
are not on the same level with the realm of the true. The idea reaches
its full reality when it knows itself, when the world is spirit. "Mind, and
mind alone, is pervious to truth, comprehending all in itself, so that all
which is beautiful can only be veritably beautiful as partaking in this
higher sphere and as begotten of the same."[51]

Let us consider in more detail Hegel's account of the three realms of
reason and how they are related. We shall follow Hegel's order, looking
first at Hegel's treatment of beauty, then morality (the good), and finally
truth.

As for the integrity and uniqueness of beauty, Hegel suggests, against
Kant, that beauty involves matter as well as form.[52] This is consistent
with Hegel's pantheism, with his holding that spirit needs matter to
perfect itself. However, beauty is a moment that is sublated by morality
and religion, and ultimately by the logical dialectic of theoretical reason.
Against Kant, Hegel says that the purpose of art is not moral. However,
neither is it its own end; rather, its purpose is ultimately to reveal the
truth by giving artistic sensuous shape to represent the idea.

> Inasmuch, however, as it is the function of art to represent the Idea to
> immediate vision in sensuous shape and not in the form of thought and
> pure spirituality . . . , the supreme level and excellence of art and the real-
> ity, which is truly consonant with its notion, will depend upon the degree
> of intimacy and union with which idea and confirmation appear together
> in elaborated fashion.[53]

Here, perhaps, is one of the origins of the typically modern notion that
art communicates ideas. If this is so, then beauty is a means to truth
and not its own unique end.

Consider next practical reason and the realm of morality (the good).
Ultimately, Hegel's ethics lacks genuine responsibility. In the first place,
moral action, according to Hegel, is driven more by passions than by
reason. As Hegel puts it, the dialectic of the idea and the passions of
human beings form the warp and woof of human history.[54] Second, Hegel

50. Hegel, *The Philosophy of Fine Art*, introduction, sec. 5, § 1, trans. F. P. B. Osmaston,
in Hofstadter and Kuhns, *Philosophies of Art and Beauty*, p. 427.

51. Ibid., introduction, sec. 1, p. 383.

52. Beauty is to be analyzed in art, not nature (ibid., introduction, sec. 1, pp. 383–84),
and art always involves the concrete (ibid., sec. 3, § 2, pp. 405–6).

53. Ibid., sec. 5, § 1, p. 427; see also p. 445.

54. *Reason in History*, ch. 3, sec. 2a, p. 29.

denies that there are any moral absolutes; all morality is conditioned by one's time.[55] Third, those great historical figures who are the means through which Absolute Spirit evolves to self-knowledge are not bound even by the morality of their time.[56] And finally, all history is the inevitable unfolding of consciousness, rather like the Neoplatonic notion of all reality coming forth necessarily from the One. Given these four points of Hegelian doctrine, there would appear to be no place in his thought for genuinely moral action, that is, action that is freely chosen and for which one is responsible. For if passions are what move us to act, then we are not free to choose how to act. If, in addition, we are determined by our own time, how can we be said to act freely or be responsible for our actions? If some individuals (perhaps oneself) transcend the morality of their time, why should others not also do the same? That is, why not embrace radically subjective moral relativism? And if we are all merely the means of Absolute Spirit coming to know itself in an inevitable process, then we are not in control of our own destinies—there is no meaningful freedom, nor therefore responsibility.

Given the apparent impossibility of freedom, it is curious that Hegel considers freedom to be both the end sought and the driving force behind the dialectic.[57] Perhaps he understands freedom in the way that Spinoza does—as belonging only to the one substance. The freedom of the individual must suffer under such a notion. Hegel, however, does not seem to be very concerned about the individual's freedom or fate. The nation states (which represent individuals in the dialectic of history) matter more than any number of individuals, and the Absolute Spirit matters more than any number of nation states. The inevitable clash between individuals and nations represents progress, and the progress of the emerging Absolute Spirit is the only good.

Thus what is is what ought to be: the worship of progress that we found in Bacon and Descartes and their successors is perfected by Hegel. The destruction of lives and nations along the way is justified by the new face of the Spirit that emerges from the destruction. As Hegel says, his philosophy is a kind of theodicy.[58] And like theodicies that try to justify all suffering and moral evil merely by reference to a future believed to be better, Hegel's is profoundly amoral.

---

55. "Whatever happens, every individual is a child of his own time; so philosophy too is its own time apprehended in thoughts." Hegel, *Philosophy of Right*, preface, trans. T. M. Knox, in *Hegel's Philosophy of Right* (Oxford: Clarendon, 1952), p. 11.

56. "The historical men, world-historical individuals, are those who grasp just such a higher universal, make it their own purpose, and realize this purpose in accordance with the higher law of the spirit" (*Reason in History*, ch. 3, sec. 2b, p. 39).

57. Ibid., ch. 3, sec. 1, pp. 22–25.

58. Ibid., ch. 2, sec. 2, p. 18.

After considering Hegel's aesthetic and moral thinking, it is time to consider the great theoretical sweep of Hegel's thought: his claim to understand the true course of history. He makes this claim explicitly: "It is not a presumption of study; it is a result which happens to be known to myself because I already know the whole."[59] The claim is, of course, rather close to claiming to know God's providence. This, in terms of Hegel's system, is only possible on the condition that the knower is God. And such, at times, seems to be Hegel's claim. Hegel clearly is in the Cartesian tradition of arguing from God to the world. Such an argument assumes that one knows what God is. Sounding very much like Spinoza, Hegel claims that all his philosophy comes out of the primary idea. "The whole course of philosophizing, being methodical, i.e., *necessary*, is nothing else but the mere *positing* of what is already contained in the concept."[60] All philosophical knowledge is analytical: there is no such thing as synthetic knowledge. The only difference between Spinoza and Hegel is one of method. Instead of geometrical deduction, Hegel uses dialectic, not only for the logical progress of ideas, but also for the march of history. Thus Hegel brings time into the definition of God. God is the perfect logical and historical process of self-realization. Every step in that progress, although not fully perfect, is the perfection of Absolute Spirit at that stage.

The only problem for Hegel is how to justify this notion of God. Where does Hegel get his idea of God as perfection? The obvious possible sources are Christian revelation, Neoplatonic philosophy, and the tradition of modern philosophy since Descartes (excluding Kant). Although the Christian notion of a perfect God may be an underlying source (as it is, perhaps, for Descartes), Hegel claims that the insight is fundamental to philosophy. For him, the notion seems to be a self-evident principle. He just accepts it and goes on from there. "That this *Idea* of *Reason* is the True, the Eternal, the Absolute Power and that it and nothing but it, its glory and majesty, manifests itself in the world—this, as we said before, has been proved in philosophy and is being presupposed here as proved."[61] Thus Hegel is drawing on philosophical sources in Neoplatonism and the modern movement. However, that one could come to any notion of perfection from mere unity is impossible, for the notion of unlimited perfection requires some kind of comparison among things of limited perfection. It is hard to see how this could issue from the purity of the logic of dialectic, beginning with the abstract notion of being, for undifferentiated being would not suggest its opposite, nonbeing (as a

59. Ibid., ch. 2, sec. 2, p. 12.
60. *The Encyclopaedia Logic*, sec. 88, p. 141.
61. *Reason in History*, ch. 2, sec. 2, p. 11.

quasi-being). Rather, it seems that one needs to begin with differences between beings in order to have a notion of nonbeing in terms of one thing not being identical to another. In other words, against Hegel's claim that all knowledge is analytical, it seems that there must be a synthetic moment to knowledge at its very inception.

This synthetic moment is the basis for traditional metaphysics that begins with experiencing and differentiating among things and concludes to the affirmation of God (the first cause of all things) and God's providence. For Aquinas, one can argue for the existence of God from the hierarchy of perfection in the world. For if things differ in terms of perfection, then one has two notions to explain: the reason for the difference (which is attributable to specific characteristics of the things) and the reason for perfection (existence, goodness, power) being distributed among things. This implies the existence of an ultimate source of all perfection, for what is unique (specific characteristics) does not explain what is common (perfection, existence, goodness, power). However, Aquinas nowhere claims to know what this ultimate perfection is. It is not that we know things as more or less perfect because we know what perfection is, as the moderns claim; rather, we begin with recognizing that some things are more perfect than others, and then understand that this implies that there must be some ultimate source of perfection transcending them all.

Aquinas argues that, since every activity depends on God, God is provident. But he does not claim to know what God's providence is. This would be impossible to know unless God tells us or unless we know the essence of God. The claim to know philosophically, as opposed to theologically, the total sweep of providence must be based on the latter claim. However, Aquinas claims repeatedly that we do not know *what* God is; we know only *that* God is, what God is not (not moved, not caused, not contingent, not limited in perfection, not ordered), and other things that are implied by such negations. Since God is the cause of all existence, God is not part of existence, for then God would be limited—a thing among other things. And if God were a thing among other things, then a further question would be raised as to the common context of the things—a question implying a further, more universal, cause.

Hegel's notion of Spirit needing matter to realize itself implies that Spirit is a part of a larger context. But if there are two elements (e.g., spirit and matter) in a common context, then we are back to the two questions requiring answers: what is the difference between spirit and matter, and how does one account for their common context (participation in existence)? The second question is answerable only by reference to a cause transcending spirit and matter. In other words, it seems that Hegel's dialectic requires a transcendent cause to explain how and why spirit and matter move toward unity. Hegel seems to imply that, since things are unfolding in such and such a way, they must be able to do so—thus locating the principle cause in potentiality.[62] But potentiality implies actuality. Only by knowing this actuality (this principle of perfection) could one predict the future course of history. Ultimately, for one to know God's providence, one must be God. Hegel, indeed, thinks he knows the mind of God and that he can explain everything in his dialectic.

To the challenge that this claim to know the sweep of history is just an unfounded assumption, such as Descartes' claim to know perfection, Hegel responds that there is empirical evidence for his claim that history is inexorably rational. After all, if the idea and the material world are necessary and complementary aspects of the coming to consciousness of Absolute Spirit, then it must be possible to prove the course of history either *a priori* or from the empirical evidence. Thus, as we have already noted, Hegel confidently explains: "It is not a presupposition of study; it is the result which happens to be known to myself because I already know the whole."[63] As powerful as Hegel's dialectic might be in interpreting history, this is a curious claim, for unless history comes to an end with Hegel, or unless Hegel is perfectly prophetic, his claim to know the whole of history empirically must fail to substantiate itself as soon as Hegel dies. There is, indeed, the inconvenience of history going on after Hegel in ways he did not envisage. All this is not to deny that there is some rational structure to the progress of history, only to warn against the claim to comprehensive knowledge of that structure: what that providence has been and—more troublesome—will be.

Let us take stock of Hegel's contribution. Hegel's claim that reality is intrinsically knowable seems right, since all attempts to limit its knowability according to some program of reason founder on the self-refuting idea that there are good reasons for regarding reason as untrustworthy. However, to say that reality is intrinsically intelligible is not the same as to say that we can give an exact account of its intelligibility. The latter project, which is Hegel's, founders on moral and theoretical absurdities. For one must abandon all essentially moral claims (including the good of explaining all reality) if one is willing to accept all manner of activity with equanimity, including loyalty and betrayal, honesty and deception, saving life and murder, simply in the name of historical progress, and Hegel's worship of the progress of history is just this. Similarly, one must abandon the serious claim to all real distinctions not only between aesthetic, moral, and theoretical insights and judgments but also between

62. Whitehead will follow Hegel on this point: see chapter 7.
63. *Reason in History*, ch. 2, p. 12.

the theoretical insights and judgments that make the dialectic intelligible; for if reason is identical with reality in some absolute unity, then all distinctions are ultimately illusory.

Extent of the Recovery

Kant and Hegel begin a recovery of reason from its reduction to the method of science by the moderns. Most obviously, both philosophers take seriously the three distinct areas of reason that we have said should be distinguished. They treat extensively the realms of truth, goodness, and beauty. In addition, each brings a special emphasis to the restoration of reason. Kant contributes the recovery of practical reasoning, insisting on the self-evidence of moral principles and their independence from the principles and method of the sciences. Hegel contributes the recovery of confidence in reason in general, arguing that there are no good reasons for the arbitrary restriction of reason to scientific method espoused by Bacon and Descartes and their disciples, or to the realm of possible experience in Kant.

Ironically, by doing this Hegel opens the way for the advancement of the sciences. Darwin's theory of evolution owes much to Hegel both in its understanding of an order occurring over time and in its claim that this ordering is not the result of a preconceived conscious plan. Darwin's evolutionary theory, in turn, proves to be very influential not just in biology but also in cosmology and physics. Contemporary science certainly owes more to Hegel's method than to the moderns' limitation of reason to empiricist or rationalist methods or to Kant's critical revolution with its *a priori* structure of knowledge.[64]

We turn, in the next chapter, to a consideration of two twentieth-century thinkers, Alfred North Whitehead and Bernard Lonergan, who were much influenced by the thought of Kant and Hegel. We shall present a more comprehensive evaluation of the contributions of Kant and Hegel at the end of that chapter, when we evaluate the contributions of all four thinkers to the recovery of reason.

---

64. Hegel's dialectic is influential in other areas as well, e.g., in political and social theory (Marx, Comte) and in theology (Kierkegaard's dialectic and process theologians).

7

Further Down the Road

Building on the work of Kant and Hegel, a number of philosophers in the twentieth century have furthered the recovery of reason. Here we shall concentrate on just two: Alfred North Whitehead and Bernard Lonergan, S.J. They not only are interested in incorporating science and modern philosophy in their work, but also are students of the history of philosophy, beginning with Plato and Aristotle and including the medievals and the moderns. Like Kant and Hegel, they are critical of the arbitrary restrictions of reason in the Renaissance and Enlightenment, but with their knowledge of and affection for the tradition of Plato and Aristotle (and in the case of Lonergan, Augustine and Aquinas), they go beyond Kant and Hegel in distinguishing the various dimensions of reason. However, even as Whitehead and Lonergan restore to reason much of what was lost in the Renaissance and Enlightenment, they still fall prey in some important respects to the temptation to restrict reason by method, which is the hallmark of the modern movement.

Whitehead

Among the philosophers of science who apply Hegelian principles to scientific theory, Alfred North Whitehead stands out. This is not only because of his metaphysical theory, which is consonant with much twentieth-century physics, but also because he is knowledgeable and

171

appreciative of the history of philosophy and wants to enrich the scope of reason beyond the mechanism of the materialists.

The first thing that should be said about Whitehead is that he is a realist: he thinks that there is something to be known and that we learn about it through experience. In this he is more like Hegel than like the tradition of idealism from Descartes to Kant. The centrality of process in Whitehead's thought also shows the clear influence of Hegel. However, unlike Hegel, Whitehead does not identify reality and thought. This is not to say that Whitehead has any doubts about the instrument of reason, as did Bacon, Descartes, Hume, or Kant; his confidence is as great as that of Aristotle or Hegel. However, while Hegel thinks that all philosophy is analytical (merely a matter of analyzing the dialectic of being), Whitehead holds a moderate empirical method rather like Locke's. Science progresses when reality forces us to change our hypotheses.

The second essential point about Whitehead is that he is deeply imbued with the history of philosophy and draws on Plato and Aristotle as well as the moderns (in particular, Bacon, Locke, and Leibniz) for his metaphysical position. Whitehead is famous for saying that the history of Western philosophy "consists of a series of footnotes to Plato."[1] He understands that something important was lost when science was made the sole way to truth. He recognizes a plurality of human interests: science, ethics, aesthetics, and religion. Here he is undoubtedly influenced by the pragmatic pluralism of William James as well as by his own wide knowledge of the history of philosophy.

Whitehead believes that, in the seventeenth and eighteenth centuries, science dominated in a way that was detrimental to the other areas of human interest.[2] The materialistic mechanism that informed this period is inadequate both to science as it has developed (life sciences, quantum mechanics, relativity theory) and to the other basic areas of human experience. According to Whitehead, the role of philosophy or metaphysics (as opposed to science) is to criticize the assumed cosmologies one inherits and formulate a more adequate one. This is his project especially in *Science and the Modern World*, but also in *Process and Reality*. "Speculative Philosophy is the endeavor to frame a coherent, logical, necessary system of general ideas in terms of which every element of our experience can be interpreted."[3]

1. Alfred North Whitehead, *Process and Reality* (New York: Free Press, 1978), p. 39.
2. See Alfred North Whitehead, *Science and the Modern World*, preface (New York: Free Press, 1967), p. vii.
3. *Process and Reality*, p. 3. "If science is not to degenerate into a medley of *ad hoc* hypotheses, it must become philosophical and must enter upon a thorough criticism of its own foundations" (*Science*, ch. 1, p. 17).

The proper philosophical cosmology must retain the strengths of those who have gone before and correct their weaknesses. Whitehead believes that the atomism of Bacon and his disciples is not completely wrong. The process introduced by Hegel and Darwin is also partially right, although it requires a reintroduction of mathematics to account for the new discoveries in physics. Thus Whitehead notes that the way is open for a new "doctrine of organism" that will involve mathematics, empirical analysis, and an attention to vitalism.[4] In some ways this could be viewed as the combination of Plato's mathematicism with Aristotle's biologism as much as the culmination of the thought of the seventeenth through nineteenth centuries. Like Hegel, Whitehead has a strong notion of progress, and he sees this progress in the development of the idea of science as each Age-Spirit reinterprets the past and adds its unique cosmological picture.[5]

Without tracing all the connections among the cosmologies that Whitehead discusses and all the hints that lead him to his theory, let us mention a few of the main ideas that he thinks are critical for understanding the historical background of his thought. First of all, Whitehead points to Bacon both for his theory of atomism and for his less well-known notion that all bodies have perception. Since this is such an important element in Whitehead's thought, let me quote part of the passage from Bacon that Whitehead cites: "It is certain that all bodies whatsoever, though they have no sense, yet they have perception; for when one body is applied to another, there is a kind of election to embrace that which is agreeable, and to exclude that which is ingrate; and whether the body be alterant or altered, evermore a perception precedeth operation; for else all bodies would be like one another."[6] Whitehead approves this theory of bodily activity over the materialistic mechanism of Descartes and Hobbes. This theory is also taken up by Locke in his moderate empiricism and by Leibniz in his theory of the monad. Whitehead calls these perceptions "feelings" in *Process and Reality*.[7]

This combination of atomic mechanism and universal vitalism is central to Whitehead's thought. Commenting on his project in *Science and the Modern World*, Whitehead writes, "I would term the doctrine of these lectures, organic mechanism. In this theory, the molecules may blindly run in accordance with the general laws, but the molecules differ in their intrinsic characters according to the general organic plans

4. *Science*, p. 36.
5. Ibid., p. 34.
6. Ibid., p. 41; Whitehead notes that the text is from the beginning of sec. 9 of Bacon's *Natural History*.
7. *Process and Reality*, pp. 40–42.

of the situations in which they find themselves."[8] Bacon speaks of the very general laws overarching the activities that occur without reference to formal structures or final purposes. Although we have noted a kind of inconsistency in holding a radical empiricism and affirming universal laws, this is the very combination of notions that Whitehead wants to establish, for it allows for exploration and explanation without enclosing reality in a deterministic system. It permits, at once, order and novelty.

Obviously influential in Whitehead's thought is the monadology of Leibniz. Here again we have an order (the universal harmony among the monads) and a lack of determinism (each monad is a microcosm of all other things, with infinite possibilities). What becomes primary is not substance, but relation. Every monad is in relation to every other monad, and these relations are intrinsic to each monad, which is a kind of microcosm. As Whitehead comments, "In a certain sense everything is everywhere at all times . . . every spatio-temporal standpoint mirrors the world."[9] For Leibniz, the things that we recognize as unities (trees, animals, human beings) are communities of monads dominated by a monad of a distinctive character. This is very like Whitehead's notion of "actual entities" as "procedures of organization."[10] Whitehead also points to the influence of the Romantic poets, in particular Wordsworth and Shelley (*Prometheus Unbound*) for the intuition of the whole inter-relatedness of nature.[11]

As to the explanation of the movement that brings these actual entities into being, the influences here are multiple. Whitehead's position is somewhat akin to Aristotle's idea of potentiality moving to actuality. However, unlike Aristotle, who holds that the final cause (the unmoved mover) is extrinsic, Whitehead's actual entities are more like Plato's self-moved movers. True, there is a notion of God as primordial act in Whitehead's thought, but this is closer to Leibniz's preestablished harmony or Hegel's unrealized idea than to Aristotle's unmoved mover.

Also influential is the vitalism of Bergson, with its roots in Darwin and Hegel. Each thing (not only the actual entities but every organic atom) has a life force by which it draws from its past relations its ever new actuality, which then becomes the potentiality from which future entities will draw their novelty, and so on. There is a kind of dialectic here, but without the destruction or determinism present in Hegel's theory. The past is preserved in the present entity through its inheritance from other

8. *Science*, p. 80.
9. Ibid., p. 91.
10. Ibid., p. 156. Whitehead also refers to these "actual entities" as "actual occasions" in *Process and Reality* (p. 18).
11. See *Science*, pp. 81–88.

entities in ways that are not predictable beforehand. Whitehead calls the process "concrescence."[12] There are no individual, isolated things, but "actuality is through and through togetherness."[13] Whitehead defines the organism as "the unit of emergent value, a real fusion of the characters of eternal objects; emerging for their own sake."[14]

Ultimately some first principle of concretion is required, and this is what Whitehead means by God. But this God, as the ground of all explanation and all rationality, is not itself rational. "God is ultimate limitation and His existence is the ultimate irrationality; . . . no reason can be given for the nature of God, because that nature is the ground of rationality."[15] Against Hegel and other idealists such as Descartes and Spinoza, Whitehead denies that we know God's nature, or that the nature of God is even knowable. Knowledge of God's essence must be drawn from experience. "The principle of empiricism depends on the principle of concretion which is not discoverable by abstract reasoning. What further can be known about God must rest on an empirical basis."[16] Empiricism requires an ultimate principle, but that principle is not open to rational analysis. In other words, Whitehead is saying (along with Aquinas) that one cannot deduce information about the world from one's knowledge of God. Hence, deductive metaphysics such as those of Descartes, Spinoza, or even Hegel must fail. In some ways this is a return to the doctrine of Aquinas, who holds that, although we know God to exist from our experience of the world, we do not (and indeed cannot) know the essence of God by natural reason. What Aquinas would not say, however, is that God is the ultimate irrationality, for although the principle of all reason cannot be proven by reason (since it is required for reason), this does not mean it is irrational. As the principle of all rationality, it could not be less than rational.

There is much to recommend Whitehead's thought. His cosmology is very subtle and handles the discoveries of modern science better than that of his ancient or modern predecessors. He is well versed in the history of philosophy and draws freely from all aspects of it, from the ancients as well as from the moderns. And he understands that there are areas of human interest besides science that can be harmed or destroyed by a faulty philosophy of science. However, there are some serious limitations

12. *Process and Reality*, p. 26. An instance of concrescence (also called an "actual occasion" or an "actual entity") is the most real entity. Such an instance is analyzed into its "prehensions," which indicate the actual entity's indefinite number of relations to an external world. See pp. 18–20.

13. *Science*, p. 174.

14. Ibid., p. 107.

15. Ibid., p. 178.

16. Ibid.

to his thought as a whole. These stem from his understanding of the role of metaphysics. Whitehead believes that the role of metaphysics (by which he means cosmology—a comprehensive and consistent theory of the way things are) is to make scientific knowledge more coherent and also to set the stage for the pursuit of other interests, such as aesthetics, ethics, or religion. On both scores, I believe he is in error.

Whitehead commends Aristotle's metaphysics in general but holds that it is ultimately defective because it is tied to a defective physics. Now there is no question that physics has made progress since the time of Aristotle and that experimentation has discovered things needing explanation that Aristotle did not know about—from the sunspots of Galileo to the molecular, atomic, and subatomic structures of matter and the four great forces of physics. However, Aristotle's metaphysics does not depend essentially on physics (at least not physics as a specialized science). Metaphysics is based on things, and the questions these things raise for us. Of course the status of "things" has been debated throughout the history of philosophy, from Plato to the present, and this word has been used in many ways. The "things" to which traditional metaphysics appeals are primarily the organic unities that we call trees and animals and human beings, with the human being as the paradigm thing.[17]

One of the great strengths of Whitehead's theory is that it recognizes these things, which he calls "actual entities" or "actual occasions" or "instances of concrescence,"[18] as real. He does not tend to mechanical reductionism in his explanations the way Hobbes does. And he is correct in holding that these creatures ("actual entities," "actual occasions," "instances of concrescence") are related in one way or another (gravity, at least) to all other things. However, these things are not just their relations to other things; there is something unique about them as living beings. Ironically, Whitehead ties metaphysics to science and thus limits metaphysics to a science of relations.

Aristotle would have said that the complex unity of an organic thing is more real than its constituent parts, or its quantitative and qualitative aspects, or its relational interdependence with other things. This notion of thing, which Aristotle called substance, is what has been constantly threatened throughout the history of philosophy. It is lost if one holds a material atomism, for then all that is real is the smallest constituent part, and it is lost if one holds an idealism, for then all that is real is the first principle: God. However, this world of things is reality as we experience it on the most obvious level.

17. Drops of water and rocks are also things, but as their individuality depends on the accident of quantity alone, they are less clearly things than living beings and so are less central to our immediate understanding of what things are.

18. *Process and Reality*, p. 211.

Although Whitehead voices concern about preserving the various levels of reality, by making the current state of physics primary in establishing his metaphysics, he runs the risk of losing this most fundamental and obvious understanding of the world.[19] For quantum mechanics and relativity theory dissolve the differences between things. Quantum mechanics and relativity theory should not be abandoned, but one should remember that they are theories *of* reality, not reality.[20] It should be granted that an understanding of things such as grounds Aristotle's metaphysics is also a theory. But as the first stage in our intellectual communion with reality before we analyze deeper levels and relations, it must be acknowledged as real, or we invite the return to skepticism born of the attempt to make things fit our theories. This is the essential problem with all attempts to dominate reality by method.

Based on this primary realistic level of meeting the world of things, distinctions appear and questions arise from these distinctions that, if pursued systematically, lead to truths about the world and ourselves that are lost when reality is seen as primarily relational. One becomes aware of the world's unity and integrity when the questions arising from our experience of things lead to the affirmation of the existence of a source of all things—what we call God.[21] As to human nature, one becomes aware of our unique place in the cosmos. In distinguishing between things and reflecting on that activity, one discovers the reality of knowledge—that knowledge is universal and timeless. What it is to be a rose and what it is to be a monkey are always and everywhere different. Actually, expressions such as "always" and "everywhere" are misleading in that they characterize knowledge as a universal presence in time and space, rather than something that transcends time and space.[22] This insight into the transcendent character of being a knower distinguishes us from the other things we experience, and in a way that cannot be attributed just to a different concretion of matter.

In addition, our participation in an existence that transcends the world of physics makes possible the attribution to ourselves of freedom in the sense required for authentic moral action. Although the freedom of actual entities to draw together relations in a novel way

19. See *Science*, p. 124.

20. Whitehead is well aware of the limitation of points of view. See his preface to *Science*.

21. Whitehead seems to arrive at the inevitability of affirming a first principle of reality (his first principle of concretion).

22. The Platonic conclusion that we are *not*, therefore, material beings would be mistaken since we are just as aware of ourselves as sensing beings, and since immateriality does not contradict materiality, there is no reason why a being may not be at once material and immaterial.

may be attributable to all things on all levels, this freedom is distinct from moral freedom. Moral freedom is a freedom *for* choice; the other is a freedom *from* determinism, a kind of uncertainty principle. To collapse the two distinct ideas into one is either to deny that human beings have moral responsibility or to attribute moral responsibility to roses and complex molecules. But the denial of human moral responsibility implies the meaninglessness of all intentional action, and the attribution of moral responsibility to roses and complex molecules is absurd. The changing face of physics does not change these insights, for they are due to our most basic encounter with the world of things, from which all realist knowledge (and hence science as Whitehead understands it) arises.

As it is not the job of metaphysics to justify a physics, neither is it the job of metaphysics to provide a foundation for understanding other areas of human interest such as ethics, aesthetics, and religion. A good metaphysics may indeed remove impediments to a proper understanding of other areas of human thought, just as a bad metaphysics may block access to these areas. For example, by revealing the existence of immaterial realities such as God and the rational soul, a good metaphysics allows one to develop a meaningful ethics or aesthetics (whose standards cannot be measured by scientific method since they are immaterial). As for a bad metaphysics, the commitment to mechanistic materialism implies the denial of freedom (and hence of a meaningful normative ethics) and even the denial of insight and judgment (and hence of a meaningful aesthetics). However, removing impediments is not the same as providing foundations. Even a good metaphysics cannot provide principles and methods for these other areas. Ethics and aesthetics require foundations other than those provided by any truth-oriented enterprise, whether it be mathematics, physics, metaphysics, or any other science.

If the principles of metaphysics are made the foundations for other disciplines, the distinctive objects and thus the essences of those disciplines are lost. Here Whitehead's thought is most seriously flawed. Although he recognizes that a cosmological explanation of the world is not the only human interest, in the end all other interests are explained by reference to this cosmological explanation. For example, when Whitehead speaks of the organism as the basic unit of "emergent value,"[23] he conflates the language of cosmology and ethics. This suggests either a metaphysical ethics (cf. Hegel) or an ethical metaphysics (cf. Kant). In either case something essential is lost, for moral obligation is not deducible from theoretical principles, however universal or true, nor is a moral concern the proper basis for establishing a cosmology.

23. *Science*, p. 107.

Let us consider how Whitehead's cosmology (metaphysics) affects his understanding of ethics, aesthetics, and religion. In ethics, Whitehead is basically a pragmatist. He admits with gratitude the influence of James and Dewey on his thought, and such influence is evident not only in the psychological basis for his cosmology (perceptions, feelings, etc.) but also in his understanding of ethics. For Whitehead, ethics does not have its own first principles as it does for Kant or Aquinas. Rather, ethics is explained in terms of human needs, the influence of one's society, and the consequences of one's particular moral actions for oneself and one's society.

The guiding principle is drawn from his metaphysical notions: since the purpose of all creation is novelty, ethical norms that constrict are bad, and those that open us to novelty and adventure are good. Like Hegel, Whitehead seems to commend novelty in ethics for its own sake. And like Hegel he has great faith in progress. Because the idea of moral absolutes does not fit this evolutionary model, Whitehead argues against what he calls the gospels of force and uniformity. Human beings have a need to wander; we need diversity as a spur to further progress (notice the psychological categories). He is less concerned with the actual outcome in terms of virtue and vice. "We must not expect, however, all the virtues. We should be satisfied if there is something odd enough to be interesting."[24] Here is a curious moral theory: the moral state of the world is acceptable if it provides some oddity of interest.

Since there is no place in Whitehead's metaphysics for constancy and stability, neither is there a place for constancy and stability in his ethics. Ultimately, Whitehead is not able to recommend a serious moral theory. Although one can piece together bits of what he would recommend (courage and tolerance, for example), he has no grounds on which to propose them as universal since he argues that there are no moral absolutes. Thus moral codes are always relative. "The moral code is the behavior-pattern which in the environment for which it is designed will promote the evolution of that environment towards its proper function."[25] Here it is clear that Whitehead's relational notion of reality influences his notions of morality, much to the detriment of the latter. For if all moral codes are relative to environment, then no moral code is certain and thus no choices or actions can be ruled out or meaningfully encouraged. "Thus the notion that there are certain regulative notions, sufficiently precise to prescribe details of conduct, for all reasonable beings on Earth, in every planet, and in every star-system, is at once to

24. Ibid., p. 207.
25. Alfred North Whitehead, *Adventures of Ideas* (New York: Free Press, 1967), p. 292.

be put aside. That is the notion of the one type of perfection at which the Universe aims. All realization of the Good is finite, and necessarily excludes certain other types."[26] The fallacy is obvious. Just because all realization of the good is particular (description), it does not follow that all obligation (prescription) is particular, especially when the prescriptions are negatives—e.g., do not kill, do not rape, do not lie.

As for Whitehead's aesthetics, the dominance of his cosmological model is again evident to the detriment of his philosophy of the beautiful. Although he does not wish to identify aesthetics with science, his model for judging what is beautiful follows his theory of the concrescence of prehensions. Just as novelty is the key characteristic of moral goodness, so it is the key characteristic of beauty. In fact, Whitehead is explicit in tracing some of the inspiration for his theory of prehensions to the Romantic poets, who themselves saw their work to be in the service of philosophy and science.[27] It is not that Wordsworth claimed to be doing science. On the contrary, he was reacting against the Enlightenment project by insisting on the need for aesthetic intuition in understanding nature. As Whitehead comments, "Both Shelley and Wordsworth emphatically bear witness that nature cannot be divorced from its aesthetic values."[28]

Hence Whitehead follows Kant here, holding that aesthetic judgment is a kind of intuition. And as the Romantics thought, the intuition of nature is more of a feeling than a rational judgment. "The habit of art is the habit of enjoying vivid values."[29] Thus Whitehead continues the Humean project of basing aesthetics on feelings. In fact, he follows Hume further in making feelings basic for all areas of thought. As Hume considers feeling and instinct to be foundational for all thought (even science), so Whitehead makes feelings fundamental for cosmology, ethics, and aesthetics.

It might even be argued that, for Whitehead, aesthetics dominates metaphysics since the idea of aesthetic appreciation is so central in his doctrine of prehension. However, in the Romantic spin given to aesthetics by Whitehead, creativity emerges as most basic, and thus

26. *Adventures*, p. 291.
27. Whitehead notes that Wordsworth, in the preface to *The Excursion*, describes the poem as a fragment of a longer projected work, "A philosophical poem containing views of Man, Nature, and Society" (*Science*, p. 81). Whitehead says that Shelley was in love with science and quotes the opening stanza of Shelley's "Mont Blanc," after which Whitehead affirms that Shelley "is here an emphatic witness to a prehensive unification as constituting the very being of nature" (*Science*, p. 86). We also noted in chapter 2 of this work the evidence for Shelley's love of science exemplified in *Prometheus Unbound*.
28. *Science*, p. 87.
29. Ibid., p. 200.

beauty's most salient feature is its novelty.[30] Progress, not intelligible beauty, takes precedence. This idea of beauty as novelty is much influenced by the work of Hegel, Darwin, and vitalism, and it is traceable to the Baconian ideal of progress. What is new is not only good in the sense of fulfilling a cosmological ideal and a technological advance, but also morally and aesthetically valuable.

In the area of technology, "new" has been nearly equivalent to "better," and it may have great explanatory power from a cosmological perspective; however, the identification of novelty with quality in the areas of ethics and aesthetics is rather dubious. The newness and freshness of a work of art, its particular success in achieving an aesthetic whole, is one of the chief features of its beauty and hence its success. However, if the work of art did not participate in intelligible qualities such as integrated order, proportion, and unity, it would not be beautiful, although it might be lively and stimulating. Novelty, whether intellectual or emotional, is not sufficient to make something beautiful.

Whitehead distinguishes religion from science by referring it to the realm of values. Science is concerned with physical phenomena while religion is "wholly wrapped up with moral and aesthetic values."[31] Basically, Whitehead's notion of religion is taken from James. Religion is the search for the vision of something beyond; it is a basic human need for adventure. As in his metaphysics, Whitehead holds that religion "persistently shows an upward trend."[32] The use of adjectives such as "higher" and "upward" are favored by Hegel, Nietzsche, and Whitehead when talking about values. Such adjectives avoid the moral commitment of such words as "better" and "right." Although higher and upward are suitable terms in a discussion of progress, they are no help in judging the value of the direction the "progress" is taking.

If one's theory is tied in with time so that temporal progress is by definition correct, then historical changes in ethics or aesthetics or religion are by definition commendable. However, although such a model of progress may fit the history of technology as introduced by Bacon and the history of biological evolution as introduced by Darwin, it is not at all clear that it fits the history of ethics or aesthetics or religion. These do not seem to be automatically improving. Only by ignoring what is essential to these areas of human experience (i.e., goodness, beauty, saving truth) can one make them fit this model. This, it seems to me, is what Whitehead is doing, and so he fails to honor the full range of

30. In some places Whitehead presents a rather traditional understanding of beauty as ordered unity. "The perfection of Beauty is defined as being the perfection of Harmony" (*Adventures*, p. 252).

31. *Science*, p. 185. Here is an example of conflation of these two areas.

32. Ibid., p. 192.

human interests that he mentions at the beginning of *Science and the Modern World*.

In the end, leaving room for adventure (novelty) is the driving theme in Whitehead's thought metaphysically, morally, and aesthetically. The new and unpredictable harmony of prehensions (beauty as novelty) is more fundamental than truth. "Truth matters because of Beauty."[33] And goodness also is ultimately a matter of beauty, again to be understood primarily as novelty. Whitehead expresses his conflation of the three distinct realms of the true, the good, and the beautiful with economy in this line: "The real world is good when it is beautiful."[34] Reality (the true) is a matter of emerging values, which are called good only insofar as they are beautiful. One could hardly ask for a neater expression of the identification of the three realms. And one could hardly think of a more confusing expression. The true is the good; the good is the beautiful; and the beautiful is the new. Bacon's ideal of progress is alive and well, as is the confusion it introduced into reason.

Lonergan

While Whitehead is certainly well versed in the history of philosophy, Father Bernard Lonergan, S.J., is even more directly imbued with the tradition I believe needs to be restored. He offers a philosophy on the scale of Kant, or Hegel, or Whitehead; that is, he proposes a philosophy that intends to deal with all aspects of reality.[35] Indeed, Lonergan is conscious of the works of these philosophers when he writes. However, Lonergan is most influenced by the thought of Augustine and Thomas Aquinas and their Greek predecessors Plato and Aristotle. Like the other philosophers we have discussed in this chapter, Lonergan has a particular method through which he brings all aspects of reality into focus. This method is arguably the most subtle and universally applicable of all those we have discussed.

Like the moderns in general, Lonergan begins with an analysis of knowing. However, when Lonergan analyzes knowing, he is not doing an epistemology but rather what he calls "intentionality analysis."[36] That

33. *Adventures*, p. 267.

34. Ibid., p. 268.

35. It should be noted that Fr. Lonergan is first and foremost a theologian, and so, like his models Augustine and Aquinas, is influenced by his faith. However, his transcendental method is grounded on the native dynamism of intelligence available to every human being.

36. Bernard Lonergan, *Method in Theology* (Toronto: University of Toronto Press, 1990), p. 340.

is, he is not trying to give a theoretical explanation of how knowledge is possible; rather, he is discussing what we do when we know. Thus, he is in the ancient/medieval tradition of beginning with act rather than with the question whether act (in this case knowing) is possible.

Like Whitehead, Lonergan is a realist: he holds that we do know some things and that it is natural for us to seek the truth. Like Aristotle, he recognizes a fundamental curiosity at the core of the human being. We have questions, and to have a question is to want to know an answer. This is fundamentally what Lonergan means when he speaks of intentionality analysis: we have a tendency, or an intention, toward knowing being. Whenever a question is answered, a new question arises because the human desire to know is insatiable, and therefore limitless. We want to know the truth. When we analyze this desire to know as it appears concretely in our knowing the world, we find that it has three levels: experience, questions for understanding, and questions for judgment.[37]

Let us examine these levels in turn and then consider how they are interrelated. Like Aristotle and the empiricists, Lonergan says that all knowledge begins in sense experience. Questions arise in us originally as we try to sort out different perceptions, to explain what we experience. Through our senses, external and internal, we are presented with data. Insights are our attempts, more or less successful, at using images and outlines to understand the data, to discover the pattern in our sense experience, to formulate the structures of things. Thus experience gives rise to questions for the understanding: What is it? Why? And how? Understanding, in turn, gives rise to questions for judgment: Is it really as we think it is? On the basis of a critical assessment of our understanding, we check whether the formulation of the understanding we have obtained is adequate to explain that aspect of the world with which we are faced.

Lonergan says that experiencing, understanding, and judging form a unity that is materially and formally dynamic.[38] He calls this unity materially dynamic because its components are not static structures but activities. Knowing is not reducible to one of these activities alone. Experience without understanding is not knowing; it is merely what animals do. However, without experience, there is nothing to understand. Understanding grasps patterns of intelligibility, but without judgment they are mere possibilities. Truth and falsity come only with the act of

37. For details of the structure of human knowing see "Cognitional Structure," *Continuum* 2 (1964): 530–42, reprinted in *Collection*, papers by Bernard Lonergan, ed. F. E. Crowe (London: Darton, Longman & Todd, and New York: Herder & Herder, 1967), pp. 221–39.
    38. "Cognitional Structure," *Collection*, pp. 222–23.

judgment. Thus, knowing is a unity of these three activities that discovers what is really so and what is not really so.

Lonergan says that knowing, beyond being materially dynamic, is also formally dynamic. By this Lonergan means that the levels of knowing are "self-assembling": experience stimulates inquiry, which leads to insights and concepts; concepts stimulate reflection when one asks whether what one thinks is true is really true; to settle the issue, one goes back to the data, either confirming one's insights or revising one's understanding and formulating new insights, which again need to be tested. Thus, knowing is an ongoing, self-correcting activity, a cumulative affair in which the dynamic parts feed off of and correct each other.

This is where Lonergan differs substantially from Kant and is rather like Whitehead. The components of experience and concept are there in Kant, but he thinks of understanding as subsuming particulars under universals rather than as grasping intelligibility in the singular and formulating concepts or definitions as possibly relevant. Because Kant does not handle the act of judgment sufficiently, Lonergan goes back to Aristotle and Aquinas. Judgment indeed has a place in Kant, but it does not refer back to the individual experience for confirmation or negation of its insight (not in metaphysics, nor in ethics, nor in aesthetics). For Kant, judgment concerns syntheses derived from the *a priori* activities of the mind; it is a pure analysis of what reason does within itself rather than an affirmation of reality based on a grasp of sufficient evidence. In the realist tradition,[39] judgment checks the formulated guesses or hypotheses (one's insights) by testing these against the data one has experienced, which gave rise to them. This gives that insight a kind of confirmed reality which is lacking in Kant, where the best one can do in terms of theoretical judgment is to judge that there must be a world of things-in-themselves, although we have no access to that world. Whitehead shares with Lonergan this implicit realism, this need to go back to the data to test one's ideas.

How does one know when one's knowing has reached the truth? What is the criterion for objectivity? Lonergan says that objectivity is the "virtually unconditioned,"[40] which is the reflective understanding's grasp that

39. Lonergan calls himself a "critical realist" as distinct from a "naive realist." He would classify Aristotle and Aquinas as critical realists, too. See Lonergan's excellent work on Aquinas's theory of knowledge, *Verbum: Word and Idea in Aquinas* (Notre Dame, IN: University of Notre Dame Press, 1967).

40. "Cognitional Structure," p. 230. This is the realm of metaphysics for Lonergan: it follows cognitional analysis. "First, in any Philosophy, it is possible to distinguish between its cognitional theory and, on the other hand, its pronouncements on metaphysical, ethical, and theological issues. Let us name the cognitional theory the basis, and the other pronouncements the expansion." Bernard Lonergan, *Insight* (New York: Philosophical Library, 1970), p. 387.

the conditions for truth formulated in the guess or hypothesis are fulfilled. Our knowing is conditioned by something other than ourselves. There is the data that need to be formulated; we are not possessed of substantive knowledge of the world prior to experience. The data raise questions for intelligence. These are answered provisionally by insights and the concepts that express them. But when absorbed and reflected upon, these insights raise new questions, questions about whether the insights accurately and sufficiently explain the way things are. In short, we test our hypotheses: we criticize our insights through reflection in order to find out whether or not they are objectively true. The conditions for objectivity (the truth) are specified by the questions raised. This is because, on the level of reflective understanding, questions intend being—what *is*. If these conditions have been met (i.e., when we are sure we have asked all the relevant questions, that the hypothesis or guess "covers" the data, so that we have no further relevant questions), then we have reached what Lonergan calls the virtually unconditioned. Once the content of knowledge is verified, we can subject the known object or reality to a metaphysical analysis.

Lonergan, following Thomas Aquinas, thinks that we never have exhaustive knowledge about the world. However, this does not mean that we do not know some things about the world with certainty. Having gathered the data, and formulated and reformulated our understanding of the data under the testing eye of reflection, we arrive at the virtually unconditioned knowledge that, as a matter of fact, a poppy is not a porpoise and that it is farther from New York to Hawaii than from Boston to Manchester, New Hampshire.

Thus Lonergan's approach is threefold: (1) to ask what we do when we know (cognitional theory); (2) to ask why the structure of knowing verified in answer to the first question is really knowing (epistemology); and (3) to unfold the fundamental structure of all that can be and is known in this fashion (metaphysics). In order to answer the first and second questions, the empirical method espoused by both Aristotle and modern science must be enlarged to include not only the data of the senses but also the data of consciousness, that is, the acts of inquiring, insight, and judgment. Lonergan calls this enlargement of experience to include consciousness "generalized empirical method."[41] The task of experiencing, understanding, and judging the structure of one's own conscious intentionality by using this method he calls "self-appropriation."[42]

One might ask how we can be sure that there are no more questions. How do we know when we have followed the method properly, that our attending to experience, our understanding of that experience, and our

41. Lonergan, *Insight*, p. 72.
42. Ibid., p. 731.

judgment of that understanding have all been up to snuff? As Lonergan was fond of saying, "insights are a dime a dozen." The patient dedication required to distinguish truth from falsity, fact from fiction, reality from myth, is not itself found in the three stages of knowing. When we come to make our judgment about whether what we understand to be the case really is the case, we are presented with two fundamental options. We could wish or hope that our insight is correct and so insist that it is, or we could patiently go back to the data, searching for evidence that would either verify or disprove our theory. The latter way is the way of a disinterested desire for knowledge. If we take it, and do so consistently, it is because we recognize that knowledge or truth is good, that it is worthwhile to take the time to get things right. We have entered the realm of moral value. Our consciousness shifts onto this level when we ask: Will I do it? The judgment to do something that ought to be done is a judgment of value. We become aware of the requirement that our deciding and doing should be consistent with our knowing. Once we know that we ought to do something, we still have to decide freely to do it.

In other words, according to Lonergan, for our conscious intentionality to unfold as it should, we must refuse to be sidetracked by disordered desire or fear or bias of any kind.[43] We must value truth. "Be attentive; be intelligent; be reasonable; be responsible." These four precepts, Lonergan says, are the core of transcendental method,[44] which makes explicit the natural spontaneities of any human consciousness that generalized empirical method discovers in the data of consciousness. Thus the questions for experience, intelligence, and judgment raise issues of moral obligation and values. There is a kind of organic movement in Lonergan's thought to the level of ethics which is missing in Whitehead.

Obeying these precepts requires one to transcend one's individual biases (one's selfishness), one's group's biases (as in classism, racism, etc.), and the general bias of one's culture, which generates the blind spots of one's education and political order. Bias causes a closure of our experiencing, understanding, and judging about the true and the real; ultimately, fighting these biases is a matter of our responsibility, our moral obligation to pursue what is good. Thus, Lonergan holds that the first three levels of transcendental method as discussed in *Insight* lead naturally to the discovery of a fourth level, the level of responsibility and choice, which is more adequately formulated in his later writings, especially *Method in Theology*. As he puts it: "In *Insight* the good was the intelligent and the reasonable. In *Method* the good is a distinct notion. It

43. Lonergan discusses the various kinds of bias that afflict human beings in *Insight*, pp. 218–32.
44. *Method*, p. 20.

is intended in questions for deliberation: Is this worthwhile? Is it truly or only apparently good? It is aspired to in the intentional response of feeling to values. It is known in judgments of value made by a virtuous or authentic person with a good conscience. It is brought about by deciding and living up to one's decisions."[45]

In his distinction of this fourth level, Lonergan shows an adequacy for dealing with the good that is lacking in Whitehead. While Whitehead conflates value and cosmology, Lonergan is careful to note the difference between the patterns we do, in fact, understand and judge in the data and our obligation to be sure that those patterns really do measure up to the way things are. In short, we must care about finding the truth. This obligation itself is not simply another concrescence.

Lonergan claims, as we mentioned above, that objectivity is achieved when the virtually unconditioned has been reached, that is, when there are no further relevant questions. But it is clear that we can and often do stifle questions, perhaps out of a desire to have our insights be true (maybe a noble enough desire in itself), perhaps out of a competitive desire to know more than others, or perhaps out of an unwillingness to make the effort we know is required to discover the truth. Cognitive self-transcendence builds on moral self-transcendence. Objectivity requires a moral dedication to the truth because objectivity is authentic subjectivity.[46] "One knows objectively just in so far as one is neither unperceptive, nor stupid, nor silly; and one does not live authentically inasmuch as one is either unperceptive or stupid or silly."[47] Self-knowledge in the sense of knowing the operations of one's knowing and what is required for these operations to achieve their end (the true and the real), is essential to achieving any knowledge of our world, whether that knowledge be in physics or mathematics or psychology or even common sense.

Lonergan calls this proper or natural unfolding of one's conscious intentionality transcendental method.[48] By "method" he means "a normative pattern of recurrent and related operations yielding cumulative and progressive results."[49] We now can see that he does not have in mind the Kantian notion of finding the grounds for rationality or moral choice; at least this is not his fundamental meaning. What he means is something rather more direct and simple. In order for us to know, we must transcend ourselves in the sense of reaching beyond our current state of ignorance; more radically, we must transcend our moral disabilities,

45. Bernard Lonergan, "Insight Revisited," in *A Second Collection*, ed. William F. J. Ryan and Bernard J. Tyrrell (London: Darton, Longman & Todd, 1974), p. 277.

46. "Cognitional Structure," *Collection*, pp. 236–38.

47. Ibid., p. 238.

48. *Method*, p. 13.

49. Ibid., pp. 13–14.

the dramatic, individual, group, and general biases we hold. The word Lonergan often uses to describe this virtuous state is "authentic." To be authentic is to be habitually attentive, intelligent, reasonable, and (with this fourth level) responsible.

Transcending of self occurs on all four levels we have discussed—attentiveness, intelligence, reasonableness, and responsibility. Lonergan says that these activities are transcendent in three different ways. First of all, they are "comprehensive in connotation."[50] Since they have their home in questions and questions can be about anything and everything, they are applicable to every field of inquiry. Second, they are "unrestricted in denotation."[51] Since our understanding of our world is never complete, there are always further formulations to be made; imperfect understanding gives rise to further questions which require more perfect answers. In the third place, they are transcendent in the sense that they are "invariant over cultural change."[52] They apply to all people, everywhere, at all times.

What Lonergan means by this last statement is that the elements of transcendental method are not subject to revision. Although insights and judgments and choices may vary depending on the situation and the data available, the pattern of coming to know and choosing is invariant.[53] Any attempt to redo the method, to improve it, must use it. If it needs to be redone, then the judgment has been made that there is this need. Why was this judged to be so? Perhaps the original insight or concept was falsely drawn from the data, or other data have been uncovered that require a new formulation, or (always a problem) perhaps there has not been sufficient care taken to attend to the data, to be intelligent, to be reasonable, to be responsible. No one at any time or place wants to be a "nonresponsible, nonreasonable, nonintelligent somnambulist."[54]

Even as these levels in the intentionality of the human spirit can be distinguished, it should not be forgotten that they are parts of a dynamic unity. As Lonergan says, "the many levels of consciousness are just successive stages in the unfolding of a single thrust, the eros of the human spirit. To know the good, it must know the real (virtually unconditioned); to know the real, it must know the true; to know the true, it must know

50. Ibid., p. 11.
51. Ibid.
52. Ibid. Here Lonergan shows how he differs from Hegel and Whitehead and how he is similar to Kant. According to Lonergan, there is something objective and universal about ethics: they are not simply a product of one's culture or era, nor are they evolving with the progress through time.
53. Lonergan, "Insight Revisited," p. 273.
54. Ibid.

the intelligible; to know the intelligible, it must attend to the data."[55] Although his choice of terms in calling the intending of the human spirit a "thrust" may lead one to think that this is an automatic, unconscious activity in its root, this is not what Lonergan means. "It is a conscious intending, ever going beyond what happens to be given or known, ever striving for a fuller and richer apprehension of the yet unknown or incompletely known totality, whole, universe."[56]

Having indicated the need for a moral component in all knowing, Lonergan points out that we would be dishonest if we did not make the obvious observation that, although we may know what we ought to do (be attentive, intelligent, reasonable, responsible), we all too often do not do it.[57] This would seem to be a rather large problem, for we have seen how knowing is a dynamic activity which requires the continued honoring of the value of truth if it is to succeed. If, in fact, we are not very reliable in our moral attentiveness (which I am afraid is the case), how is it that we can be successful in following the method and grasping the true and the good? This leads us to the last level of consciousness uncovered by Lonergan's cognitional analysis.

We may know that we *ought* to be disinterested in our pursuit of the truth; to actually *be* disinterested is quite another story. What with passions, laziness, pride, and individual and cultural biases, there are plenty of factors to divert us from following what we may know to be the correct plan of action. To be successful in carrying out our projects, we need help. We need to be in love. At this point in Lonergan's thought, we leave the realm not only of being proportionate to human knowing but even of the transcendent being unconditioned by space and time that is in principle accessible to natural human knowledge. The love required for sustained authenticity that can help us transcend our selfishness and pride is a gift from God, and it pertains to the realm of special transcendence or the supernatural.[58]

Just as transcendental method (working properly) is an ongoing, cumulative affair, ever producing new insights, improved formulations, and correct judgments about the way the world is and about the

55. *Method*, p. 13. Again, this notion concerns our conceptual grasp of the object; it is not necessary to reach the virtually unconditioned to know that there is objective reality to be known. This reality breaks in upon us, raising questions whose pursuit is the ongoing life of science and ethics insofar as prudence is concerned (that is, the application of first principles to particular situations where success requires experience).

56. Ibid.

57. Although we cannot be absolutely sure about the motivations of others, we have direct insight into our own, where we find this tendency to do what we know we ought not to do, or not to do what we know we ought to do.

58. This does not mean that the love is unnatural, for it is clear that it is natural (even if somewhat rare) for people to love the truth and each other.

ways we should act in it, biases can snowball in the other direction. This "cumulative decline" can happen on the individual, group, or cultural level.[59] When inattentiveness, oversight, unreasonableness, and irresponsibility are allowed to lead the way, individuals and societies build up a momentum of bias. And when this happens, it becomes very difficult to change the direction of decline by rational argument, or by merely human willpower. The less we pay attention to data, to making intelligent formulations of meaning, to judging by the evidence, and to deciding and acting in accordance with reason, the less power reason and will have to turn us from our ways.[60] As Lonergan says, such an individual or civilization in decline "cannot be argued out of its self-destructive ways, for argument has a theoretical major premise, theoretical premises are asked to conform to matters of fact, and the facts of the situation produced by decline more and more are the absurdities that proceed from inattention, oversight, unreasonableness and irresponsibility."[61] When a situation Lonergan calls "moral impotence"[62] obtains, the answer is not more reasons (although the reasons may be sound) or more human willing, but love. The grace of God, both as immediately present to the individual and as mediated by the beliefs of religious communities, makes possible the overcoming of moral impotence and the turning from bias to the open pursuit of the true and the good.

As for the role of religious beliefs, any religion that promotes selfless dedication to the truth and to concern for others can help reverse the tendency in the human condition to selfishness and the blindness and injustice such selfishness brings. On this score, Lonergan says Christianity can be particularly effective. "We may note that a religion that promotes self-transcendence to the point, not merely of justice, but of self-sacrificing love, will have a redemptive role in human society inasmuch as such love can undo the mischief and restore the cumulative process of progress."[63]

Within the even more universal realm of religious experience, the possibility for healing through love is open to all. Although not all believe in the Christian God, all are (as Christians believe) offered grace from such a God. Lonergan says that to be in love with God is to be in love in an unrestricted way. If there is an unrestricted desire to know in the human spirit, then this desire is fulfilled by being in God's love. "Just

59. *Method*, p. 55.
60. This is very like Aristotle's theory of the virtues, where he says that our actions create a second nature in us (character) which is difficult to change. See *NE* 3.7.1114a12–22.
61. *Method*, p. 55.
62. *Insight*, pp. 627–30.
63. *Method*, p. 55.

as unrestricted questioning is our capacity for self-transcendence, so being in love in an unrestricted fashion is the proper fulfillment of that capacity."[64] Lonergan is not saying that we know God in the sense of knowing God's essence: in this life, that is impossible. However, we may experience God's love for us. When we are conscious of being loved by God, yet not of knowing what God is, we are in the presence of a mystery. We are conscious, Lonergan, says, of "having undergone a conversion."[65] This conversion to the mystery of love enables the moral attentiveness and dedication necessary for authentic knowing to take place. Being-in-love is the foundation for living in accordance with the requirements of morality. "So the gift of God's Love occupies the ground and root of the fourth and highest level of man's intentional consciousness."[66] And as the fourth level is the ground and root of the other three levels, love is the foundation for the moral and intellectual life of the human being.

Lonergan's thought provides two very important contributions. The first he makes explicit; the second is implied quite obviously by what he says. As to the first, wherever the intellectual activities of knowing and choosing occur, the levels of self-transcendence made explicit in Lonergan's transcendental method are enacted. Whatever one's field of endeavor, one must be attentive, intelligent, reasonable, responsible, and (on the deepest level) in love if one would succeed. The mind always operates through the activities of attending to data, making insights, and judging whether those insights are correct; for the mind to perform these duties well, one must value truth, and to be confirmed and constant in our respect for the value of truth, we must be in love with the truth. Thus, Lonergan would say that where truth sets the direction of one's living, there is love; that is, the grace of God is also at work. Although each discipline has its own special methods, all disciplines share this common structure of knowing. "However true it is to say that one attends, understands, judges, decides differently in the natural sciences, in the human sciences, and in theology, still these differences in no way imply or suggest a transition from attention to inattention, from intelligence to stupidity, from reasonableness to silliness, from responsibility to irresponsibility."[67]

As to the second important contribution, not only do the requirements of transcendental method promote success in any intellectual field, but

64. Ibid., p. 106. Notice the Aristotelian potency/act formulation, and also note that Aristotle refers to God as love: "it [the final cause] causes motion as something which is loved, and that which is moved moves the others" (*Metaphysics* 13.7.1072b4, trans. Hippocrates G. Apostle [Grinnell, IA: Peripatetic Press, 1979], p. 205).

65. *Method*, p. 106.

66. Ibid.

67. Ibid., p. 23.

also the commitment to true value on the fourth level and the response to grace of the fifth level (call it love or faith) reveal the search for truth as an activity that rejoices in growth and cooperation. If truth is good, then it is good wherever it is found and should be respected and welcomed for its own sake. Thus there is no good reason why, for example, a theologian should denigrate the scientist's knowledge, or the scientist the theologian's. As valuers of truth, experts in the various disciplines share a common ground beyond their specialties. If they were to become aware of this ground through the self-knowledge gained by attending to, understanding, and judging what it is to be a knower, they would welcome each other's insights. And of course, if one's awareness is freed in some measure from pride, fear, and biases, one is able to pursue the truth in pureness of purpose; that is, the awareness of being in love supports the pure, unrestricted, and disinterested desire to know. One is able to be thankful both for what one has been allowed to accomplish and for what others have brought to light. Thus the close relationship between knowledge, value, and God's gift of grace in faith and love, which Lonergan clarifies in his cognitional analysis, grounds a cooperative venture into discovering the many-sided fullness of what it is to be human. This ideal of cooperation and collaboration is at odds with the modern ideal of individualism, of discovering a method by which one can single-handedly solve all the problems of mankind.

Since the primary thesis of this book is to recover this many-sided fullness of being human, I am in full agreement with the intention of Lonergan's project. His work is indeed impressive in its comprehensiveness and intelligence. However, I am not sure that Lonergan's project always fulfills the promise of his thought, in particular with regard to his handling of the realms of the good and the beautiful. With Whitehead, his method is able to deal with questions arising from contemporary physics in ways that the methods of Kant and Hegel (and certainly of the early modern thinkers) could not. And Lonergan's method is far less committed to supporting a physics than is Whitehead's. However, the method's primary focus remains theoretical: it explains what we do when we experience, know, judge, and choose. Any philosophy, of course, would be deficient if it did not attempt to offer a theoretical explanation of everything, including moral obligation and aesthetic appreciation. However, the theoretical enterprise of uncovering the psychological structure of our knowing does not get to the heart of what is most distinctive about moral obligation and aesthetic appreciation.

Lonergan certainly makes clear his intention to distinguish systematically the three naturally human realms of intelligibility—truth, goodness, and beauty. In the first chapter of *Method in Theology*, he lays out this intention explicitly, emphasizing the unity of transcendental method but also our ability to distinguish specialized intelligent activities.

> Indeed, so intimate is the relation between the successive transcendental notions, that it is only by a specialized differentiation of consciousness that we withdraw from more ordinary ways of living to devote ourselves to a moral pursuit of goodness, a philosophical pursuit of truth, a scientific pursuit of understanding, an artistic pursuit of beauty.[68]

The distinctions here are very much those I wish to make. However, I believe that essential distinctions between these realms are sometimes missed in Lonergan's account. This may be due to his insistence on the single thrust of the human spirit. "The many levels of consciousness are just successive stages in the unfolding of a single thrust, the eros of the human spirit."[69] Clearly, this is correct in that one does not have many intellects, and one is a unity. On this unification, he writes:

> Finally, this doubly dynamic pattern . . . is a conscious intending, ever going beyond what happens to be given or known, ever striving for a fuller and richer apprehension of the yet unknown or incompletely known totality, whole, universe.[70]

This passage admirably summarizes the search for truth, whether philosophic or scientific. However, it is limited to being a theoretical explanation, which is but one aspect of our intelligence, not the whole of it. After all, although it may be true that we have this thrust of spirit, we do not always follow it. As Lonergan often notes, it is not automatic for us to pursue the truth in such a disinterested fashion. More often than not, we let various biases deflect us. Thus the thirst for the truth is something that we *ought* to follow. But why should we? The answer to this question is not found in any psychological analysis of what we, in fact, do.[71] The realm of the moral good (that which ought to be pursued and not violated), with the freedom and responsibility it brings, is a distinct dimension of reason. So, too, the appreciation of beauty and the creation of art are not reducible to, nor merely in the service of, either theoretical or moral intelligence.[72]

68. Ibid., p. 13.
69. Ibid.
70. Ibid.
71. As David Hume so ably pointed out, from propositions of fact, no propositions of value can validly be deduced.
72. Lonergan would seem to agree with this position in general. After all, he distinguishes the level of decision from the first three levels. And when he discusses art, he gives it a place on the level of experience, distinct from theoretical knowing and judging, and from moral decision-making.

One way of distinguishing my position from Lonergan's may be to revisit his explanation of what he is doing in his method. He wants to get away from the faculty psychology of the scholastics (particularly the textbook approach in which explanations are organized in a deductive order). This is well and good, and I agree that the closed essentialist explanation of human nature as a universal substance with distinct faculties from which can be deduced physical, moral, and aesthetic conclusions is a dead end. For this reason, Lonergan emphasizes an analysis of the activities in which we engage when we know. This is very much in the spirit of Aquinas. As Aquinas says, we know the faculty only by knowing the habits, and we know the habits only by knowing the activities. But Aquinas goes on to say that the activities are specified by objects.[73] Thus before we know that we have a single thrust of the spirit (i.e., a single power or faculty of intellect) we are engaged in activities characterized by distinct objects. My concern is that we not lose the distinctiveness of these objects (and thus their activities) in our assertion of the truth that there is a single thrust of the spirit toward transcendence.

Let us consider the moral realm first. In *Insight*, Lonergan proposes a parallel between metaphysics and ethics. "Just as the dynamic structure of our knowing grounds a metaphysics, so the prolongation of that structure into human doing grounds an ethics."[74] He claims his transcendental method works equally well for ethics as it does for metaphysics. "Essentially the same method is available for ethics. . . . For the root of ethics, as the root of metaphysics, lies neither in sentences nor in propositions nor in judgments but in the dynamic structure of rational self-consciousness."[75] As his metaphysics develops out of the dynamism of progressive patterns of consciousness, so too does his ethics. Lonergan speaks of ethics, like metaphysics, as "a system on the move."[76] When speaking of natural right, Lonergan does not think that it is to be grounded in self-evident propositions.

> It [natural right] may be placed in universal propositions, self-evident truths, naturally known certitudes. On the other hand, it may be placed in nature itself, in nature not as abstractly conceived, but as concretely operating. It is, I believe, the second alternative that has to be envisaged if we are to determine norms in historicity.[77]

73. *ST* 1.77.3.
74. *Insight*, p. 602.
75. Ibid, p. 604.
76. "Theories of Inquiry," in *Second Collection*, p. 40.
77. "Natural Right and Historical Mindedness," *A Third Collection*, ed. Frederick E. Crowe (New York/London: Paulist Press/Geoffrey Chapman, 1985), p. 172. "It is quite true . . . that I do not base a code of conclusions upon a code of verbal propositions named first principles" ("Theories of Inquiry," *Second Collection*, p. 39).

Lonergan wants to avoid legalism and bring his theory into line with the progress of modern thought,[78] and he thinks that his transcendental method avoids both legalism and relativism.[79] There are good reasons to avoid legalism, for morality exists in the world not in written words but in human persons. And the idea of "ethics on the move" as indicating process and progress in the moral life makes good sense, for we do not stay the same: if we are not growing in virtue and grace, then we are falling away. However, an ethics "on the move" in *all* ways makes no sense. As Chesterton often remarked, there can be no progress if there is no end (or ends) toward which we are progressing.

Lonergan wants to avoid the objectivity which holds that reality and morality are somehow "out there."[80] But the objectivity of moral absolutes does not require that they be "out there." At issue is not the origin of the self-evident principles (whether from outside or from within) but the fact of their self-evidence. Of course, not all of ethics is self-evident, and so we cannot have a purely deductive system of moral decision-making. But neither does it make sense to say that moral obligation can operate apart from the presence of self-evident principles in the mind of every mature rational being. It makes no sense to hold people responsible for their actions unless they could know better, and the only way that all could know better is if all have direct access to moral principles. If morality is wholly a matter of upbringing, culture, or common agreement at some historical moment, then those who lack the appropriate upbringing or culture, or who have not caught on to the moral consensus of the time, are not to blame for their evil actions. But except for very unusual circumstances (e.g., extreme youth, brainwashing, insanity), we do hold people responsible for their actions.

Thus the content of Lonergan's ethical theory is somewhat slim on moral precepts. Lonergan says that, because the human being is in process,[81] it is difficult to make universal judgments about behavior. Just as intending the truth does not presuppose that one already knows what is true, so intending the good does not presuppose that one knows what one should do. "When I ask whether this or that project or undertaking really is worthwhile, I intend the good, but as yet I do not know what

78. "Transition from a Classicist World-view," *Second Collection*, pp. 6–7.

79. "The stock objections that historical-mindedness involves one in relativism and situation ethics are to be met by adverting to the distinction just drawn. One cannot ground a concrete historical apprehension of man on abstract foundations: but this does not establish the inadequacy of the quite different foundations provided by a transcendental method" ("Transition from a Classicist World-view," p. 6).

80. "Theories of Inquiry," p. 39.

81. "The concrete being of man, then, is being in process" (*Insight*, p. 625).

would be good and in that sense worthwhile."[82] If Lonergan means by
this that one does not know the precise value of this particular project, or
that one does not know the complete and final good, then he is certainly
correct. But if he means that one knows nothing certain about what is
good, then he is mistaken. As Aquinas says, there are some goods that
we immediately see are good in themselves, such as life, knowledge,
and friendship.[83] We know that pursuing them is worthwhile and that
violating them is wrong. It is true that there is no absolute rule about
pursuing these goods. This is because there are many different ways to
fulfill them and, since each is self-evidently good, no one of them is better
in all respects than the others. So it is true that there is no single good
project that we must pursue. However, we do know that some intentional
actions are always and everywhere wrong—like intending to violate the
goods of life, knowledge, and friendship. It is the negative norms that
are universal and absolute, not the affirmative ones.

Lonergan's method does do quite well in explaining how virtues and
vices arise, that is, how our ability to honor what is good is developed
or hindered. In the Aristotelian tradition, Lonergan is committed to the
experiential origin of ethics. As to the matter which gives rise to moral
insight, he suggests feelings.[84] "Intermediate between judgments of fact
and judgments of value lie apprehensions of value. Such apprehensions
are given in feelings."[85] "Feelings reveal values to us."[86] It is true that
reason takes feelings as data and orders them according to appropriate
patterns; this is the traditional doctrine of the moral virtues. Thus there
is this level of empirical data.

However, the obligation to be virtuous is not itself derived from feelings. Lonergan clearly thinks that there are absolute obligations in his
transcendental commands—be attentive, be intelligent, be reasonable,
be responsible, and be in love. It is difficult to see how these commands
could be drawn out of experiential data. Certainly, it is on the occasion
of interactions with others that we become aware of our obligations
to them, and certainly in judging a particular moral action, we must
attend to the situation, which for us (as embodied) will always involve
an experiential dimension. But these matters do not reach the essence
of moral obligation. There seems to be no essential causal connection
between feelings and obligation, such that feelings can always be counted
on to direct our choices in a morally good way. In the virtuous person,

82. "Natural Right and Historical Mindedness," *Third Collection*, p. 174.
83. See Aquinas, *ST* 1–2.94.2.
84. *Method*, pp. 30–34.
85. Ibid., p. 37. According to Lonergan, feelings are the experiential stage of cognitional
structure that leads to judgments about the good.
86. "Natural Right and Historical Mindedness," *Third Collection*, p. 173.

feelings run in accord with obligation and hence are reliable moral guides. However, this is not so in the vicious individual, who may not feel any regret in wrongdoing, and may even delight in it. In fact, being good seems to mean not letting feelings or passion deflect us from what reason tells us we should or should not do. Lonergan himself makes this point in *Insight*. "Accordingly, it will not be amiss to assert emphatically that the identification of being and the good by-passes human feelings and sentiments to take its stand exclusively upon intelligible order and rational value."[87]

Virtue ethics and prescriptive natural-law ethics are not incompatible. In fact, they ought to be together.[88] But the "ought" is not implied in any empirical foundation, whether external or internal. Nor is it deduced from theoretical premises. The virtues grow in us only through the direction of practical reason guided by these self-evident principles. Aristotle, directly after discussing what might be called an "ethics on the move" (the moral virtues, which depend on a mean determined by reason, taking into account all the details of the circumstances—doing the right thing at the right time, to the right extent, to the right person, with the right instrument, etc.) declares that there are some actions that are always and everywhere wrong.

> Not every action nor every feeling, however, admits of the mean, for some of them have names which directly include badness, e.g., such feelings as malicious gladness, shamelessness, and envy, and, in the case of actions, adultery, theft, and murder; for all of these and others like them are blameworthy for being bad, not just their excesses or deficiencies. Accordingly, one is never right in performing these but is always mistaken.[89]

It should be said that Lonergan is aware of most of these criticisms, and that he intends his moral theory to yield moral precepts. In a response to Michael Novak, who points to the lack of clear moral precepts in his account of ethics, Lonergan admits that he did not work out the implications of a complete ethical theory. He claims that he worked out a metaphysics of proportionate being but not an ethics of proportionate good. Although he insists that his basis for ethics in cognitional analysis leaves open a historical development of morals, he does not think that

---

87. *Insight*, p. 606. However, in making feelings the experiential (though not the ultimate) stage of the morally self-assembling person in *Method*, Lonergan opens the door to a process ethics to match his process metaphysics.

88. On this point, see chapter 6 of my book on ethics, *The Quest for Moral Foundations* (Washington, DC: Georgetown University Press, 1996).

89. Aristotle, *NE* 2.6.1107a9–15, p. 29.

his theory necessarily rules out traditional ethics, with its clear moral precepts.

> Though I did not in *Insight* feel called upon to work out a code of ethics, neither did I exclude such a code. On the contrary, I drew a parallel between ethics and metaphysics. In metaphysics I not only assigned a basis in invariant structures but also derived from that basis a metaphysics with a marked family resemblance to traditional views. A similar family resemblance, I believe, would be found to exist between traditional ethics and an ethics that, like the metaphysics, was explicitly aware of itself as a system on the move.[90]

Perhaps it is only that Lonergan did not complete his intention of arriving at the code of moral precepts that would mirror that of Aquinas and the natural law tradition. I do not argue here that this would be impossible (although I do see it as problematic), only that I do not see it done.

Let us consider briefly how Lonergan's method handles beauty. As we mentioned above, Lonergan clearly distinguishes the realms of the true, the good, and the beautiful according to levels of consciousness. In such a scheme, he relates the artistic pursuit of beauty to the first level (attending to data), the scientific pursuit of understanding to the second level (understanding insight), the philosophic pursuit of truth to the third level (judging what is), and the moral pursuit of goodness to the fourth level (deciding what to do).[91] As to beauty's place in this scheme, Lonergan is certainly right on two counts. First, Lonergan insists on the element of experience in our appreciation of beauty. Second, he recognizes that the appreciation and creation of beauty is an intellectual activity. It is a dimension of meaning.[92]

Most of Lonergan's attention to the aesthetic realm, and thus to beauty, is found in his discussions about art. Art, he says, is "the objectification of a purely experiential pattern."[93] As a *pure* pattern, art is not instrumental but is for its own sake. It is not for science, nor is it understood in terms of a psychological or epistemological theory.[94] As a *pattern*, it

---

90. "Theories of Inquiry: Responses to a Symposium," *Second Collection*, pp. 39-40.
91. *Method*, p. 13.
92. Ibid., p. 64. Here Lonergan's basic method is more adequate than that of Kant for whom beauty is subjective. Against Kant's account, it seems clear that aesthetic judgment involves experience and understanding that experience.
93. Ibid., p. 61. Lonergan attributes this definition to Susanne K. Langer in *Feeling and Form* (New York: Scribner, 1953), whose theory of art he follows. See also the more complete treatment of art in *Topics in Education*, vol. 10 of *Collected Works of Bernard Lonergan* (Toronto: University of Toronto Press, 1993), pp. 208–32.
94. "Art," in *Topics for Education*, p. 213; see also *Insight*, pp. 184–85, where Lonergan insists that art is for its own sake, requires freedom, and involves the sense and intellect.

has to do with reason. As *experiential*, it has to do with sensation. In this definition, Lonergan does clearly distinguish the realm of the beautiful from that of the true and the good. He insists that the patterns of art are not instrumental, not for pragmatic or technical purposes, nor for scientific or metaphysical understanding. These latter patterns of sense experience are alien to the pure pattern that is art.[95] Nor is art at the service of morality. "Not only are alien patterns to be excluded but also the pattern must be purely experiential. . . . Out of them [colors, shapes, sounds] may rise a lesson, but into them a lesson may not be intruded in the manner of didacticism, moralism, or social realism."[96] In short, the realm of the beautiful cannot be accounted for by the other areas of differentiated consciousness. These areas present alien patterns that can account for certain aspects of an appreciation or creation of art, but they can never get to the heart of the matter.

Despite the many good insights to be found in his discussions of art, Lonergan fails to give full force to the distinctiveness and essence of the aesthetic realm, which is found in our appreciation of beauty. In his transcendental method, he rightly focuses on the activity (here the making of art) rather than some static habit of first principles in a faculty psychology. But it seems that he does not focus sufficiently on the object that specifies the activity—beauty. Because Lonergan's discussions of aesthetic value focus on art rather than an analysis of the beautiful, some of the distinctiveness of beauty vis-à-vis truth and goodness is lost.

The problem is that the creative arts involve a number of objects, depending on the intentions of the artist, the kind of art, and the context. Some artists explicitly intend their art to reflect reality, to communicate truth, or to make a moral or political statement. Even without such explicit intention, works of art involve multiple objects. This is especially true of a literary work of art, which (most clearly in the longer forms) presents a kind of worldview (metaphysics) and a morality (the motivations of the characters). Lonergan sometimes ends up explaining the value and uniqueness of art in terms of these other objects which are foreign to art's essential characteristic—beauty.

For example, he says that art is much like other disciplines in that it involves a withdrawal from the world and a return.

> It is a withdrawal from practical living to explore possibilities of fuller living in a richer world. Just as a mathematician explores the possibilities of what physics can be, so the artist explores possibilities of what life, ordinary living, can be. There is an artistic element in all consciousness, in

95. *Method*, pp. 61–62.
96. Ibid., p. 62.

all living. . . . We ourselves are products of artistic creation in our concrete living, and art is an exploration of potentiality.[97]

Just as mathematics may be ordered (and thus be instrumental in some way) to the enrichment of physics, art may be ordered (and thus be instrumental in some way) to the enrichment of ordinary living. The instrumentalism that he intends to rule out in his definition of art is creeping in here. I do, however, agree that there is beauty in a well-lived life. One's character is, in many ways, one's free creation. And a well-ordered and integrated life has a certain beauty to it. In *Insight*, Lonergan speaks of the dramatic pattern of experience. "Not only, then, is man capable of aesthetic liberation and artistic creativity, but his first work of art is his own living. The fair, the beautiful, the admirable is embodied by man in his own body and actions before it is given a still freer realization in painting and sculpture, in music and poetry."[98] Perhaps the beauty of a well-ordered life is prior to artistic creation, but such a dramatic pattern is not the prime analogue for beauty. Beauty is first recognized in the material things we experience. It comes to us from the integrated unity of things other than us, and it brings to us aesthetic delight. Only secondarily and by analogy do we reflect on the beauty of a well-ordered life or turn to the creation of beautiful artistic objects which may further enrich our lives.

Lonergan also suggests that art gives us deeper truth. "In a sense, it [art] is truer than experience, leaner, more effective, more to the point."[99] Here, art (if not beauty) is commended as a vehicle for achieving truth, as a means of revealing reality more effectively than other ways such as science or metaphysics. Perhaps art can be an effective truth-bearer, but again, I would argue that this is a secondary or accidental feature of art, whose most distinctive and essential characteristic is beauty. Although there is undoubtedly an intelligible aspect of appreciating beauty or of creating art, this does not mean that beauty is a vehicle for truth, for intelligibility can be theoretical, moral, or aesthetic.

There is, as well, sometimes a moral flavor to Lonergan's account of the value of what the artist is doing. Art is communication between the artist and others. As such, it has a communal aspect. "It is grasping what is of seems significant, of moment, of concern, of import to man in the experience."[100] Lonergan sees art as having a purpose of communicating

97. "Art," p. 217. Lonergan discusses the beauty of well-ordered life in terms of the dramatic pattern of experience in *Insight*, pp. 187–89. Again, I do not think that he is wrong here, only that beauty must first be analyzed in itself, and only by analogy applied to the creativity of living good lives.

98. *Insight*, p. 187.

99. "Art," p. 218.

100. Ibid.

something of importance, i.e., something of moral value. Again, I do not wish to deny that art has this kind of value, only that it is not the same thing as aesthetic value, which is essentially a matter of beauty.

Finally, as Lonergan emphasizes the experiential in ethics, so does he emphasize it in art. Art, he says, has a close relation to feelings. He does not mean that the artist's depth or intensity of feeling translates into good art. In fact, he explicitly denies this. "All that revelation of experience is not art, but simply the symptoms of the experience itself. One moves to art when the actor, understanding how a person would feel, puts forth deliberately those symptoms."[101] Thus the artist orders feelings for self and others. "Thinking about art helps us think, too, about exploring the full freedom of our ways of feeling and perceiving."[102] This is true, nor is it irrelevant to art: consider Aristotle's famous point about the role of catharsis in great tragedy.[103] But again, the focus here is more on the importance of psychic health (moral realm) than on beauty.

Thus the application of Lonergan's method to matters of beauty seems to me to be at least problematic. Critical realism may characterize our work in science and metaphysics. The questions that are raised for us (so long as we are open to the requirement to find sufficient answers to them) do move us to a more and more adequate account of the truth about reality. And one can get at the nature of knowing and its requirements by cognitional analysis. However, aesthetic appreciation seems to require the acceptance on our part of something that transcends us from the beginning. It is a beautiful thing that shows us beauty. It is the bird in flight, or the face of the beloved. We do not work up to these things by responding to questions that they raise for us. They come to us in their integrity. As Hans Urs von Balthasar so nicely puts it: "The beautiful brings with it a self-evidence that enlightens without mediation."[104] For Lonergan, the world is one mediated by meaning. It seems, however, that for the experience of beauty there is no mediation: the beautiful breaks in upon us. True enough, there is a process of question and answer that goes on, on some level, for the artist producing a beautiful work of art, but this production is secondary to the artist's knowledge of what beauty is. This he or she gains by direct experience. And true enough, we can attain a deeper level of aesthetic appreciation by critical reflection. But it is hard to see how the initial appreciation of beauty could be explained as anything other than a direct encounter with the beautiful thing in its

101. Ibid.
102. Ibid., 232.
103. Aristotle, *Poetics*, 6.1449b23–28.
104. Hans Urs von Balthasar, *The Glory of the Lord: A Theological Aesthetics*, trans. Erasmo Leiva-Merikakis (San Francisco: Ignatius, 1982), p. 37.

integrity. The appreciation of beauty implies a realism unmediated by any critique of consciousness.

As in my comments on Lonergan's moral theory, so here I do not wish to say that Lonergan misses the point completely. Far from it; there is much of value in his discussions of art and the insights into aesthetics there developed. My concern is that what is most essential to great art and to our aesthetic experience of nature—beauty—not be lost in the intricacies of an experiential analysis of artistic creation.

Evaluation of Reason's Recovery

In these last two chapters, we have focused on four thinkers who try to restore to reason some of the splendor that was stripped from it by Bacon and Descartes and their followers. In Kant, Hegel, Whitehead, and Lonergan, one finds systematic philosophies of an impressive range. Gone is the mechanical materialism found in the early empiricists; gone too is the static mathematical modeling of reality presented by the early rationalists. Each of these four thinkers attempts to recover the range of reason that had been seriously restricted by the narrow methods of the early modern thinkers. Indeed, each of these thinkers pays substantial attention to the three realms of reason that we have been claiming were collapsed into scientific method by Bacon and Descartes and their disciples. Kant has his three *Critiques* in which theoretical matters, practical matters, and aesthetical matters are dealt with systematically. Hegel's dialectic treats of art, morality, and the philosophical idea. Whitehead is conscious of trying to recover not only the vitalism ruled out by material mechanism but also the areas of morality, art, and religion that had been systematically excluded. Lonergan incorporates within his treatment of the levels of cognitional structure attention to the true, the good, and the beautiful. Thus in some ways all four work toward the restoration of reason for which I am arguing.

However, although all the philosophers address the three different realms of human reason, each fails to meet one or more of them on its own terms. One realm with its distinctive method dominates each philosopher's thought. As sophisticated as these methods are (particularly compared to the empirical or mathematical methods of the early moderns), they are not able to incorporate successfully what is essential in each of the three realms.

When Kant makes his Copernican Revolution and suggests that reality conforms to our thought (except for a world of things-in-themselves to which we have no access), he immediately skews the essence of scientific and metaphysical reason, as well as aesthetics. This is not to say that he is wrong in all that he says about these areas: on the contrary, it is amazing how many insightful things he has to say about them. However, once he denies any direct access to "things," he has lost an essential aspect of physics (the ability to respond to new discoveries), metaphysics (the possibility of arguing from things and their limitations to a real cause of them independent of our formative powers), and aesthetics (the objective concreteness and particularity of the beautiful thing).

If, as seems plausible, the Copernican Revolution was in the service of morality, then Kant's philosophy suffers from the domination of practical reason over theoretical and aesthetic reason. Kant correctly sees that if the paradigm of reason is scientific method with its demand for sense verification, then moral obligation is at an end. He is also correct in his insistence that reason, as practical, has its own first principles which provide us with universal moral imperatives. However, the further step of denying theoretical reason its proper role in knowing the world and the existence of the cause of the world is mistaken. Kant's moral realism does not sit well with his theoretical and aesthetic idealism. And even his ethical theory suffers, for without the admission that character is ultimately bound up with both the ability to respond freely to duty and with dispositions of the body, Kant can give no adequate account of the virtues.

Hegel denies Kant's distinction between things-as-they-appear and things-in-themselves, insisting that we have direct access to reality. Reality is intrinsically intelligible down to the level of the last detail. Every particular thing is embraced by the dialectic (logical and historical) of the Absolute Spirit coming to self-consciousness.

However, although Hegel restores confidence in reason's ability to know the true, he fails to account for the distinctive realm of the good— moral obligation. Of course, on one level he does account for it by his historical dialectic: ethics are conditioned by one's time, and ultimately (like everything else) by the inevitable progress of Absolute Spirit coming to know itself. However, this misses the essence of ethics, which is not a description of when or why people do what they do but the obligation to honor and not violate certain fundamental human goods, regardless of time or place or psychological state. Most obviously, Hegel's dialectic ignores the ultimate value of human life since individuals and nations must be destroyed in the Absolute Spirit's necessary march toward self-realization.

Within the dialectic, beauty suffers too. Hegel does insist on the concrete aspect of the beautiful thing. However, as a mere stage in the inevitable progress of the dialectic, the particular beautiful thing (just as the particular individual person or nation) does not matter. But, as Kant rightly sees, the essence of the beautiful is that it is enjoyed for its own sake and not for the sake of some future added perfection. In Hegel's scheme, all distinctions prove to be ultimately illusory, as reality is nothing but the one Absolute Spirit coming to self-consciousness. Even the high degree of self-consciousness exhibited by Hegel in reflecting on reality and developing his philosophical dialectic is ultimately but a stage to be sublated in an inevitable progress of a not-yet-conscious Mind.

The realism of Whitehead restores the place of extramental reality in our knowledge. Reality is neither informed by our mind as Kant held, nor just the necessary reflection of the cosmic mind as Hegel held. Whitehead's is a much humbler position, not indeed the radical empiricism of the materialists (for Whitehead insists on the importance of mathematics and vitalism), but the scientific ideal of progress made by hypothesis and verification. If reality is not what we think it is, then we need to change our model. All scientific models are just that—models. They are not to be mistaken for the fullness of reality.

Although clearly superior to Kant and Hegel in its ability to handle the changes in contemporary science, Whitehead's philosophical method has problems getting to the heart of moral goodness and beauty. Like Hegel, he sees morality as progressing, as reflecting the novelty of the age. If this is true, then there are no moral absolutes and so no moral obligation; for all stages are by definition new and hence, arguably, might demand new moral norms. Also, by making relation primary and substance nearly nonexistence, Whitehead has a hard time distinguishing between things, especially between things that we would say vary significantly—e.g., mouse and human being. Unless there is something substantially different about the human being that allows for its freedom of choice and hence moral responsibility, there is no reason to attribute to us any more freedom or responsibility than to a mouse. In a similar way, Whitehead's process metaphysics distorts his understanding of beauty and art. For Whitehead it is not the intrinsic, integrated unity of a thing that makes it beautiful but rather its being new and innovative. Again process of progress dominates content.

Along with attention to the theoretical disciplines of science and metaphysics, Lonergan carefully accounts for the distinct character of moral obligation and aesthetic appreciation. In his method of cognitional analysis, they are associated with distinct levels of consciousness. Responsibility is found on the fourth level: one ought to be attentive, intelligent, and reasonable. These are moral obligations, not reducible to the theoretical components of our reason found on the first three levels. Aesthetic appreciation is found on the first level, that of immediate experience: the appreciation of beauty is not to be confused with insight, judgment, or obligation. However, Lonergan's method is ultimately a method of theoretical reason, which reflects on how insights are developed out of attention to data and judgments go back to the data for verification. Such a model is eminently suitable for pursuing the truth about the way the world is, especially empirically (scientific method), though also metaphysically. However, it does not apply equally well to the realms of the good and the beautiful.[105]

Lonergan's model applies only imperfectly to morality, for his "ethics on the move" cannot adequately account for moral precepts, without which moral judgment (and hence responsibility) is impossible, and without which praise, blame, reward, and punishment are either meaningless or unfair. Lonergan's analysis goes a long way toward explaining how people *are* motivated, but why people *ought* to act against certain motivations and in favor of others (and Lonergan is adamant, unlike Hegel and Whitehead, that they should) is not so clear.

Even more than the good, it seems that the beautiful transcends us and presents itself to us immediately. Beauty breaks in upon us. It is not composed of judgments patiently built up from insights abstracted from data. The beautiful thing is there as an integral whole, calling us to respond in appreciation. Recognizing that judgments of beauty are not the same as judgments of truth (third level) or moral judgments (fourth level), Lonergan seeks in his schema a unique place for aesthetic judgment. In this he is right. However, in specifying the uniqueness of art, he often focuses on the experience of the artist creating something new and unique that serves to move us to a richer level of living by presenting to us deeper truths about reality or important paradigms to be imitated or absorbed. It seems that the role of the artist is subsumed under the true (the unique pattern of truth) and the good (the pattern as a paradigm for living), with the result that the unique character of beauty is in danger of being overlooked.

105. Even metaphysically, I would disagree somewhat with Lonergan's account. It seems to me that metaphysical knowledge begins immediately upon our exercising reason, that it does not appear on the scene only upon the advent of the virtually unconditioned. Or perhaps it does, but the virtually unconditioned appears, to some degree, at the outset. In a way, I think that Lonergan would agree with this, for he emphasizes the role of judgment in knowledge, and judgment reflects back on our experience of things. This act of reflection leads to progress in knowledge as we reformulate our insights to fit our experience of things. Thus as soon as there are some confirmed distinctions among things, the traditional metaphysics of Aristotle and Aquinas begins. What Lonergan says, following Aristotle—that our natural desire to know leads us in our quest to understand reality—is certainly right. However, this natural desire does not operate in a vacuum but always in relation to a world of things. Aristotle also says, famously, that philosophy begins in wonder (*Metaphysics* 1.2.982b12–14). But we wonder about things, not just data. This is particularly true if we consider our knowledge of other human beings. It seems odd to consider other people real merely insofar as they are "virtually unconditioned," for another person is not real only insofar as I am attentive, intelligent, reasonable, and responsible, that is, on the condition that I am authentically subjective.

Considering these four thinkers in broad terms, it seems clear that Hegel and Whitehead presuppose the principles of theoretical reason (the realm of the true) in their methods and that Kant presupposes the principles of practical reason (the realm of the good) in his.[106] Given these presuppositions, it is inevitable that the realm of reason, given second or third place, will suffer by being forced to fit under inappropriate principles and method. This we have seen to be the case. Lonergan's transcendental method is a bit different, for it discovers all three realms in our consciousness. However, the analysis itself is an attempt to explain the structure of intentionality in terms of a single thrust of the human spirit, and as such is a theoretical enterprise—worthy in itself, but not the entirety of intelligence.

If we would avoid these distortions of reason, we must keep in mind Aristotle's simple but profound insight that distinct subject areas (objects) require distinct methods. Although these subject areas may resemble each other and even overlap in some ways, the attempt to reduce them to one area with one transcendent method must fail. Because we know that the human being is one and that there is a single source of all reality, we have a natural desire to reduce the realms of the true, the good, and the beautiful to unity. But since we know human nature only by reflecting on our multiple activities, and since we know the existence of a creator only by studying the many things we experience, our idea of unity must never be undifferentiated. The tendency to reductionism must be very carefully avoided.

Clearly there are reasons to affirm unity, but we must distinguish how much unity we know from how much unity we desire and so project. Bacon was right in cautioning against our tendency to jump hastily to conclusions and to project more unity than is warranted. Particularly dangerous is our tendency to reduce reality to what can be understood through one model or method. In the next two chapters, we shall lay out the essential differences found in the three realms of reason (chapter 8) and the distinctions necessary when affirming the reason's unity (chapter 9).

---

106. It might, perhaps, be said that aesthetics as understood by Hume and Nietzsche (i.e., as feeling and novelty) dominates the thought of Hegel and Whitehead, but such an aesthetics is closely linked to (one might say distorted by) a metaphysics of novelty and process.

8

The Restoration of Reason

In contrast to the narrow view of reason taken by the early modern philosophers whereby reason is confined to empirical and mathematical functions, the view of the ancient and medieval tradition, which this book seeks to restore, understands reason as a much broader enterprise. This tradition includes in the purview of reason the realms of the true, the good, and the beautiful. In addition to the mathematical and empirical functions of reason found in the moderns, the realm of the true includes a metaphysics of existing things that are not just constructions of our minds and that lead us to affirm the existence of immaterial realities. In addition to the expanded insight into the truth about being, reason knows the good and directs us to pursue what ought to be (ethics and politics). Reason also knows the beautiful (aesthetic appreciation and art).

Given the diversity of these disciplines, one's reaction to the thesis that reason applies to all three may be incredulity. Surely we do not judge the objects of mathematics, ethics, and aesthetics in the same way. If mathematics is a matter of reason, surely ethics and aesthetics are not. The insight that these various fields are not judged in the same way is certainly true (and, in fact, the major thesis of this book). However, this insight need not mean that the various fields are not judged by reason, only that reason has distinct acts appropriate to distinct fields of inquiry.

We discussed this tradition in chapter 3 when examining why the ancient and medieval worlds did not emphasize technology, and we have referred to it elsewhere in our criticisms of the moderns. Now it is time to present more systematically the tradition's distinction between the realms of the true, the good, and the beautiful. In doing so, we shall exemplify our main points by referring to the backbone of that tradition: Plato, Aristotle, Augustine, and Aquinas. We shall draw most directly on Aristotle and Aquinas, for they make these distinctions explicitly, but I shall also point to texts in their masters that support the same distinctions.[1] Because the tradition is less systematic in distinguishing the realm of the beautiful from the other two realms, this part of the discussion will be quite a bit longer, for it is necessary to draw together insights from a number of places. However, in the process of clarifying the uniqueness of the realm of the beautiful, we shall also amplify our explanations of the distinctive features of the realms of the true and the good.

If there are distinct realms of reason, then each must have its own first principles that are not derived from either of the other two or from both. As first, these principles must be self-evident. Here we shall focus on the self-evident principles of knowledge, not primarily as psychological explanations of how knowledge comes to be, but rather as principles of reason that must be primary if there is any human knowledge at all.

My thesis is that such principles are irreducibly multiple, corresponding to distinct operations of the intellect. Thus the first principles of a philosophy of the true (the so-called theoretical sciences—mathematics, the sciences, and metaphysics), the first principles of a philosophy of

---

1. On the one hand, one might argue that Plato and Augustine do not belong on this list since their metaphysics of unity tends to blur the distinctions between disciplines. Plato claims that all reality can be deduced from one principle, the Good (*Republic* 6.508b–509c), and that the Good and the Beautiful are the same (*Lysis* 216d, *Phaedo* 48b, and *Symposium* 212a). Thus, he might be said to conflate the three realms, reducing them all to one metaphysical principle. Augustine, in addition to being a Platonist and hence falling prey to many of the same tendencies as Plato, is first and foremost a theologian, interested in the multiple aspects of human knowing primarily insofar as they lead to God. This fact might cause him to ignore the intrinsic differences between the realms of natural reason in the face of a transcendent supernatural object: God. Although these objections are not without some truth, they are not decisive. The principal insights that form the clear distinctions found in Aristotle and Aquinas concerning these three realms of reason can all be found in the writings of Plato and Augustine as well. Hence the latter thinkers clearly belong in this tradition.

On the other hand, one might object that this list too short. Cicero, Boethius, and Anselm, for example, are certainly in the tradition, and each recognizes the distinct areas of reason of which we speak. However, someone like Cicero is clearly derivative in his thought, drawing largely from Plato and Aristotle (as well as from the Stoics who themselves were influenced by Plato and Aristotle). Boethius and Anselm are heavily influenced both by the ancients and by Augustine. To support my thesis, the texts cited from Plato, Aristotle, Augustine, and Aquinas are sufficient.

the good (ethics and politics), and the first principles of a philosophy of the beautiful (aesthetics and art) are distinct from each other, no set being reducible to another or to the other two.[2] However, although these first principles are distinct, human reason is not to be divided into three separate powers (as one would distinguish reason from imagination and sense). For truth, goodness, and beauty are all objects of knowledge and, as such, have common characteristics—chief among them being universality. Additionally, the three areas of human intelligence overlap and are, in some sense, mutually inclusive. This unity and overlapping will be the subject of the next chapter.

In order to distinguish the three realms of reason clearly, we shall begin with a general discussion of first principles and then turn to the grounds for insisting on three kinds of first principles. Thus we shall first define our terms, explaining the nature of primary principles and their place within the structure of the soul. This done, we shall turn to the task of explaining why three realms of reason, each with its own first principles, should be distinguished. For this job we require a model very different from that of the rationalists. Instead of deducing distinct powers from the unity of the soul, and then distinct principles from the

2. Numerous interpreters of the tradition would disagree with this point, some (e.g., Henry Veatch, Ralph McInerny, Russell Hittinger, Jean Porter) holding that ethics are grounded in metaphysics, others (e.g., Umberto Eco and Mark Jordan) holding that the philosophy of the beautiful is grounded in metaphysics. On metaphysics grounding ethics, see Henry B. Veatch in his *For an Ontology of Morals* (Evanston, IL: Northwestern University Press, 1971), Ralph McInerny in his *Ethica Thomistica: The Moral Philosophy of Thomas Aquinas* (Washington, DC: Catholic University of America Press, 1982), Russell Hittinger in his *Critique of the New Natural Law Theory* (Notre Dame, IN: University of Notre Dame Press, 1987), and Jean Porter in *The Recovery of Virtue: The Relevance of Aquinas for Christian Ethics* (Louisville, KY: Westminster/John Knox, 1990). On metaphysics grounding a theory of beauty, see Umberto Eco, *Art and Beauty in the Middle Ages*, trans. Hugh Bredin (New Haven, CT: Yale University Press, 1986), and Mark Jordan, "The Evidence of Transcendentals and the Place of Beauty in Thomas Aquinas," *International Philosophical Quarterly* 29, no. 4 (1989): 393–407. A position more like the one I am proposing is to be found in the writings of Germain Grisez and John Finnis. See Germain Grisez, *The Way of the Lord Jesus: Christian Moral Principles* (Chicago: Franciscan Herald, 1983), and John Finnis, *Natural Law and Natural Rights* (Oxford: Clarendon, 1980). See also the joint article by Germain Grisez, John Finnis, and Joseph Boyle, "Practical Principles, Moral Truth, and Ultimate Ends," *American Journal of Jurisprudence* 32 (1987): 99–151. Also influential on my thought is the work of Francis Kovach, both in terms of the distinction between the three realms and in his interpretation of aesthetics. In essay 19, "Lie and Protective Statement: Nature and Morality," in Francis Kovach, *Scholastic Challenges to Some Medieval and Modern Ideas* (Stillwater, OK: Western Publications, 1987), Kovach distinguishes three roles for language: epistemic, aesthetic, and moral (protective statements); implied in such a distinction is the idea that reason works in three essentially different ways. In his *Philosophy of Beauty* (Norman: University of Oklahoma Press, 1974), Kovach develops an extensive theory of beauty based on the tradition that I am articulating.

one power of reason, we must begin with the distinct objects that are immediately intelligible to us and argue to distinct activities, principles, powers, and only then to the unity of the soul. This is how all legitimate learning takes place, for we must begin with what is better known to us, not with an unknown (though necessary) cause or principle that must be operating if we are learning. By knowing different objects and reflecting on this knowing we become aware of the distinct rational operations that logically require distinct habits of first principles. From the fact that all these activities share a common feature (they are all acts of knowing), we come to say that they belong to one power of the soul, the intellectual power or reason.[3] And from reflecting on the unity of the agent who knows, senses, and grows, we become aware of the unity of a soul with various powers.[4] Thus the unity of reason and the unity of the soul are the last things we know, not the first.

First Principles

Aristotle and Aquinas call the knowledge of first principles dispositions or habits of reason, that is, of the soul's intellectual power.[5] They are natural habits, as distinct from the acquired habits that modify our personalities or characters.[6] The habits of first principles differ from acquired habits in that we cannot help but have these habits of first principles. They are not innate in the sense that Plato or Descartes might have held, for all knowledge begins in the senses. But they are self-evident; that is, they are immediately known in the act of knowing anything. As Thomas says, "There necessarily are some things in our intellect which it knows naturally, namely, first principles—even though in us this knowledge is not caused unless we receive something through our senses."[7] First principles are known not by acts of reasoning (as if demonstrated) but directly by the understanding.[8] Aristotle refers to the

3. Aristotle, *De Anima* 2.6 and 3.4; Thomas Aquinas, *ST* 1.79.8 and 11; *De Veritate* (hereafter, *DV*) 16.1 ad 13. Reason as we are using it in this book is basically equivalent to this idea of an intellectual power. Thus it is more than just the ability to think logically. It also involves intuition of first principles, insight, and judgment.

4. *ST* 1.78.1. For Aristotle and Aquinas, philosophical explanation for the existence of causes is always from multiplicity to unity, never a deduction from one to the many.

5. *NE* 6.6; *ST* 1.79.12; *DV* 15.1; Thomas Aquinas, *Commentary on Nicomachean Ethics* (hereafter, *Comm. NE*) 6.5.1179.

6. *DV* 10.13 and 8.15; *Comm. NE* 2.4.286; *Summa contra gentiles* (hereafter *CG*) 2.82.1 and 83.31.

7. *DV* 8.15.c in *The Disputed Questions on Truth*, trans. Robert W. Mulligan (Chicago: Henry Regency Co., 1952), vol. 1, p. 393.

8. Ibid., 15.1.c.

grasping of first principles as intuition. "Intuition, too, is of ultimates, and in both directions, for of both the primary terms and the ultimate particulars there is intuition and not reasoning."[9]

That we have such principles obviously cannot be proven through demonstration from prior principles, for there are no principles prior to first principles. Rather, from the fact that we make judgments of certain kinds, we know that there must be principles on which such judgments depend. "Primary things cannot be understood by anything anterior to them, but by something consequent, as causes are understood through their proper effects."[10]

The nature of first principles can be explained only negatively, that is, by denying the need for a further explanation. According to Aristotle, principles of demonstration are immediate (i.e., not mediated); thus an immediate premise or principle has no other prior to it.[11] Or put another way (also negatively), if any proposition is meaningful, there must not be an infinite regress of principles on which that proposition depends.[12]

First principles have three fundamental characteristics: (1) they are presupposed to all other knowledge; (2) they are more certain than any other knowledge; and (3) they are self-evident. If any particular knowledge is certain, it must be based on universal principles that are certain.[13] If the particular knowledge is based on such principles, the principles must evidently be more certain than the knowledge, since it is to the principles that one refers in justifying the knowledge.[14] And if the particular knowledge is to be justified, the principles on which it rests must be not only more certain than the conclusion but also absolutely certain (self-evident).[15] For if the principles were not self-evident, then the meaningfulness of the conclusion could be called into question. Why should one accept a conclusion based on principles that can be doubted? As Augustine says, we begin with the fact that we do make such and such judgments and then seek to explain the principles that are necessary if such judgments can be made. "Searching into why it was that I gave approval to the beauty of bodies, whether in heaven or on earth, and what helped me to make such judgments, and to say 'This should be thus and so, and not that,' searching, then,

9. *NE* 6.12.1143b1–3, p. 112.

10. *Comm. NE* 1.1.9.

11. Aristotle, *Posterior Analytics* (hereafter, *PA*) 1.2.72a6–8; see also Thomas Aquinas, *Commentary on Posterior Analytics* (hereafter, *Comm. PA*) 1.5.

12. *Comm. NE* 6.5.1177.

13. *DV* 15.2 and 16.1; *Comm. NE* 1.2.20.

14. *DV* 8.15 and 12.12 ad 8; *Comm. NE* 6.4.1164; *Comm. PA* 2.20.

15. *ST* 1–2.57.2 and 94.2; Thomas also calls these principles indemonstrable: *Comm. NE* 6.5.1175 and 1177.

into why I passed such judgments, for I did pass them, I had found that immutable, true, and eternal truth, which exists above my change-able mind."[16]

Aristotle and Aquinas discuss self-evidence in numerous prominent places.[17] A proposition is self-evident if its meaning is clear as soon as the meaning of its terms is known. However, it is important to distin-guish between propositions that are self-evident in themselves but not to us (such as "God exists") and those that are self-evident in themselves and to us (such as the whole is greater than its part).[18] Here we must be concerned with the latter; for clearly, if the first principles of knowledge are not self-evident to us, then we can never justify any conclusions by them.

Such self-evident principles are present in the natural light of reason that makes all knowledge possible. Whereas for Hume human intelli-gence is limited to manipulating materials given by passion or instinct or custom, for Aristotle and Aquinas it is part of our intellectual nature to be able to grasp first principles by direct understanding or intuition.[19] If there are habits of first principles in Hume's thought, they are habits formed below the level of intelligent activity, habits of feeling. As habits of feeling, they cannot be known to be true. As Hume says, the best we can do is estimate their probability based on our experience. In con-trast, the first principles of Aristotle and Aquinas are intelligible. They are known to be true not indeed by deduction from prior premises but by seeing the absurdity of denying them. These self-evident principles must be presupposed to any knowledge we gain about the world or ourselves. They cannot be doubted. "It is impossible for the soul of a man to be deprived of the light of the agent intellect, through which first principles in speculative and practical matters are made known to us. For this light belongs to the nature of the soul, since by reason of this the soul is intellectual."[20]

However, the fact that Aristotle and Aquinas consider first principles to be habits indicates that these principles have some relation to experi-

16. Augustine, *Confessions* 7.17, trans. John K. Ryan (Garden City, NY: Image Books, 1960), p. 175.

17. Aristotle, *PA* 1.2 and 3; *NE* 6.3 and 6; *Metaphysics* 2.2.996b26–997a16; Aquinas, *ST* 1.2.1; 1–2.94.2.

18. Aristotle, *PA* 1.2.72a1–5, *NE* 1.2; Aquinas, *ST* 1.2.1; 1–2.94.2.

19. See Aristotle, *NE* 6.6.1141a9 and *PA* 2.19.100b14, and Aquinas, *Comm. NE* 6.5.1179, and *Comm. PA* 1.19.

20. Thomas Aquinas, *DV* 16.3.c in *Disputed Questions on Truth*, trans. James V. Mc-Glynn (Chicago: Henry Regency, 1953), vol. 1, p. 312. In the same work, Aquinas writes, "Knowledge in a certain sense is implanted in us from the beginning (since we have the light of the agent intellect) through the medium of universal conceptions which are im-mediately known by the light of the agent intellect" (*DV* 10.6, vol. 2, p. 28).

ence.[21] As Aquinas says, if we did not know what a whole or a part was (and this knowledge we gain through sense experience of material things), we would not be aware of the principle that a whole is greater than its part.[22] Aristotle is very clear on this point: the habit of first principles is not *a priori*. Rather, the habits of first principles arise in the activity of sensation.[23] It is the human being, not the mind, that knows; thus all knowledge comes to be out of, or perhaps in, sense experience. In any case, the essential point about first principles is that they are self-evident, not how they come to be or where they come from. Logically, they do not require explanation. Although it is interesting to speculate about their origins, it is really irrelevant to the status of such principles as first in the various ways of knowing. Aquinas, commenting on a passage by Aristotle, writes:

> Hence he concludes that there do not pre-exist any habits of first principles in the sense of being determinate and complete; neither do they come to exist anew from other better known pre-existing principles in the way that a scientific habit is generated in us from previously known principles; rather the habits of principles come to exist in us from pre-existing sense.[24]

Although we do not know the principles *a priori*, we do have, *a priori*, a power able to know such principles: reason.[25] The sense experience is thus the occasion of our becoming aware of these first principles, but it is not their cause in the sense of origin. If we were not oriented toward making fundamental distinctions, we would not recognize whole and part in our experience; that is, our experience would not (indeed, could not) be intelligible. Our grasping of first principles such as this one is not like induction, where experience of many similar relations gives us knowledge of a universal kind. Nor is it like the gaining of virtuous habits, where repeated actions form certain dispositions in one's character. One case of recognizing a whole and a part (thus understanding the terms) is all that is required for one to understand that any whole is greater than one of its parts.[26] How experience figures in our awareness of these first principles differs according as we are dealing with the true, the good, or the beautiful; this will become clearer as we discuss the three realms in more detail.

---

21. *ST* 1–2.51.1; *DV* 8.15; *Comm. NE* 6.5.1179; *Comm. PA* 2.20.
22. *ST* 1–2.51.1; *CG* 2.82.32.
23. See *Comm. PA* 2.19 [100a10–15].
24. *Comm. PA* 2.20, trans. F. R. Larcher (Albany, NY: Magi, 1970), p. 238.
25. *Comm. PA* 2.19.99b28–34.
26. As Aristotle says, the universal is grasped in the first instance of experiencing a particular. *PA* 2.19.100a15–100b2.

Multiple Principles

Having considered in a general way the place of first principles in our rational life, let us now turn to the claim that our reason is guided by more than one set of first principles. Aristotle and Aquinas typically distinguish theoretical reason from practical reason[27] and then go on to argue for two (not three) appropriate kinds of first principles. However, this way of dividing reason can lead to irrelevant categorizations. I shall propose a different way of distinguishing that is compatible with the Aristotelian/Thomistic approach, but that I believe to be more fundamental.

By their root meanings, theoretical reason has to do with "seeing" what is the case (from the Greek word *theorein*, to look at), and practical reason has to do with "acting" (from the Greek *prassein*, to do or to act). According to Aristotle, theoretical reason includes such subjects as logic, mathematics, the various sciences, and metaphysics. Under practical reason fall such subjects as ethics, politics, and art. These distinctions seem to give Aristotle a basis for distinguishing the three areas of human reason that I wish to discuss: the true (theoretical reason), the good (practical reason as doing), and the beautiful (practical reason as making).[28] The last fits least well since the appreciation of beauty and the activity of art are not identical.

In fact, however, there seem to be theoretical and practical components of each of the three areas. Consider the subject areas of theoretical reason. Although theoretical reason clearly seeks to discover the truth about things, such a seeking (the act of questioning) is itself an act of practical reason—a good to be done or pursued. And any method of understanding things is chosen for the sake of achieving truth and is thus a practical matter. Or consider the subject areas of practical reason. Here one can distinguish between the theoretical component of knowing the truth about what is good and what ought or ought not to be done, and the practical component of choosing the particular acts that will lead to the acquisition of virtuous or vicious habits.[29] Finally, consider the last of the three areas, practical reason as making. Besides the making

27. See Aristotle, *Metaphysics* 6.1; *NE* 6.2; Aquinas, *ST* 1–2.94.2.
28. Aristotle, *NE* 1.1.
29. For the knowledge of first principles, see Aquinas's treatise on law, esp., *ST* 1–2.94.2. For particular acts of will and habits, see his treatise on the virtues, *ST* 1–2.49–65. This distinction is less clearly drawn in Aristotle, but it is there. The most obvious place where Aristotle insists on inviolable principles is *NE* 2.6. Having just defined ethical virtue in terms of finding the mean between extremes, which involves all sorts of qualifications (the right amount at the right time to the right person, etc.), he insists that some things are clearly wrong in themselves (always and everywhere) and therefore do not admit of a mean.

that is art, there clearly must be principles (like the first principles of ethics) by which we distinguish good art from bad art—the beautiful from the ugly. What is more, the appreciation of beauty does not fit the model of practical reason as oriented toward action: it is more like contemplation (an act of theoretical reason) where the beautiful thing is appreciated for its own sake.

Therefore I propose to analyze the distinct realms of human reason by focusing on three distinct objects. These objects specify three distinct activities, which in turn are guided by three distinct habits of first principles. That is, I shall distinguish between the true, the good, and the beautiful. The clearest texts in support of the distinction between the realms of the true and the good, the activities that respond to these objects, and their distinct first principles, are found in Aquinas. Those texts making the clearest case for a distinct realm of the beautiful with its own activities and first principles are to be found in Aristotle. Thus for the first distinction, I shall focus on Aquinas and for the second on Aristotle. However, as I mentioned above, the distinction of the three areas can be found in both Aristotle and Aquinas, as well as in the writings of Plato and Augustine, and I shall draw on materials from all four thinkers.

The True

Let us begin by distinguishing between the principles applicable to understanding what is true and those applicable to choosing what is good. A well-known locus for this distinction is *Summa theologiae* 1–2.94.2. Here, Aquinas's purpose is to distinguish the foundations of natural law. To clarify his position he compares the first principles applicable to understanding the truth about being with those applicable to understanding what ought to be pursued and not violated—i.e., the good. Thus he begins by specifying distinct objects of reason: being (what truly is) and goodness. Just as there is a first principle grounding our knowledge of being by which we make judgments of truth and falsity, so there is a first principle concerning our knowledge of the good by which we make judgments of value and know what we ought to do. The first principle of knowing being is: something cannot be and not be at the same time and in the same respect (the law of noncontradiction).[30] The first principle of knowing the good is: good is to be done and pursued

30. This principle is clearly formulated by Plato in *Republic* 4.436b, and more explicitly by Aristotle, *Metaphysics* 4.3.1005b19–21.

and evil avoided (the first principle of practical reason).[31] Each of these principles is self-evident to us. This means that neither is derived from the other, or from any other principle. Although propositions about what should or should not be done must assume the law of noncontradiction or be meaningless, the meaning of such propositions is not reducible to statements about what is or is not the case. There is no implication of obligation in statements of truth. The mathematical equation $2 + 2 = 4$ and the scientific proposition "the speed of light is constant" do not tell us what we ought to do. But implicit in our understanding of good is that it ought to be pursued and not violated.

> Now as *being* is the first thing that falls under the apprehension simply, so *good* is the first thing that falls under the apprehension of the practical reason, which is directed to action: since every agent acts for an end under the aspect of good. Consequently the first principle in the practical reason is one founded on the notion of good, viz., that *good is that which all things seek after*. Hence this is the first precept of law, that *good is to be done and pursued and evil is to be avoided*. All other precepts of the natural law are based on this.[32]

Aquinas goes on to identify other self-evident propositions regarding what is true and what is good. Although these propositions are secondary in the sense that they make use of the first principle, they are equally self-evident. Thus it is self-evident that the whole is greater than its part;

31. This principle is found in Plato, Aristotle, and Augustine as well as in Aquinas. Plato writes in the *Republic*, "All men want good things" (*Republic* 4.438a, trans. G. M. A. Grube [Indianapolis: Hackett, 1979], p. 102), and Aristotle opens his *Nicomachean Ethics* with the following words: "Every art and every inquiry, and similarly, every action and every intention is thought to aim at some good; hence men have expressed themselves well in declaring the good to be that at which all things aim" (*NE* 1.1.1094a1–4, p. 1). It might be objected that Plato's and Aristotle's point is more metaphysical here than properly moral; that is, they declare that all actions *do* aim at good rather than that they *should*. However, there are many other places in Plato's writings where he insists on the obligation to do good. Consider, as an example, the following passage from the *Apology*: "You are wrong, sir, if you think that a man who is any good at all should take into account the risk of life or death; he should look to this only in his actions, whether what he does is right or wrong, whether he is acting like a good or a bad man" (*Apology* 28bc, in *Five Dialogues*, trans. G. M. A. Grube [Indianapolis: Hackett, 1987], p. 33). See also *Crito* and *Republic* 2, where he talks about the greatest of goods being what we should seek. And when Aristotle declares that "men have spoken well" in speaking of the good as the object of choice, he shows that we are able to make evaluative judgments (and asks us to do so in agreeing with him) as well as descriptive ones. Augustine writes, "Since knowledge and activity render a man happy, error in knowledge must be avoided, just as sin is to be shunned in our actions" (*On Christian Combat* 13, in *The Fathers of the Church*, vol. 4, trans. Robert P. Russell [New York: CIMA Publishing, 1947], p. 331).

32. *ST* 1–2.94.2, vol. 2, p. 1009.

as soon as the meaning of the terms is known, the proposition is known to be true. Likewise, as soon as the terms life, procreation, knowledge, and friendship are understood, it is evident that they ought to be pursued and promoted and not violated. That is because life, procreation, knowledge, and friendship are self-evidently good; they are not just good as means to, or as aspects of, other goods but good in themselves. Aquinas, in the course of his writings, will indicate other basic goods besides these, the most important being beauty (which we shall discuss in some detail later in this chapter) and religion.[33] In presenting these goods as self-evident dimensions of human flourishing, he is squarely in the tradition of his predecessors.[34]

In numerous places Thomas discusses the principles and subject matter of the knowledge of being, not only distinguishing its principles from those of the good, but also showing how it operates in three distinct areas: physical science, mathematics, and metaphysics.[35] Here he follows Aristotle, who distinguishes these three theoretical sciences in terms of different levels of abstraction.[36] Abstraction is the consideration

33. Aquinas considers all Ten Commandments (including the first three having to do with God) as under the natural law (*ST* 1–2.100.1), and he holds that religion is a natural virtue (*ST* 2–2.85.5 ad 3).

34. One can find the basic goods in the other three thinkers, as well. See Plato, *Republic* 2.367d, where he speaks of justice, knowledge, and health; *Phaedo* 61d–62c, where he forbids suicide (affirms life); and *Laws* 4 and 5, where he speaks of various fundamental goods—procreation, religion, health, and friendship. Aristotle mentions all the goods spoken of by Aquinas in his *Nicomachean Ethics*. First, note that out of ten books in his *Nicomachean Ethics*, Aristotle devotes two (8 and 9) to the good of friendship. Note also that Aristotle's final word on human happiness (10.7) identifies it with contemplation (knowledge of the truth). On the good of life, see 9.4.1166a9–23 and 9.9.1170a19–b8; on procreation and family, see 8.12.1162a14–32; on obligations to parents and elders, see 8.12.1162a4–9 and 9.2.1165a21–30; on religion, see 8.12.1162a4–9 and 8.14.1163b13–30. One can find similar goods in the writings of Augustine: "Surely we must see that God gives us some goods which are to be sought for their own sake, such as wisdom, health, friendship" (*The Good of Marriage* 9, in *Treatises on Marriage and Other Subjects*, Fathers of the Church 27, trans. Charles T. Wilcox [Washington, DC: Catholic University of America Press, 1955], p. 21). The argument against suicide, in *City of God* 1, indicates Augustine's concern for the good of life. Other goods he mentions are procreation (*The Good of Marriage* 3), beauty (*City of God* 22.24), filial piety (*City of God* 10.1), and religion or *latreia* (*City of God* 10.3).

35. *Opusc. XVI, Expositio, Super librum De Trinitate Boethii* 5.1; *ST* 1.81.1 ad 2.

36. *Metaphysics* 6.1. These distinctions are found more or less in Plato and his disciple Augustine, although in Plato, at least, they are not considered as degrees of abstraction. Consider the divided line in *Republic* 6, where Plato distinguishes levels of being and knowing derived from the first principle of the Good: images (imagination), objects of sense (opinion), mathematical realities (reasoning), and forms (understanding) (terms follow Grube, pp. 164–66). Such distinctions can also be found in Augustine's work. It is easy to find examples of Augustine using metaphysics. He commends the Platonists for acknowledging God as "the author of all being, the light of truth, and the giver of bless-

of some intelligible content of a thing, leaving out of consideration other aspects of the thing's reality. Knowledge is always universal, while sense experience is of particular things.

Physical science, whose formulations are universals abstracted from particulars, always retains reference to the physical, and so abstracts from particular matter, but not common matter. Thus we understand a dog to have internal organs, but our understanding is general and does not fix on the organs of a particular dog. We know that a pine tree must have roots, bark, and needles (or more generally, cellulose), but we do not think that every pine tree has these particular roots, bark, and needles (or this quantity of cellulose).

Mathematics gets its content through abstracting the quantitative aspect from physical things, thus ignoring both kinds of physical matter (particular and common), but keeping the notion of intelligible matter (time for arithmetic and space for geometry). Once this abstraction is complete, there is no further reference to the physical. Thus, a triangle is not made out of any kind of matter, although it is a spatial figure and hence involves what Aquinas calls intelligible matter.

Metaphysics, although drawing its subject matter from our experience of the physical world, considers being as being, without reference to the limitations of physical things or to intelligible matter. Its objects—being, power, act, God—are defined without reference to any matter, physical or intelligible.[37] Metaphysical principles such as act and potency have no intrinsic relation to matter of any sort, even though all acts are accompanied by some potency (apart, that is, from the first principle, God, who is pure act). Thus Aristotle and Aquinas speak of act and potency within the intellect (distinguishing a passive and an active intellect), even though the intellect is not material. Even more radically, Aquinas speaks of the real distinction between essence (potency) and existence

---

edness" (*City of God* 8.5, p. 151). Basically, Augustine follows Plato in his arguments for the existence of God, arguing from the imperfect to the perfect, from the changing to the unchanging, from the activity of the mind to the need for an immaterial and intelligent cause of everything (*City of God* 8.5; *On Free Choice of the Will* 2.12–16; *Confessions* 8). Likewise, it is easy to find passages in which Augustine talks about the objects of mathematics. Augustine follows Plato in thinking that they are constitutive of things (*On Free Choice of the Will* 2.16; *Literal Commentary on Genesis* 6.3.7; cf. Plato's *Timaeus*) and that they are of mystical importance (*Literal Commentary on Genesis* 6.3.7; *On the Trinity* 4.4–6). Although Augustine spends little time studying natural things for their own sake, he makes use of them to prove the existence of God (*Of True Religion* 24.25), and he insists that they have their own natures that we can understand. "They are impelled by their own weights; they seek their own places" (*Confessions* 13.6, p. 341).

37. For a focused account of the three levels of abstraction, see Aquinas, *ST* 1.85.1, esp. ad 2.

(act) in every created being, even in the immaterial separate substances (angels).

One important consequence of this theory of abstraction is that our knowledge of even the simplest physical thing (and all knowledge begins with material things) is imperfect; for we do not have direct access to the essences of material things, nor can we exhaust the particularity of any individual. We become more and more aware of the essential differences among things through our study of the differences among them that we experience through the senses (what Aristotle and Aquinas call accidental differences). "Even in sensible things essential differences themselves are unknown. They are, therefore, signified through accidental differences which arise from essential ones, just as a cause is signified by its effect."[38] Beyond this, we know that each physical thing has its own individuality irreducible to that of other things of its kind, yet we do not know that individuality as individual. Always our knowledge of a thing abstracts from its individuality.

The unity of the human being as sensing and knowing (specifically, our ability to judge whether or not our idea is true through referring back to the original sense experience of a thing) reminds us that our knowledge of any individual thing is never exhaustive. Physical knowledge of things, gained through abstraction, is real (albeit limited) knowledge. The same can be said for mathematical and metaphysical knowledge of things. It may even be that mathematical knowledge of things is more important than physical knowledge, and that metaphysical knowledge is more important than mathematical. Indeed, it would seem that metaphysical knowledge is the most real since it penetrates most deeply into the heart of any thing's being. However, this does not mean that it is comprehensive knowledge or that the other levels of intelligibility are unreal and hence may be ignored. We must not overstate our claim to knowledge within these areas of the true and also, of course, within the greater arena of knowledge in general, which also includes the good and the beautiful.

It should be noted that for Aristotle and Aquinas, logic does not count as one of the sciences of being; rather, it is presupposed by these sciences.[39] In the beginning of his *Prior Analytics*, Aristotle defines logic as the science of demonstration.[40] It is not a science of what is known or what is to be demonstrated, but the science of how to demonstrate. This is in marked contrast to what Hegel says about the nature of logic, or what Bacon assumes by making his method

38. Thomas Aquinas, *On Being and Essence*, in *Selected Writings of St. Thomas Aquinas*, trans. Robert P. Goodwin (Indianapolis: Bobbs-Merrill, 1977), p. 60.

39. See Aquinas, *Exposition, de Trinitate*, 5.1 ad 2.

40. *Prior Analytics* 1.1.

of induction the way to all truth. For both Bacon and Hegel, logic is a science of being: what they count as real is what conforms to their logical methods.

These two mistakes—the counting of our conceptions of things as exhaustive, and the counting of logical structures of thought as the content of reality—are closely related, and ultimately identical. Once one says that what we know are only our conceptions, one is committed to a logicism. Aquinas is very careful to insist that what is known is the material thing, and that our thought (idea, species, impression, conception) is that by which the thing is known.

> Some have asserted that our intellectual faculties know only the impression made on them. . . . This is, however, manifestly false for two reasons. First, because the things we understand are the objects of science; therefore if what we understand is merely the intelligible species in the soul, it would follow that every science would not be concerned with objects outside the soul, but only with the intelligible species within the soul. . . . Secondly, it is untrue, because it would lead to the opinion of the ancients who maintained that *whatever seems, is true*, and that consequently contradictories are true simultaneously. For if the faculty knows its own impression only, it can judge of that only.[41]

The possibility of progress in science obviously depends on this distinction. As Whitehead points out so well, the scientist must have recourse to sense experience not just for verification but also for reinvigoration and inspiration. Reality has a way of surprising us, of throwing anomalies at us, forcing us to reconsider our prior conceptions.

This kind of realism is essential not only for science but also for the possibility of any kind of truth at all. If truth has no relation to objective reality, but is only about what each of us thinks, then the truth is destroyed. Sometimes we disagree, holding contradictory opinions about some subject. If truth is simply what each of us thinks it is, then contradictory positions would both be true—a violation of the first principle of being and knowing, the law of noncontradiction. In other words, the theory that what one knows are one's impressions or ideas leads to absurdity, to the impossibility of meaningful communication or even common human sanity. If all one knows are one's own ideas or impressions, then one is cut off from participation in any meaningful relation with the world of things or with other human beings. In short, one ends up with solipsism (all one can know is oneself) and finally skepticism (nothing can be known) since one has no idea why one has ideas or how to justify them as legitimate.

41. *ST* 1.85.2, vol. 1, p. 433.

The Good

Having considered the richness of the realm of the true (theoretical reason), let us consider the distinct realm of the good (practical reason). Aquinas discusses the first principles of knowing the good at some length. He gives the name *synderesis* to the understanding of these first principles. This understanding is a natural habit belonging to the power of reason. "The first practical principles, bestowed on us by nature, do not belong to a special power, but to a special natural habit, which we call *synderesis*."[42] The first principles of moral obligation are not learned from any other content, not within the realm of obligation (since they are first in this order) and not from any other order (such as physics, metaphysics, or aesthetics). They are known by nature and are self-evident.

Unlike the sciences of being, ethics is not a matter of abstraction. It is true that moral virtue, which is a participation of reason in our emotional and appetitive lives,[43] is built up by many actions in a way similar to Aristotle's account of the origin of knowledge in the *Posterior Analytics*.[44] By making choices, we develop certain dispositions of character—good ones from making good choices, bad ones from making bad ones. However, we do not gain knowledge of what is good and ought to be done by abstraction. Why something is right or wrong, and hence that one ought to pursue or avoid it, cannot be derived by abstracting universals from particular feelings or experiences. For the moral life is, most centrally, the refusal to let feelings deflect us from doing what reason tells us we ought to do. True enough, our responses to feelings and experiences may create habits (either good or bad) and thus be a theoretical explanation of how we *do* act, but how we *ought to* act cannot be explained by reference to physical or emotional facts. The knowledge that one ought to do good and avoid evil cannot be deduced from the principles of theoretical reason.

This insight is echoed by Hume in his famous dictum that there is no getting "ought" (value) from "is" (facts), which we discussed in chapter 4. Recall that Hume's point is a simple logical one. In order for an

---

42. Ibid., 1.79.12, vol. 1, p. 401; *DV* 16. Texts suggesting the existence of such a principle are easily found in Plato, Aristotle, and Augustine. Plato, in his *Apology*, states (and shows by Socrates' actions) that there is a principle of moral action that is never to be compromised. This is reiterated in his *Crito*, the *Republic*, and the *Laws*. Aristotle's "right reason" in his definition of moral virtue speaks to the same point (*NE* 2.6.1106b–1107a2). And Augustine mentions in several places that there are natural principles of morality. "His fundamental duty is to look out for his own home, for both by natural and human law he has an easier and readier access to their requirements" (*City of God* 19.14, p. 460); see also, *City of God* 19.1 and 12 and *On Order* 2.9.26.

43. See Aristotle, *NE* 1.13 and Aquinas, *Comm. NE* 1.20.243.

44. Aristotle, *PA* 2.19; cf. Aquinas, *Comm. PA* 2.20.

argument to be valid, nothing may appear in the conclusion that is not found in the premises. If all premises are from the realm of the true (science, mathematics, or metaphysics), then it is invalid to conclude within the realm of the good (with a statement about how one ought to act). In other words, propositions of obligation (imperatives) are not logically derivable from propositions of fact (indicatives). Any specific conclusion of moral obligation requires a general premise of obligation. Hume thought that there were no general premises of obligation (since he limited reason to relations of ideas and matters of fact) and so reverted to an emotivism to explain human behavior. But Aquinas and the tradition understand that, because it is clear that some particular choices violate moral obligation (such as killing innocent children for fun), there must be principles of moral obligation that are absolutely certain. Such certainty can be found only in self-evidence. Therefore, the principles of moral knowledge are self-evident.

Just as the rich life of understanding reality (physics, mathematics, and metaphysics) follows from the first principles of theoretical reason, so the rich life of moral decision-making and virtue follows from the first principles of practical reason. As we noted above, not only is the obligation to pursue what is good and avoid what is evil self-evident to us, but so also is the meaning of human good found in such fundamental human goods as life, procreation, knowledge, friendship, and beauty. These goods are good in themselves, not just means to other ends or instances of other goods. When we judge some action to violate these goods (whether it is an action that has happened or one about which we are deliberating), we know that it is wrong and should not be done.[45]

Beyond this restriction, we have a general obligation to honor and promote these goods. This general requirement to pursue what is good is much less specific than the strict obligation not to violate it. The reason for this is that there are several basic goods, each good in itself and infinitely worthy of our attention and participation. There is no precise formula for how much of each good any individual should pursue.

Implied by this obligation to pursue good and avoid evil is freedom of choice, an essential concomitant of practical reason. Clearly, there can

---

45. Without getting into the intricacies of moral reasoning about tough cases, it is essential to distinguish between intentionally choosing to violate a basic good and accepting damage to a basic good as an inevitable yet unintended side-effect of a good action. The key text is Thomas Aquinas's discussion of the permissibility of killing in self-defense (*ST* 2–2.64.7). He says that it is never permissible to intend to kill another, even if that other is trying to kill you, since such an action would violate the good of life. However, one does have the right and even the duty to protect one's own life. Thus it is permissible to protect one's life by an act that has the unintended side-effect of killing the attacker, but only if one uses the least force possible. To use more force than necessary indicates an intention to harm the other, which is evil and should never be willed.

be no natural obligations if we are not free to fulfill them. It is absurd to commend or criticize people for their actions if they predetermined.[46] Thus freedom of choice is a kind of first principle (not of content but of operation) of practical reason. Much ink has been spilled in the history of philosophy trying to prove or disprove that we are free according to some criterion of theoretical reason (physics or metaphysics). Such discussions may be interesting studies, but they are irrelevant. We can never prove from theoretical reason that we are free. Descartes was right to admit the possibility that, when we think we are acting freely, we are really just being deceived into thinking this by some higher being (or a materialist might say, some subrational biological or physical force).[47] We cannot definitively rule out this possibility. Of course, neither can it be proved by theoretical reason that we are not free, except by assuming that God or matter determines all our actions. But since such an assumption amounts to assuming that we do not have freedom, the argument begs the question (i.e., assumes what it claims to prove). Thus, as far as theoretical reason goes, we cannot settle the issue. The only proof that we are free is the practical proof drawn for the absurdity of denying our own acting selves. We simply cannot believe that our actions (those we choose) are determined by forces other than ourselves. To believe this would be to hold that our actions are not our actions—an obvious contradiction.

Freedom of choice is a prerequisite for moral action. Since we know that we are obliged to honor and not violate basic goods such as life, knowledge, and friendship, we know that we are free to choose so to honor them (or dishonor them, as the case may be). Thus we are morally restricted in our behavior. That is, if we would be good, there are some things we must not do: we must never intentionally violate any of the basic goods. However, there is another implication for freedom in our recognition of a plurality of basic goods that must not be forgotten. When it comes to pursuing and promoting good in the world (which we are also obliged to do), we are completely free to choose how to go about this. Since the basic goods are all self-evidently good (not derived from other more basic goods nor from each other), they are all worth pursuing, even to the extent of dedicating one's life to that pursuit. Hence, how we go about this part of the ethical project is up to us. We are free to choose how we want to live our lives: whether being a doctor promoting life, or a scientist pursuing knowledge, or an artist creating beauty, or a social worker or politician promoting the public good, or a parent

46. "Man has free will: otherwise counsels, exhortations, commands, prohibitions, rewards and punishments would be in vain." Aquinas, *ST* 1.83.1, vol. 1, p. 418.
47. See Descartes, *Meditations on First Philosophy*, meditation 1.

raising children, etc. There is no best life. The playing field is wide open for creative freedom.

The freedom of choice implied by practical reason distinguishes it from theoretical reason.[48] We are not free to create truth.[49] What is, is, and what is not, is not. But we are free to create the kind of life we shall lead and the kind of person we shall be. And so long as we do not violate basic goods, this moral creativity, however expressed, is good.[50]

The Beautiful

In our discussion of beauty as an object distinct from truth and goodness, we shall follow Aristotle primarily, for he is most explicit about giving to beauty its own set of principles, which are reducible neither to the theoretical disciplines (whose object is the truth about what is) nor to the practical disciplines (which have the good as their object). In general, Aristotle is ever careful to distinguish between disciplines according to subject matter (object) and the methods appropriate to each. Different disciplines have different objects, and therefore have different principles and require different methods. Since mathematics, biology, physics, metaphysics, ethics, and aesthetics are about different subject matters, one would do violence to them by treating them all under one method.[51]

One of the best texts on this essential point is Aristotle's *Poetics*. Here Aristotle explains what he takes to be essential to good literature, that is, to beauty in creative writing. Although his remarks in this work are apropos most directly of how one ought (and ought not) to judge literature, the same general point about focusing on what is essential is applicable to studying any field. Because literature involves propositions of various kinds, and so is the most liable of the arts to be interpreted in terms of the criteria of truth and goodness, it offers us an excellent opportunity to clarify the distinction between disciplines. We are less likely to think that the purpose of painting or music is to disseminate truth or morality (although there have been those who have thought so).

Speaking of art in general, Aristotle says that our response to beauty and art is natural (not derived from some other aspect of human nature)

48. Freedom of choice is also a feature of aesthetic reason.

49. The exception is in the making of artificial things, whose essences conform to our ideas. Cf. Thomas Aquinas, *DV* 1.2.

50. Of course, once we have made some choices, we have committed ourselves to fulfill some obligations and our choices are morally limited. For example, once one chooses to marry and have a family, one should not spend endless nights away from home playing music or studying Aristotle. Or once one commits to a college education, one should not spend all one's time socializing with friends. But these are obligations we freely choose.

51. See *On the Soul* 1.1; *Metaphysics* 2.1; *NE* 1.1.

and that the essence of beauty and art is that they delight. Thus we enjoy making and appreciating art for two reasons: "imitating is innate in men from childhood . . . and all men enjoy works of imitation."[52] Whether or not art involves truth or moral goodness is irrelevant to its essence.

As for literary art, Aristotle says that a good piece of literature ought to evoke wonder and delight.[53] If literature (or art in general) does not evoke wonder and delight, then it has failed, even if it has given accurate historical, physical, metaphysical, or ethical information. Although issues of truth and morality do occur in stories, they are not of central concern in judging the aesthetic quality of the work. Consider this key text.

> Correctness for the poetic art is not the same as for politics or any other art. Within the poetic art itself mistakes are of two kinds: (a) essential and (b) accidental. . . . If the poet describes an impossible object in relation to the art itself, he makes a mistake. But the description is correct, provided that the end of the poetic art is attained; for the end is enhanced, if in this way that description makes the corresponding part or some other part of the poem more striking.[54]

The essential purpose of the poetic art is not to provide information, whether historical, or physical/metaphysical, or ethical. Thus the principles of good literature are not those of history. "Its compositions should not be like those histories which must present not a single action but all the chance and unrelated happenings to one or more persons during a single period."[55] Nor are the principles of good literature those of physical or metaphysical accuracy. "With respect to the making of poetry, a convincing impossibility is preferable to an unconvincing possibility."[56] It is better to get one's facts wrong than to violate the principles of beauty. Finally, the principles of good literature are not those of the ethical/political realm. "As to whether something was nobly or ignobly said or done, one should examine the problem by attending not only to whether the thing done or said was good or bad, but also to the man who performed the deed or spoke."[57] The words and actions should fit the character and help to perfect the literary work as a whole, for the essential goodness of a piece of literary art is not moral goodness (whether of the character or the reader/viewer), but goodness of beauty.

52. Aristotle, *Poetics* 4.1488b5–9 in *Selected Works*, trans. Hippocrates G. Apostle and Lloyd P. Gerson (Grinnell, IA: Peripatetic Press, 1982), p. 635. See Plato on the natural charm of poetry, *Republic* 10.601b, and *Hippias Major* 297e.

53. *Poetics* 4.1488b5–19 and 24.1460a12–18.

54. Ibid., 25.1460b15–27, p. 660.

55. Ibid., 23.1459a22–25, p. 657.

56. Ibid., 25.1461b12–13, p. 662.

57. Ibid., 25.1461a5–8, p. 661.

The focus in the *Poetics* is tragedy, which Aristotle defines as "an imitation of an action which is serious and complete and has a proper magnitude, rendered with speech made pleasing separately in the parts of each of its different divisions, presented dramatically and not by means of narrative, and ending in, by means of pity and fear, catharsis of such emotions."[58] The parts Aristotle has in mind are: plot, character, thought, language, sung lyrics, and spectacle.[59]

Given this definition of tragedy, one might accuse Aristotle of violating his own principles, for he seems to be making catharsis the ultimate principle of tragedy. This would appear to make emotion or psychological health the main purpose of tragedy. Perhaps Aristotle is responding to Plato's challenge in book 10 of the *Republic*, where Plato argues for the banishment of art from the state until someone can show how art could be good for the people, that it might have some "healthy or true purpose."[60] However, although Aristotle does mention catharsis as something good that comes out of tragedy, catharsis does not seem to be part of his defense of beauty and art in general. In his treatment of art in the *Poetics*, this idea of catharsis is not emphasized; in fact, it appears only in this passage. This makes perfect sense, for unless one wants to reduce the importance of art to a psychological cleansing (which can be understood as either a factual consequence of art or an obligation on the part of the artist to promote the good of health), then the importance of art must lie elsewhere. I suggest that instead of reading "end" here ("ending in, by means of pity and fear, catharsis of such emotions") as indicating the ultimate purpose of tragedy, one should read it as indicating a temporal sequence of events: a psychological insight into the effects of tragedy on the audience.

Recall that Aristotle says that a good piece of literature evokes wonder and delight. These are simultaneous with and essential to the appreciation, not consequences of such an experience in another order, whether of truth, morality, or psychology. Thus they are intrinsic to our participation in beauty, appreciated for their own sakes. Wonder seems to indicate the intellectual aspect, and delight the sensual aspect, of our appreciation of beauty. Together, wonder and delight refer to the fullness of aesthetic appreciation, which is an appreciation by the whole human being. The

58. Ibid., 6.1449b24–28, p. 638.

59. Ibid., 6.1550a8–10, p. 638. Comedy would seem to have all the same parts as tragedy but to lack its serious theme and the catharsis by means of pity and fear. Comedies such as those of Shakespeare do, in fact, involve serious themes in parts, as well as tensions of fear and pity; these tensions are, however, resolved in the end in a happy way. Aristotle says that epic has the same parts as tragedy (including the reversals, recognitions, and sufferings that bring about pity and fear), excepting song and spectacle (*Poetics* 24.1459b8–14).

60. *Republic* 10.603b, p. 247; see also 10.607b–608b.

catharsis of pity and fear is not essential to the artistic quality of the play since catharsis is related to psychological or physiological health, not beauty. Like history, physics, metaphysics, and ethics, catharsis is irrelevant to beauty. It may be true that a great tragedy is cathartic, and it may be good for us to have our emotions purged, but catharsis is not what ultimately makes a play great. A play that moves one emotionally is not, for that reason, a beautiful piece of art. Nor does appreciation of a play need to involve emotion to be genuine.

Of the parts of tragedy, plot is the most important element, since it is upon the quality of the plot that the success of the work of literature depends. "The plot, then, is the principle and, as it were, the soul of tragedy."[61] Each of the other parts belongs essentially to another field and is used by the artist in the service of tragedy's proper end. Thus character is essentially a matter for ethics; thought for logic, rhetoric, and dialectic; language for grammar; sung lyrics for music; and spectacle for the visual arts.

A good plot has a clear beginning, middle, and end and is unified around one action, which is as complex and of as great a magnitude as the unity of the plot allows. Key to a good plot are reversals and recognitions since these are surprising and hence the source of wonder and delight. In the best plot these reversals and recognitions come about by necessity, that is, by the necessity set up by the story. The other parts (character, thought, language, sung lyrics, and spectacle) also contribute to the quality of the play and are listed in order of importance.

This attention to plot is consistent with what Aristotle says in the *Metaphysics* about beauty, that beauty is found most of all in "order, symmetry, and definiteness."[62] Structure and form are most essential to the beautiful, and in a piece of literature the plot provides these most of all. Aristotle goes so far as to say that the greatness of a tragedy comes across when it is read as well as performed, for the structure or plot remains the same, even if all the spectacle and song be taken away. This is not to say that the other parts are unimportant, just that they are secondary to and in the service of the plot. In fact, one reason why Aristotle thinks that tragedy is superior to epic is that it involves sung lyrics and spectacle. Although least important to the tragedy, they are a source of delight and hence a part of what is artistic about a play. But if any of these lesser parts claims its own due apart from its relation to the plot, then the beauty of the play as a whole is diminished.

61. *Poetics* 6.1450a39, p. 639.
62. *Metaphysics* 13.9. Here he also insists that the good is distinct from the beautiful, "for the good is always in action but the beautiful may also be in what is immovable" (1078a32–33, p. 218).

Thus character and thought are successful in a play or story not by themselves but insofar as they support the plot. For example, when Aristotle says that the main character in both tragedy and epic poetry should be as good as or better than we are,[63] this is not in order to teach us morality, but so that the work may have its proper effect of arousing wonder and delight. So also the reasonableness of the thought process is important for making the plot plausible and hence powerful, not for the sake of teaching us logic or how to reason correctly about the things of this world. Although Aristotle says that it is "right to censure a poet for using what is unreasonable or evil without any necessity,"[64] this does not mean that quality of thought and the moral goodness of characters are in themselves tests of the greatness of a tragedy. Rather it means that bad reasoning or immorality, if not necessitated by the plot, provides suitable grounds for criticizing a play. If, however, either were to serve the plot, then the poor reasoning or immoral action would not be suitable grounds for negative criticism.

Although Aquinas commented on Aristotle's *Posterior Analytics*, *Physics*, *Metaphysics*, *Nicomachean Ethics*, and *Politics*, and so was well-versed in Aristotle's thought concerning the realms of the true and the good, there is no evidence that he had ever read Aristotle's *Poetics*. Aquinas's philosophy of beauty owes more to Augustine and Augustine's roots in the Neoplatonists and Cicero.[65] Aquinas never wrote a systematic account of the beautiful, but it is clear that he thinks it is known by a distinct act of reason whose principles differ from those of the true and the good.

The case for Aquinas recognizing the realm of the beautiful as distinct from the realms of the true and the good can be made in two ways. One way is to look at his discussion of beauty as a transcendental (a metaphysical approach following the order of nature). The other is to consider what he says about beautiful things (an experiential approach following the order of discovery). This second approach is ultimately the basis for the first. Following it, one finds that appreciating things as beautiful is not the same as discovering the truth about them or understanding what makes them good.

Because of its clarity of expression, let us begin with Aquinas's account of beauty as a transcendental. Like truth and goodness (and the other transcendentals, being and oneness), beauty can be predicated of everything.[66] That is, the recognition of beauty is as universal as that of

63. *Poetics* 2.

64. Ibid., 25.1461b19–20, p. 663.

65. See Augustine, *Of True Religion* 29.54–30.55 and *City of God* 11.22–23; cf. Cicero, *On Moral Obligation* 4.

66. On the so-called transcendentals, see *ST* 1.2.3; *DV* 21.4.c and ad 4. This is a traditional Platonic point. See, in particular, Plato's *Symposium* 206c–212a. Cf. Augustine, *Confessions* 11.4 and *City of God* 12.5.

truth or goodness. Adopting Plato's notion of participation, Thomas says that every particular thing insofar as it participates in being participates also in goodness.[67] Good adds to being the notion of desirability, for everything that is can be desired and so be said to be good. Following Pseudo-Dionysius, Aquinas recognizes that beauty has the same extension as goodness.[68] Everything that is, is also good and beautiful. As Thomas says, "Beauty and goodness in a thing are identical fundamentally, for they are based upon the same thing, namely, the form."[69] If everything participates in goodness, then everything participates in beauty. However, goodness and beauty differ in meaning since the good is the object of desire and hence is related to the will, while beauty is the object of appreciation and so related to the power of knowing. In other words, good is related to final cause (a purpose or end to be sought), while beauty is related to formal cause (something intelligible).[70] Again, the recognition of good moves the rational appetite, while the recognition of beauty stills it.[71] Knowledge of the beautiful is contemplative rather than practical, a matter of appreciating something for its own sake rather than desiring to possess it. "Beauty . . . consists in a certain clarity and due proportion. Now each of these is found radically in the reason because both the light that makes the beauty seen, and the establishing of due proportion among things, belong to reason. Hence since the contemplative life consists in an act of the reason, there is beauty in it by its very nature and essence."[72]

Let us turn now to Thomas's account of the original character of beauty found in the physical things that are the natural objects of our knowledge.[73] Like Aristotle, Thomas says that the essence of beauty is that it delights. It is valued, but unlike the good as a principle of ethics, it is not valued because of how it guides our actions. Rather, it is enjoyed for its own sake. "For beautiful things are those which please when

67. *ST* 1.6.4.

68. *Opusc. XIV, Expositio de divinis nominibus* 4.5.

69. *ST* 1.5.4 ad 1, vol. 1, p. 26. In *Lysis* 216d, Plato identifies the good and the beautiful; in *Crito* 48b Plato says that the good, the beautiful, and the just life are the same; and in *Republic* 6, Plato speaks of the Good as the ultimate source of—and as more beautiful than—knowledge and truth. "The Good is not being but superior to and beyond being in dignity and power" (*Republic* 6.509b, p. 163). As a criterion for judging that the Good is beyond being, beauty must be beyond being, as well.

70. *ST* 1.5.4.1 ad 1. Recall that these are the two causes rejected by Bacon and the modern tradition, which rejection led to the absurdities of that tradition in trying to deal with moral and aesthetic issues.

71. *ST* 1–2.27.1 ad 3. Aristotle says in *Metaphysics* 13.9 that while the good is always in action the beautiful may be in what is immovable.

72. *ST* 2–2.180.2 ad 3, vol. 4, p. 1926.

73. Ibid., 1.85.1.

seen."[74] According to Aquinas, beauty is characterized by three essential properties. "Beauty includes three conditions: *integrity* or *perfection*, since those things which are impaired are by that very fact ugly; due *proportion* or *harmony*; and lastly, *brightness*, or *clarity*, whence things are called beautiful which have a bright color."[75]

Although the characteristics of integrity, perfection, due proportion, and harmony can, in some way, be said to belong to all three realms (the true, the good, and the beautiful), they are essential only to the realm of the beautiful. One can speak about the integrated and well-ordered truth of complex theoretical knowledge and about the requirement to integrate and harmonize one's own intentions or those of individuals within a social group; however, neither reason for the sake of the truth nor reason for the sake of the good considers integrity, perfection, proportion, or harmony in themselves, but rather in the truth to be known or the moral goodness to be attained. To judge something beautiful is not to judge its scientific or metaphysical status, or to judge its value as something to be pursued.

When trying to articulate the first principles of beauty, one runs into a bit of a problem, for there is no tidy first principle such as the law of noncontradiction in the realm of the true or the first principle of practical reason in the realm of the good. We found these realms dramatically differentiated by mood as well as object: thus the true is about "is" (indicative mood) and the good is about "ought" (imperative mood). This distinction is helpful because it is embedded in the way we use language, and language refers to thought. When it comes to demarcating the first principle of beauty, however, we have no such convenient formulation or easy way of distinguishing. Perhaps this is due to the fact that the appreciation of beauty includes the particular thing as particular. Although there are some rational principles to guide us in our aesthetic judgments, the uniqueness of the integral unity of the beautiful thing renders a precise formulation impossible. However, by clarifying how beauty is like and unlike the other realms, we may succeed, if not in arriving at a neat formulation of the first principle of aesthetic reason, at least in making room for beauty as a distinct object

74. Ibid., 1.5.4 ad 1, vol. 1, p. 26. Besides these key texts and some others where Aquinas speaks of beauty, many of his texts on art are helpful in distinguishing activities (and hence the habits of first principles presupposed by these activities) that differ in kind from those whose purpose is the discovery of truth or the achievement of good. Thus, like Aristotle, Aquinas distinguishes between the essence of art and morality by showing that a bad artist is one who fails in his proper task, which is to make a beautiful thing, while a morally bad person is one who fails at being good (not one who is ugly). See *ST* 1–2.21.2 ad 2; 57.3 and 5; *Comm. NE* 6.4.1172–73.

75. *ST* 1.39.8.c, vol. 1, p. 201.

of intelligibility that, as distinct, must have its own first principles and its own method.

Beauty shares with truth the characteristic of being concerned with formal cause, and so is an object of contemplation rather than action. It even involves a kind of abstraction, for one can say something about what all beautiful things share—e.g., order, integrity, proportion. However, the contemplation of beauty differs from the contemplation of truth in that the former involves essentially, in its paradigm case, sense experience. The knowledge whose object is the truth about being involves levels of abstraction, and its ultimate object is the first principle of all reality, which is pure, immaterial intelligibility. Although such knowledge begins with sense experience and returns to sense experience to test its judgment, the sense experience is not important for its own sake, but for the sake of knowing the truth about things.

In contrast to this, sense experience is integral to the appreciation or contemplation of a beautiful object. This is emphasized by Thomas's third characteristic of beauty: brightness or clarity. One could, perhaps, interpret this third characteristic as an element of intelligibility rather than sensual delight, but to reduce beauty entirely to intelligibility would be to destroy the notion of the beautiful thing as itself beautiful. Beauty is not just a response to unity, integrity, proportion, and order. It is also rooted in sense experience. One wants to remain in the presence of the beautiful object. One does not want just to know what it is (object of theoretical reason) or to achieve it (object of practical reason), but to let it be and to be with it. Although one could say that we are delighted by the truth and by what is good, and so scientific theorems and moral character could be called beautiful, these are beautiful by analogy with the prime analogue: the beauty of a physical thing, grasped by the unity of sense and reason.

This is not to say that the essence of the appreciation of beauty lies in feeling. This is the modern error, arising perhaps from taking science as the paradigm for knowing: if only what can be verified by sense experience is to be accounted real knowledge, then other judgments must be of sense or sentiment. However, this restriction of reason to scientific method is unwarranted, and certainly Plato, Aristotle, Augustine, and Aquinas all think that judgments about beauty are matters of intellect as well as sense. Consider the following quotation from Aquinas: "Beauty, as stated above, consists in a certain clarity and due proportion. Now each of these is found radically in the reason because both the light that makes beauty seen and the establishing of due proportion among things belong to reason."[76]

76. Ibid., 2–2.180.2 ad 3, vol. 4, p. 1926.

Beauty also shares with the good, as distinct from the true, a practical mode: art. Whereas we are passive in our recognition of the truth of being (the mind conforms to what is), beauty involves an active mode: we can be creators as well as appreciators of beauty. Applying an understanding of the principles of beauty and an aesthetic sensibility, we can produce a new beautiful particular, just as we can produce a particular act of goodness from an understanding of moral principles and from a virtuous character. However, the ends of art and virtuous action are different. Although both involve free will (as against the knowledge of truth), the purpose of art is not moral goodness, nor is the purpose of virtuous action the creation of beautiful objects to be contemplated.

In sum, although it shares certain characteristics with the realms of the true and the good, the realm of the beautiful is distinct in principles and method. This must be so, since the object of aesthetic reason (beauty) is distinct from the object of theoretical reason (truth) and the object of practical reason (goodness). Although we may not be able to formulate neatly a first principle of aesthetic reason (as we did for theoretical reason and for practical reason), we must not, on that account, deny to aesthetic reason its own distinct domain. We must remember that the power of reason is known by the habits (first principles), which are known by the activities, which are specified by the objects. Clearly, the objects—truth, beauty, and goodness—are not identical. Therefore, neither are the activities, habits, and methods by which the objects are known.

All these features in Aquinas's account of beauty can be found in Aristotle, Plato, and Augustine. The most immediate source for Aquinas is Augustine, who freely acknowledges the influence of the Neoplatonists and Cicero. Insofar as the Neoplatonists considered that their work was an integration of Plato and Aristotle, there is also the clear possibility of an influence from Aristotle on the Neoplatonic theory of beauty and hence ultimately on Augustine.

In various texts in Aristotle outside the *Poetics*, one can find principles similar to those of Aquinas. As we noted above, Aristotle distinguishes clearly between the good and the beautiful; "for the good is always in action but the beautiful may also be in what is immovable."[77] In the same passage, he goes on to describe the beautiful in terms of "order, symmetry, and definiteness."[78] The element that Aquinas calls brightness and clarity can be inferred from Aristotle's assertion in the *Poetics* that tragedy is ultimately better than epic since it possesses all the structural elements of epic plus elements of sensuous delight. "Tragedy is superior

77. *Metaphysics* 13.3.1078a32, p. 218.
78. Ibid., 13.3.1079b1, p. 218.

to epic because it has all the essential parts which epic has; furthermore, no small part of it consists in music and spectacle, through which pleasures are most vividly reinforced."[79]

In Augustine, one finds essentially the same terms as in Aquinas. Unity, symmetry, and proportion are recurring principles in Augustine's discussions of the beautiful. "In all the arts it is symmetry which gives pleasure, preserving unity and making the whole beautiful."[80] And again, "Beauty is not a matter of bulk but of the symmetry and proportion of members."[81] One also finds the idea that beauty is found in clarity or brightness in Augustine: he speaks of things that are "beautiful to the senses,"[82] the "luster of beauty,"[83] and the "brightness of light."[84]

What is perhaps more surprising than finding Aquinas's principles in Aristotle and Augustine is to find them in Plato himself, given Plato's penchant for reducing all things to the metaphysical unity of the Good and his skepticism about the value of the poet's art.[85] However, despite this tendency toward metaphysical dominance, it is quite clear that Plato distinguishes beauty from truth and goodness. The great beauty of his dialogues in proportion, diction, and integrated unity is clear evidence that Plato cares for beauty. Beyond this, Plato distinguishes in various dialogues the characteristics of beauty that one finds in Augustine and Aquinas. Even in book 10 of the *Republic*, where he moves to banish the poet from the *polis*, it is clear that Plato understands the difference between the true, the good, and the beautiful and has a deep appreciation for beauty.

In the *Republic* Plato is worried that the young might take the fables of the poet for reality and believe them to be accurate descriptions of the way things are (realm of the true) or ought to be (realm of the good); that is, he is worried about poetry being taken for something that it is not. Admittedly, poetry may not have any "true or healthy purpose," but its place is not to lead to a better understanding of the world, or a more virtuous life; it is to be enjoyed for its own sake. It is the fact that people mistakenly think that beauty in art or poetry is a vehicle for truth or morality that is the problem, not that beauty is somehow of itself misleading in terms of truth or corrupting in terms of pursuing what is good. Beauty has its own essential part to play in our lives,

79. *Poetics* 26.1462a14–16, p. 664.

80. Augustine, *Of True Religion* 30.55, trans. J. H. S. Burleigh (South Bend, IN: Regency/Gateway, 1959), pp. 51–52.

81. *City of God* 11.22, p. 229. See also *On the Trinity* 9.6; *City of God* 11.27, 12.4 and 22.20; and *On Eighty-Three Different Questions* 78.

82. *Of True Religion* 30.56, p. 52.

83. *City of God* 11.23, p. 231.

84. *Of True Religion* 29.52; cf. *On the Trinity* 8.2.

85. See *Republic* 10, where Plato bans poets from the republic until someone can make the case for their inclusion.

not as truth-bearing or virtue-developing but as delightful. Nor is this delight merely pleasure in the physical sense. Given that beauty involves order and structure, it is appreciated by an act of intellect as well as by a bodily act. There is, of course, nothing wrong in making moral judgments about how one's children ought to be educated, as Plato does: in fact, we have an obligation to think carefully about this. But if, as seems clear, the beautiful is not the same as the good, then to judge the beautiful by the principles of the good and not by its own principles is a violation of reason.

Indeed, it seems clear that Plato understands the essential difference between the appreciation of beauty and metaphysics or morality. Even in the *Republic* Plato commends Homer as the greatest of the poets and admits the charm of poetry.[86] In the *Phaedo*, when he explains why he took up writing verses while in jail, Socrates makes clear that the poet's job is not to write about things as they are: "I realized that a poet, if he is to be a poet, must compose fables, not arguments."[87]

Not only does Plato clearly recognize that beauty is distinct from truth and goodness; he also presents principles of beauty drawn from our experience of material things. Beauty, for Plato (as for Aristotle, Augustine, and Aquinas), involves both intellect and sense. Consider the following texts from which one can create a robust theory of the beautiful as essentially distinct from the true and the good. In the *Philebus*, Plato speaks of the beautiful as having "qualities of measure and proportion."[88] And elsewhere he states that the beautiful orders all things in loveliness.[89] Like Aristotle, Plato holds that beautiful things are objects of delight. We have access to the beautiful through the senses; "for beauty alone this has been ordained, to be most manifest to sense and most lovely of them all."[90] However, although beauty involves sensual experience essentially, the appropriate sensual experience is limited to that which is seen and heard. "Beauty is the pleasant which comes through the senses of hearing and sight."[91] These senses are closest to intelligence and fitted to transmit the intelligible qualities of the beautiful object. Even the idea of beauty as brightness can be found in Plato. "Now beauty, as we said,

86. *Republic* 10.606e–607a.
87. *Phaedo* 61b, in *Five Dialogues*, trans. Grube, p. 97.
88. *Philebus* 64e, trans. R. Hackforth in *Collected Dialogues*, ed. Edith Hamilton and Huntington Cairns (Princeton, NJ: Princeton University Press, 1978), p. 1147; see also 65a and 66a–b.
89. *Greater Hippias* 289e.
90. *Phaedrus* 250d, trans. R. Hackforth, in *Collected Dialogues*, p. 497.
91. *Greater Hippias* 298a, trans. Benjamin Jowett, in *Collected Dialogues*, pp. 1551–52. Note the difference between this theory of how the senses are related to beauty and that of Hume and Nietzsche, for whom the aesthetic is most closely related to taste and touch (feeling).

shone bright amidst these visions, and in this world below we apprehend it through the clearest of our senses, clear and resplendent."[92]

Thus, although Plato often uses beauty as a metaphysical principle equivalent to the true and the good, he also distinguishes beauty from the other two realms, giving it concrete expression based in the material things of this world. And like Aristotle and Aquinas, Plato distinguishes beauty from the other objects of human reason, both according to the order of nature and according to the order of discovery.

Full Breadth of Reason

We have seen in this chapter how the tradition of Plato, Aristotle, Augustine, and Aquinas distinguishes three fundamentally different realms of reason according to three distinct objects: the true, the good, and the beautiful. Reason, indeed, is one power, as we shall emphasize in the next chapter; however, it is oriented to the world in three different ways. Thus it operates according to three quite different methods guided by three sets of first principles. As these first principles are all self-evident, no set of principles is derived from any other. The good cannot be essentially grasped through the principles that govern our knowledge of truth or beauty. The essence of beauty cannot be explained through the first principles of truth or those of goodness. Nor, of course, can one reduce claims about what is true to moral or aesthetic categories.

To confuse the three realms by using the method or invoking the principles appropriate to one in order to account for the others is to render meaningless whole realms of intelligibility. This was the great temptation and false step of the Renaissance and Enlightenment philosophers. And it is the great sanity of the philosophers of the ancient/medieval tradition that they did not try to do this. Although one can find places where each of our models—Plato, Aristotle, Augustine, and Aquinas—fails to distinguish properly between the three realms and lets one set of principles or method do the work of another, none of these thinkers sees such a reductionism as a virtue (as do the moderns) and so never settles into the absurdity of a consistent misapplication of method.

In an age where the scientific/technological paradigm with its demands for specialization tends to dominate, there is the grave danger of adopting one set of principles or one viewpoint for everything. To understand that the essence of ethics cannot be reached by scientific method, that great literature is not reducible to ethical or political themes, that history is not reducible to metaphysics, nor metaphysics to historical conditions,

92. *Phaedrus* 250d, p. 497.

is to guard against the enslavement of the human spirit. To understand the proper limits of disciplines is to prevent the hegemony of any one method—a hegemony which, since it obviously cannot handle all the aspects of our intellectual life, must lead to mental confusion and frustration and perhaps to the loss of trust in reason. Although this loss of trust may be the current state of affairs, it is not warranted. To restore the full life of reason is to recover great riches of our humanity and the world.

9

Reason's Threefold Unity

For eight chapters now, we have stressed the importance of differentiating the distinctive principles and methods appropriate to understanding truth, pursuing goodness, and appreciating beauty. Again and again we have seen how philosophers let one rational activity dominate the others, and we have tried to show how this domination is both unwarranted and bad for human reason. Still, the attempt to unify these realms of reason does seem reasonable, for presumably the same human intelligence is ordered to these three distinct objects. We are self-aware: we know that we understand what is true, pursue what is good, and appreciate what is beautiful, and we know that it is the same knowing self in each case. Hence there is a legitimate need to talk about the unity of reason. How are these three realms of reason related? Is there a transcendent principle that grounds these distinct realms and a universal method that integrates them?

That the realms of the true, the good, and the beautiful are related is a metaphysical necessity, for just as propositions within each realm presuppose the habit of first principles of that field, so the three distinct habits we have been discussing presuppose one power of reason.[1] All three kinds of judgment involve the application of universals, even though the origin and character of the universal are different in each case. Even the aesthetic judgment, which includes the appreciation of the particular as particular, involves universal criteria such as unity,

---

1. See Aquinas, *ST* 1.79.8 and 11; *DV* 15.1.c and ad 5; *CG* 2.83.31.

integrity, and proportion. But common features suggest a common cause. Hence all three judgments are grounded in a common source or cause: the power of reason.

However, to explain how the three habits we have distinguished can be deduced from one power is beyond the scope of reason. We can say *that* there must be one power, but we are unable to say *what* that one power is. This is rather like what Aquinas says about God the Creator: we can know that all things are created (that they are dependent on a first cause of existence), but we cannot know how this cause creates. Since we can know only *that* there is a God, not *what* God is, there is no possibility of deducing truths about the world from an understanding of the essence of the Creator. In a similar way, we can know *that* the three distinct habits of first principles have their origin in one self-aware intelligence, but we cannot know how these habits of first principles are born from that intelligence. Since we do not know *what* the power of reason is in itself, we cannot deduce the distinct principles and methods from that power.

An authentic metaphysics of existence always argues from effect to cause, not from cause to effect. We know first the distinct objects: the true, the good, and the beautiful. These objects specify three distinct activities, with three habits of first principles. Reflecting on the fact that these three activities are activities of reason guided by self-evident principles, we come to the conclusion that there is one power of reason. However, we cannot argue from the one power of reason to the distinct principles, activities, and objects (from cause to effect) because we do not know the essence of the power of reason. That is, we cannot define reason. To do this, we would have to step outside reason in order to get a view of reason as a whole, and this we cannot do. Reason, though not limited to any single realm, always works in one or the other. We have no access to principles higher than those self-evident principles of truth, goodness, and beauty that we have discussed. Because our insights and judgments are always of truth, goodness, or beauty, they cannot grasp the transcendent essence of our intelligence. We are not in a position to define the power of reason. Thus any attempt at definition would (as we have seen in the moderns) restrict reason arbitrarily, much to our intellectual detriment.

Just as Aristotle says that it is not helpful to try to explain the goods we seek by affirming the existence of a transcendent good,[2] so it is not helpful to try to explain the three distinct activities of reason by affirming a transcendent activity of reason. In each case intelligibility moves from knowing diverse (essentially distinct) elements to knowing that a

2. Aristotle, *NE* 1.4.

source of these elements exists, not from the essence of the source to the existence or essence of the diverse elements. In other words, we do not know more about the basic goods or the activities of reason by knowing that they have a transcendent source.

However, although we cannot define the transcendent principle of all reason, we can say something about how the three realms of reason are related. When we reflect on the realms of the true, the good, and the beautiful, we find that they are in some sense mutually inclusive. Each realm, in a way, embraces and unifies the scope of human reason.

All three are unified within the realm of the true. Propositions about what is good or beautiful must make use of the law of noncontradiction, the first principle of truth. Insofar as goods and beautiful things are beings, they fall under the principles of logical and metaphysical truth. The good and the beautiful are two of the so-called transcendentals, characteristics that belong to everything that is. Thus the realm of the true does include the realms of the good and beautiful in a way.

But all three are also unified within the realm of the good. Truth and beauty are desirable; that is, they are goods. And they are not good merely as means to or as aspects of other goods: they are good in themselves, ultimate goods. Truth and beauty are two of the self-evident principles of goodness that provide some specificity to the first principle of practical reason (good is to be done and pursued and evil avoided). Thus the realm of the good includes, in a way, the realms of the true and the beautiful.

Finally, all three are unified within the realm of the beautiful. A true judgment about the way things are, insofar as it is complete, ordered, and unified, is beautiful. The character of a person in whom the virtues are well ordered and in whom particular choices and actions are consistent with a unified good purpose (and this is the most real locus of goodness in this world) is beautiful.[3] And so the realm of the beautiful includes, in a way, the realms of the true and the good.

Of course, this book itself is an exercise in theoretical reason insofar as it is an attempt to explain the nature of human intelligence. So one might say that this kind of theoretical explanation takes priority. On the contrary, the book would never have been written if I had not thought that it would be a good thing to explain the multidimensionality of reason and that I therefore ought to do it. From this perspective, purpose and practical reason are prior. Less obvious is my appreciation of the integrated order of human intelligence and my intention to present this integrated order in a pleasing form. Were this book a successful piece of fiction, this point would be clearer. But even as it is, I take into account matters of aesthetics when I write this book. I try to order the

3. See *ST* 2–2.145.2.c.

book in such a way that it holds together as a coherent whole, to make the chapters about the right length, and to write in a clear and pleasing style. Thus the book can be viewed from three different standpoints: its content, its purpose, and its intrinsic order and unity.

However, even as we reflect on how the three realms of reason seem to include one another, let us not forget the essential distinctions between them. The fact that each realm in some sense includes the other two is not an argument for reducing them all to one; quite to the contrary, it is an argument against such a reduction. In discussing the basic human goods in his book *Natural Law and Natural Rights*, John Finnis argues that they are equally fundamental.[4] Each is self-evidently good, and none can be understood as a mere aspect of another. One way of showing this is to argue that each good can reasonably be held to be the most important. If each can, from a certain perspective, be considered the most important, none is absolutely the most important. Our discussion here leads to the same conclusion. Because any one of the three realms can be said to include the other two, there is no reason to say that any one of the realms does include the other two in all respects.

Let us remind ourselves of the distinction between what is essential and what is accidental to each of the realms. Essential to the realm of the true is the activity of judging whether propositions about reality are true or false. But the fact that statements about goodness and beauty are true or false is accidental to what goodness and beauty are. For what is good ought to be pursued, not just affirmed as true. It is not enough merely to note that people can help each other; since helping others is good, we ought to help each other. And what is beautiful cannot be reduced to the simple clarity of theoretical propositions; rather, a beautiful object invites appreciation, contemplation, and delight.

Essential to the realm of the good is the activity of judging that some things ought to be done (because they are good) and other things ought not to be done (because they are evil). However, it is accidental to truth and beauty that they be goods. Truth in and of itself is an insight or judgment with no immediate implications for action. "$3 \times 4 = 12$" and "cheetahs run faster than horses" are not intrinsically moral propositions; they do not oblige one to act. Beauty in and of itself is an object of contemplation and delight. What makes a work of nature or of art beautiful is not its moral worth, but its aesthetic quality. Thus one can have a beautiful play about an immoral character—*Macbeth* or *Richard III*.

Essential to the realm of the beautiful is the activity of appreciating the harmonies and integrated unity of some object (or creating such an

---

4. Finnis, *Natural Law and Natural Right*, p. 92.

object in art). But it is accidental to truth claims that they be beautifully formulated. Whether the fact that oak is a stronger wood than pine be conveyed in poetry or technical prose is irrelevant to its truth. The simplicity and unity of Hobbes's mechanistic philosophy does not make it any less false. And it is accidental to moral judgments or actions that they be aesthetically pleasing. The beauty of a well-orchestrated robbery does not render it any less wrong

To be human is a complex and mysterious affair. We find ourselves in a world of meaning that is irreducibly multifaceted: we are aware of knowing things and their relations; we are aware of choosing among things more or less worthy of our attention; and we are aware of appreciating things for their own sake. In short, we respond to truth, goodness, and beauty. In turn, these three realms of knowing are multifaceted. The first includes truths within such diverse fields as logic, mathematics, the various sciences, and metaphysics, but also truths about what is good and what is beautiful. The second concerns all those goods worth pursuing for oneself and for those who share one's various circles of community. Among these goods are truth and beauty. The third sphere involves the appreciation of natural beauty and the appreciation and/or creation of artistic beauty. Included within such a sphere of appreciation and creation are the integrated wholes of true accounts of reality or of individual characters or communities.

Although each of these realms of meaning can be said to include, in a way, all things (so that its principles might seem able to explain the other realms in its own terms), we must resist the temptation to reduce them all to one. Not only would such a reductionism destroy the essential features of the two realms that were explained away; it would also be bad for the favored realm.

A reductionism to the realm of the true would be bad for metaphysics, for the movement toward unity of explanation begins with diversity, with the many things of our experience, among which are the recognitions of things as good and beautiful. To argue that the diversity is unreal because it implies a unified first principle is illegitimate, since the implication that there is such a first principle comes only through the recognition of diversity and the questions such diversity raises.[5] Again, this is like arguing for the existence of one God from the diversity of things and activities that we experience (the structure of all of Aquinas's five ways) and then turning around and arguing that, because God is one, all the diversity we find in the things we experience is really just an illusion. Such a way of arguing is illegitimate and self-destructive.

5. This mistake, of course, is the source of the metaphysical muddle of the moderns, from Descartes to Hegel.

A reductionism to the realm of the good would be bad for ethics, for among the things that are recognized as good in themselves are such things as truth and beauty, which are to be sought for their own sakes and not just as means to one transcendent end. The fact that we have a single word for human fulfillment—happiness—should not fool us into thinking that we understand some monolithic principle of good to which every other good is reducible or that we have some moral obligation to which all other obligations must give way. One ought not to deny the goodness of anything. Hence, if there are goods, such as truth and beauty, which cannot be said to be merely means to or aspects of other more fundamental goods but are intrinsically good, then it would be wrong to reduce their status to being mere ancillaries to the moral life of fulfilling obligations. The judgment that there must be an ultimate end or purpose of the diversity of human goods is metaphysically true. However, since we do not know what that transcendent purpose is, we cannot be strictly obliged to honor it above all else. Therefore, to subjugate the distinctive basic goods of truth and beauty to such a transcendent moral duty would violate what we do know clearly to be good.

And a reductionism of all intelligibility to the realm of beauty would be bad for aesthetics, for the appreciation of beauty is rooted in the apprehension of a particular thing as particular. Both intellect and sense are involved essentially in a judgment about beauty. In the act of universalizing the idea of beauty sufficiently to include both the universals of truth and the universals of obligation, one would be forgetting an inextricable characteristic of beauty: that it includes particularity in its very essence. For a philosophy of beauty to claim that its principles are foundational for those of metaphysics and ethics would be to renounce its delight in the particular as particular.

No one single principle or habit of first principles can adequately ground all human meaning. The fact that consciousness reveals to us a unified self should not lead us to deny the diverse objects of our knowing, for a single knower does not imply a single object known. The awareness of oneself as knower presupposes something known, and to know something is to distinguish it from some other thing or things. The truth is that to understand, to pursue, and to appreciate are three distinct activities of the human being as rational, corresponding to three distinct objects: the true, the good, and the beautiful. We ought always to keep this truth in mind lest we cripple our intelligence, renounce our freedom and responsibility, and turn our backs on the beauty that surrounds us. Not only is human intelligence open to these three realms of reason so that we ought to guard against shutting down this openness; there is also great delight in appreciating the diverse riches of these three realms of human intellectual activity.

Bibliography

Aeschylus. *Prometheus Bound*. Translated by David Grene. Vol. 1 of *Greek Tragedies*. Edited by David Grene and Richmond Lattimore. Chicago and London: University of Chicago Press, 1968.

Alexander of Hales. *Summa Theologica*. 4 vols. Quaracchi: Collegium S. Bonaventurae, 1924–48.

Arendt, Hannah. *The Human Condition*. Chicago: University of Chicago Press, 1958.

Aristotle. *Metaphysics*. Translated by Hippocrates G. Apostle. Grinnell, IA: Peripatetic Press, 1979.

———. *Nicomachean Ethics*. Translated by Hippocrates G. Apostle. Grinnell, IA: Peripatetic Press, 1984.

———. *On Parts of Animals*. In *Selected Works*, pp. 310–23.

———. *On the Soul*. Translated by Hippocrates G. Apostle. Grinnell, IA: Peripatetic Press, 1981.

———. *Physics*. Translated by Hippocrates G. Apostle. Grinnell, IA: Peripatetic Press, 1980.

———. *Poetics*. In *Selected Works*, pp. 631–64.

———. *Politics*. Translated by T. A. Sinclair. Middlesex, England: Penguin, 1976.

———. *Posterior Analytics*. Translated by Hippocrates G. Apostle. Grinnell, IA: Peripatetic Press, 1981.

———. *Selected Works*. Translated by Hippocrates G. Apostle and Lloyd P. Gerson. Grinnell, IA: Peripatetic Press, 1982.

Augros, Robert M., and George N. Stanciu. *The New Story of Science*. New York: Bantam, 1986.

Augustine. *The Christian Combat*. Translated by Robert P. Russell. In *Selections*, pp. 307–53. Fathers of the Church 4. New York: Fathers of the Church, 1947.

243

————. *City of God*. Translated by Gerald G. Walsh et al. Garden City, NY: Image Books, 1958.

————. *Confessions*. Translated by John K. Ryan. Garden City, NY: Image Books, 1960.

————. *Divine Providence and the Problem of Evil* [*De ordine*]. Translated by Robert P. Russell. In *Selections*, pp. 227–332. Fathers of the Church 5. New York: Cima, 1948.

————. *Eighty-Three Different Questions*. Translated by David L Mosher. Washington, DC: Catholic University of America Press, 1982.

————. *The Good of Marriage*. Translated by Charles T. Wilcox. In *Treatises on Marriage and Other Subjects*, pp. 9–51. Fathers of the Church 27. New York: Fathers of the Church, 1955.

————. *The Literal Meaning of Genesis*. Translated by John Hammond Taylor. Ancient Christian Writers 41–42. New York: Newman, 1982.

————. *Of True Religion*. Translated by J. H. S. Burleigh. South Bend, IN: Gateway, 1959.

————. *On Free Choice of the Will*. Translated by Anna S. Benjamin and L. H. Hackstaff. Indianapolis: Bobbs-Merrill, 1964.

————. *The Trinity*. Translated by Stephen McKenna. Fathers of the Church 45. Washington, DC: Catholic University of America Press, 1963.

Bacon, Francis. *The Great Instauration*. In *The New Organon and Related Writings*, pp. 3–29.

————. *The New Organon and Related Writings*. Edited by Fulton H. Anderson. Translated by James Spedding, Robert Leslie Ellis, and Douglas Denon Heath. New York: Liberal Arts Press, 1960.

————. *The New Organon or True Directions Concerning the Interpretation of Nature*. In *The New Organon and Related Writings*, pp. 33–268.

————. "Of Beauty." In *Selected Writings of Francis Bacon*, pp. 112–13.

————. "Of Building." In *Selected Writings of Francis Bacon*, pp. 114–17.

————. *Of the Proficience and Advancement of Learning, Divine and Human*. In *Selected Writings of Francis Bacon*, pp. 155–392.

————. *On the Interpretation of Nature, proem*. In *Selected Writings of Francis Bacon*, pp. 150–54.

————. *Preparative Toward Natural and Experimental History*. In *The New Organon and Related Writings*, pp. 269–92.

————. *Selected Writings of Francis Bacon*. Edited by Hugh G. Dick. New York: Modern Library, 1955.

Balthasar, Hans Urs von. *The Glory of the Lord: A Theological Aesthetics*. Translated by Erasmo Leiva-Merikakis. San Francisco: Ignatius, 1982.

Beardsley, M. C., ed. *European Philosophers from Descartes to Nietzsche*. New York: Modern Library, 1960.

Beck, Lewis White, ed. *Eighteenth-Century Philosophy*. New York: Free Press, 1966.

Berkeley, George. *A Treatise Concerning the Principles of Human Knowledge*. Edited by Colin M. Turbayne. Indianapolis: Bobbs-Merrill, 1979.

Bonaventure. *Commentaria in quatuor libros Sententiarum Petri Lombardi*. Vols. 1–4 of *Opera Omnia*. 10 vols. Quaracchi: Collegium S. Bonaventurae, 1882–1902.

Cicero. *On Moral Obligation*. Translated by John Higginbotham. Berkeley: University of California Press, 1967.

Copernicus, Nicolaus. *On the Revolutions of the Heavenly Spheres*. Translated by A. M. Duncan. New York: Barnes & Noble, 1976.

Dante Alighieri. *The Divine Comedy*. Translated by Allen Mandelbaum. 3 vols. New York: Bantam, 1982–1986.

Descartes, René. *Discourse on the Method of Rightly Conducting One's Reason and of Seeking Truth in the Sciences*. Translated by Donald A. Cress. Indianapolis: Hackett, 1980.

———. *Meditations on First Philosophy: In Which the Existence of God and the Distinction of the Soul from the Body Are Demonstrated*. Translated by Donald A. Cress. Indianapolis: Hackett, 1979.

———. *The Passions of the Soul*. In *Philosophical Works*, vol. 1, pp. 331–427.

———. *Philosophical Works*. Translated by Elizabeth S. Haldane and G. R. T. Ross. 2 vols. Cambridge: Cambridge University Press, 1981.

———. René Descartes to Mersenne, March 18, 1630. In Tatarkiewicz, *History of Aesthetics*, vol. 3, p. 373.

———. René Descartes to Princesse Elizabeth of the Palatinate, February 22, 1649. In Tatarkiewicz, *History of Aesthetics*, vol. 3, p. 374.

Dick, O. L., ed. *Aubrey's Brief Lives*. London: Secher & Warburg, 1950.

Duns Scotus, John. *Quaestiones super libros Sententiarum* [Ordinatio, also known as Opus Oxoniense]. In *Opera omnia*, vols. 8–21. 26 vols. Paris: Vivès, 1891–1895.

Eco, Umberto. *Art and Beauty in the Middle Ages*. Translated by Hugh Bredin. New Haven, CT: Yale University Press, 1986.

Erasmus, Desiderius. *Praise of Folly*. Translated by Betty Radice. Middlesex, England: Penguin, 1985.

Euclid. *The Thirteen Books of Euclid's Elements*. Translated by Sir Thomas L. Heath. New York: Dover, 1956.

Finnis, John. *Moral Absolutes*. Washington, DC: Catholic University of America Press, 1991.

———. *Natural Law and Natural Rights*. Oxford: Clarendon, 1980.

Galilei, Galileo. *The Assayer*. In *Discoveries and Opinions of Galileo*, pp. 229–80.

———. *Discoveries and Opinions of Galileo*. Edited and translated by Stillman Drake. Garden City, NY: Doubleday Anchor, 1957.

———. "Letters on Sunspots." In *Discoveries and Opinions of Galileo*, pp. 87–144.

Gardiner, Patrick L., ed. *Nineteenth-Century Philosophy*. New York: Free Press, 1969.

Gilson, Etienne. *The Unity of Philosophical Experience*. New York: Charles Scribner's Sons, 1937.

Grabo, Carl. *A Newton among Poets: Shelley's Use of Science in "Prometheus Unbound."* New York: Cooper Square, 1968.

Grisez, Germain. *The Way of the Lord Jesus: Christian Moral Principles*. 3 vols. Chicago: Franciscan Herald, 1983–1997.

Grisez, Germain, John Finnis, and Joseph Boyle. "Practical Principles, Moral Truth, and Ultimate Ends." *American Journal of Jurisprudence* 32 (1987): 99–151.

Hegel, Georg Wilhelm Friedrich. *The Philosophy of Fine Art*. Translated by F. P. B. Osmaston. In Hofstadter, *Philosophies of Art and Beauty*, pp. 382–445.

———. *Hegel's Philosophy of Right*. Translated by T. M. Knox. Oxford: Clarendon, 1952.

———. *Reason in History*. Translated by Robert S. Hartman. Indianapolis: Bobbs-Merrill, 1953.

———. *The Science of Logic*. Part 1 of *The Encyclopaedia Logic*. Translated by T. F. Geraets, W. A. Suchting, and H. S. Harris. Indianapolis: Hackett, 1991.

———. *The Science of Logic*. Translated by W. H. Johnston and L. G. Struthers. London: George Allen & Unwin, 1966.

Hesiod. *The Poems of Hesiod*. Edited by R. M. Frazer. Norman: University of Oklahoma Press, 1983.

———. *Theogony*. In *The Poems of Hesiod*, pp. 21–90.

———. *Works and Days*. In *The Poems of Hesiod*, pp. 91–142.

Hittinger, Russell. *A Critique of the New Natural Law Theory*. Notre Dame, IN: University of Notre Dame Press, 1987.

Hobbes, Thomas. "The Answer to Davenant, 1650." In Tatarkiewicz, *History of Aesthetics*, vol. 3, p. 381.

———. *Leviathan*. Edited by C. B. Macpherson. London: Penguin, 1985.

Hofstadter, Albert, and Richard Huhns, eds. *Philosophies of Art and Beauty*. Chicago: University of Chicago Press, 1964.

Hughes, Philip. *A Popular History of the Catholic Church*. New York: MacMillan, 1966.

Hume, David. *Dialogues Concerning Natural Religion*. Edited by Henry D. Aiken. New York: Hafner, 1951.

———. *An Enquiry Concerning Human Understanding*. Edited by Eric Steinberg. Indianapolis: Hackett, 1980.

———. "Letter from a Gentleman to His Friend in Edinburgh." In *An Enquiry Concerning Human Understanding*, pp. 115–24.

———. *A Treatise of Human Nature*. Edited by L. A. Selby-Bigge. 2nd ed. Revised by P. H. Nidditch. Oxford: Clarendon, 1978.

Jordan, Mark. "The Evidence of Transcendentals and the Place of Beauty in Thomas Aquinas." *International Philosophical Quarterly* 29 (1989): 393–407.

Kant, Immanuel. *Critique of Judgment*. Translated by Werner S. Pluhar. Indianapolis: Hackett, 1987.

————. *Critique of Pure Reason*. Translated by Werner S. Pluhar. Indianapolis: Hackett, 1996.

————. *Groundwork of the Metaphysics of Morals*. Translated by H. J. Patton. New York: Harper & Row, 1964.

————. *Kant: Selections*. Edited by Theodore M. Greene. New York: Scribner, 1957.

————. *Lectures on Ethics*. Translated by Louis Infield. Indianapolis: Hackett, 1963.

————. *Prolegomena to Any Future Metaphysics*. Translated by James W. Ellington. Indianapolis: Hackett, 1977.

Kepler, Johannes. *The Harmonies of the World*. Translated by Charles Glenn Wallis. In *Great Books of the Western World*, vol. 15, pp. 1005–85. Edited by Mortimer J. Adler. 2nd ed. Chicago: Encyclopaedia Britannica, 1990.

Kovach, Francis. *Philosophy of Beauty*. Norman: University of Oklahoma Press, 1974.

————. *Scholastic Challenges to Some Medieval and Modern Ideas*. Stillwater, OK: Western Publications, 1987.

Langer, Susanne K. *Feeling and Form: A Theory of Art*. New York: Scribner, 1953.

Leibniz, G. W. "Letter to Simon Foucher." In Popkin, *The Philosophy of the Sixteenth and Seventeenth Centuries*, pp. 303–10.

————. *Meditationes de cognitione, veritate et ideis*, 1684. In Tatarkiewicz, *History of Aesthetics*, vol. 3, pp. 381–82.

————. *New System of Nature and of the Communication of Substance, as Well as of the Union of Soul and Body*. In Popkin, *The Philosophy of the Sixteenth and Seventeenth Centuries*, pp. 323–31.

————. *On True Method in Philosophy and Theology*. In Popkin, *The Philosophy of the Sixteenth and Seventeenth Centuries*, pp. 310–15.

————. *Principes de la nature et de la grace*. In Tatarkiewicz, *History of Aesthetics*, vol. 3, p. 382.

————. *The Principles of Philosophy, or the Monadology*. In *Discourse on Metaphysics and Other Essays*, pp. 68–81. Translated by Daniel Garber and Roger Ariew. Indianapolis: Hackett, 1991.

————. *Second Explanation of the System of the Communication of Substances*. In Popkin, *The Philosophy of the Sixteenth and Seventeenth Centuries*, pp. 332–33.

————. *Theodicy*. In Popkin, *The Philosophy of the Sixteenth and Seventeenth Centuries*, pp. 333–39.

Locke, John. *An Essay Concerning Human Understanding*. Edited by A. S. Pringle-Pattison. Oxford: Clarendon, 1969.

———. "Language and its Proper Use." In *Selections*, pp. 26–42.

———. *Second Treatise of Government*. Edited by C. B. Macpherson. Indianapolis: Hackett, 1980.

———. *Selections*. Edited by Sterling P. Lamprecht. New York: Scribners, 1928.

———. "Some Thoughts Concerning Education." In *Selections*, pp. 3–15.

———. "The Spirit of Toleration." In *Selections*, pp. 43–51.

Lonergan, Bernard J. F. "Art," in *Topics in Education*, pp. 208–32.

———. "Cognitional Structure." *Continuum* 2 (1964): 530–42.

———. *Collection: Papers by Bernard Lonergan*. Edited by F. E. Crowe. London: Darton, Longman & Todd, and New York: Herder and Herder, 1967.

———. *Insight*. New York: Philosophical Library, 1970.

———. "Insight Revisited." In *A Second Collection*, pp. 263–78.

———. *Method in Theology*. Toronto: University of Toronto Press, 1990.

———. "Natural Right and Historical Mindedness." In *A Third Collection*, pp. 169–83.

———. *A Second Collection: Papers by Bernard Lonergan*. Edited by William F. J. Ryan and Bernard J. Tyrrell. London: Darton, Longman & Todd, 1974.

———. "Theories of Inquiry: Responses to a Symposium." In A *Second Collection*, pp. 33–42.

———. *A Third Collection*. Edited by Frederick E. Crowe. New York: Paulist Press, 1985.

———. *Topics in Education*. Vol. 10 of *Collected Works of Bernard Lonergan*. Toronto: University of Toronto Press, 1993.

———. "Transition from a Classicist World-view." In *A Second Collection*, pp. 1–9.

———. *Verbum: Word and Idea in Aquinas*. Notre Dame, IN: University of Notre Dame Press, 1967.

Machiavelli, Niccolò. *The Prince*. Translated by George Bull. Middlesex, England: Penguin, 1921.

Malebranche, Nicolas. *Christian Meditations*. In Tatarkiewicz, *History of Aesthetics*, vol. 3, pp. 367–68.

———. *Dialogues on Metaphysics*. Translated by Willis Doney. New York: Abaris Books, 1980.

———. *The Search after Truth*. Translated by Thomas M. Lennon and Paul J. Olscamp. Columbus: Ohio State University Press, 1980.

———. *Treatise on Morality*. In Tatarkiewicz, *History of Aesthetics*, vol. 3, p. 379.

McInerny, Ralph. *Ethica Thomistica: The Moral Philosophy of Thomas Aquinas*. Washington, DC: Catholic University of America Press, 1982.

Montaigne, Michel de. *An Apology for Raymond Sebond*. Translated by M. A. Screech. London: Penguin, 1993.

———. *Essays*. Translated by J. M. Cohen. London: Penguin, 1988.

Nagel, Thomas. *The Last Word*. Oxford: Oxford University Press, 1997.

Newman, John Henry. *The Idea of a University*. Edited by Martin J. Svaglic. Notre Dame, IN: University of Notre Dame Press, 1982.

Nietzsche, Friedrich. *Beyond Good and Evil*. Translated by Walter Kaufmann. New York: Vintage, 1966.

———. *The Will to Power*. Translated by Walter Kaufmann and R. J. Hollingdale. London: Weidenfeld & Nicolson, 1968.

Pascal, Blaise. *Pensées*. Translated by W. F. Trotter. New York: E. P. Dutton, 1931.

Plato. *Apology*. In *Five Dialogues*, pp. 23–44.

———. *The Collected Dialogues of Plato*. Edited by Edith Hamilton and Huntington Cairns. Princeton, NJ: Princeton University Press, 1978.

———. *Crito*. In *Five Dialogues*, pp. 45–58.

———. *Five Dialogues*. Translated by G. M. A. Grube. Indianapolis: Hackett, 1981.

———. *Greater Hippias*. Translated by Benjamin Jowett. In *Collected Dialogues*, pp. 1534–59.

———. *Laws*. Translated by Trevor J. Saunders. Middlesex, England: Penguin, 1970.

———. *Lysis*. Translated by J. Wright. In *Collected Dialogues*, pp. 145–68.

———. *Phaedo*. In *Five Dialogues*, pp. 93–155.

———. *Phaedrus*. Translated by R. Hackforth. In *Collected Dialogues*, pp. 475–525.

———. *Philebus*. Translated by R. Hackforth. In *Collected Dialogues*, pp. 1086–1150.

———. *Republic*. Translated by G. M. A. Grube. Indianapolis: Hackett, 1985.

———. *Symposium*. Translated by Alexander Nehemas and Paul Woodruff. Indianapolis: Hackett, 1989.

Popkin, Richard H. *The Philosophy of the Sixteenth and Seventeenth Centuries*. New York: Free Press, 1966.

Porter, Jean. *The Recovery of Virtue: The Relevance of Aquinas for Christian Ethics*. Louisville, KY: Westminster/John Knox, 1990.

Rorty, Richard. "Does Academic Freedom Have Philosophical Presuppositions?" *Academe* (November–December 1994): 56–57.

Schelling, Friedrich Wilhelm Joseph von. *System of Transcendental Idealism*. Translated by Albert Hofstadter. In Hofstadter, *Philosophies of Art and Beauty*, pp. 347–77.

Shelley, Percy Bysshe. *Prometheus Unbound*. In *Shelley's Prometheus Unbound: The Text and the Drafts*. Edited by Lawrence John Zillman. New Haven, CT, and London: Yale University Press, 1968.

Spinoza, Baruch. "Epistola LVIII." In Tatarkiewicz, *History of Aesthetics*, vol. 3, p. 380.

———. *The Ethics*. Translated by Samuel Shirley. Indianapolis: Hackett, 1982.

———. *Theologico-Political Treatise*. In *Chief Works of Benedict de Spinoza*. Translated by R. H. M. Elwes. New York: Dover, 1951.

Tatarkiewicz, Wladyslaw. *History of Aesthetics*. Translated by Adam and Ann Czerniawski. 3 vols. The Hague: Mouton, 1974.

Tertullian. *Prescription against Heretics*. Translated by P. Holmes. In *Ante-Nicene Fathers*, vol. 15, pp. 243–67. Grand Rapids: Eerdmans, 1951.

Thomas à Kempis. *Imitation of Christ*. Translated by Edgar Daplan. New York: Sheed and Ward, 1950.

Thomas Aquinas. *Commentary on Nicomachean Ethics*. Translated by C. I. Litzinger. 2 vols. Chicago: Regency, 1964.

———. *Commentary on Posterior Analytics*. Translated by F. R. Larcher. Albany, NY: Magi, 1970.

———. *Compendium Theologiae*. Translated by Cyril Vollert, S.J. St. Louis: B. Herder, 1958.

———. *The Disputed Questions on Truth*. Translated by Robert W. Mulligan. 2 vols. Chicago: Henry Regency, 1952.

———. *An Exposition on the Hebdomads of Boethius*. Translated by Janice L. Schultz and Edward A. Synan. Washington, DC: Catholic University of America Press, 2001.

———. *In librum beati Dionysii De divinis nominibus*. Edited by C. Pera. Taurini: Marietti, 1950.

———. *On Being and Essence*. In *Selected Writings of St. Thomas Aquinas*, pp. 33–67.

———. *On the Truth of the Catholic Faith: Summa Contra Gentiles*. Translated by Anton C. Pegis, James F. Anderson, Vernon J. Bourke, and Charles J. O'Neil. 5 vols. Garden City, NY: Image Books, 1955–1957.

———. *Selected Writings of St. Thomas Aquinas*. Translated by Robert. P. Goodwin. Indianapolis: Bobbs-Merrill, 1977.

———. *Summa Theologica*. Translated by the Fathers of the English Dominican Province. 5 vols. Westminster, MD: Christian Classics, 1981.

Veatch, Henry B. *For an Ontology of Morals*. Evanston, IL: Northwestern University Press, 1971.

Whitehead, Alfred North. *Adventures of Ideas*. New York: Free Press, 1967.

———. *Process and Reality*. New York: Free Press, 1978.

———. *Science and the Modern World*. New York: Free Press, 1967.

William of Ockham. *Quaestiones in librum quartum Sententiarum*. Edited by Rega Wood and Gedeon Gál. St. Bonaventure, NY: St. Bonaventure University, 1984.

Index

abstraction, 149, 217–19; three levels of, 217–19
act and potency, 218–19; and Aristotle 218; and Aquinas, 218–19,
Aeschylus, 66–67; on ambivalence about technology, 67
Alexander of Hales, 49–50
ancient and medieval tradition: Plato, Aristotle, Augustine, and Aquinas, 207–208, 235–36
Anselm, Saint, 49, 208n1
anthropomorphism, 78–79
Aquinas. *See* Thomas Aquinas, Saint
Aristotle: on abstraction, 149, 217–19; on abstraction's three levels, 217–19; on act and potency, 218; on activity/function, 77; on aesthetic objections to emphasis on science and technology, 83–84; on aesthetics, 224–28; on art, 224–28; against the atomists, 76–78; and basic goods, 217n34; on beauty, 224–28, 232–33; and catharsis, 226; on beauty as order, symmetry, and definiteness, 227, 232–33; on beauty's relationship to wonder and delight, 225–28; distinguishes disciplines by objects, 224; distinguishes between theoretical and practical reason, 214; and first principle of practical reason, 216n31; on first principles, 90, 210–13; on four causes, 75–78; on freedom, 79–80; and Hegel, 157–61; on human being as, in a way, all things, 80–81; on human being as paradigm of reality, 78–80; and law of noncontradiction, 215n30; on literary art, 225–28; on logic, 20, 22n19, 23–24, 219–20; on mathematics, 95n29, 218; on metaphysics, 75–81, 176–77, 205n105, 218–19; on method, 87n1; on mind as a blank tablet, 18; and moral absolutes, 197; on moral and political objections to emphasis on technology, 70–71; and natural law, 197; on natural philosophy, 75–79; and new science, 11; on physical science, 217–19; and realism, 96–97; on substance, 76, 78; on theoretical objections to emphasis on science and technology, 75–81; on tragedy, 201; on unmoved mover, 61; and virtue, 71, 197; and Whitehead, 172–74, 176–77; and wonder, 52
Arendt, Hannah, on freedom in politics, 71n21
art, 232; and Aquinas, 230n74; and Aristotle, 224–28; and Bacon, 27; and Descartes, 32; and free will; and Hegel, 163–64; and Hobbes, 41; and Kant, 153–54; and Lonergan, 193, 198–202; and novelty, 27, 143, 180–91; and Schelling, 163; and Whitehead, 181
atomism, 21, 76–78; Hobbes's material, 131; Leibniz's immaterial, 131; and Whitehead, 173–74